Eats of Eden

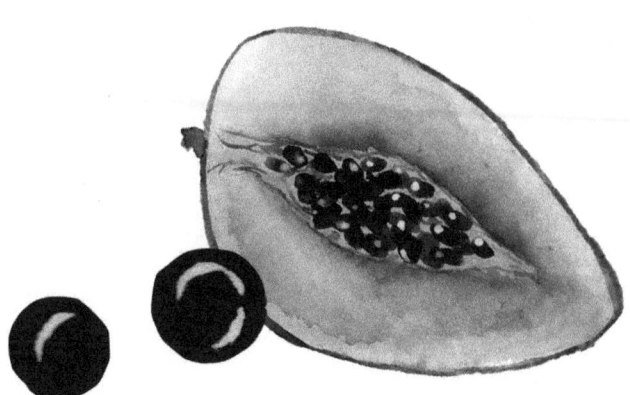

TABITHA BLANKENBILLER

a foodoir

Alternating Current Press
Boulder, Colorado

Eats of Eden
Tabitha Blankenbiller
©2018 Alternating Current Press

Alternating Current
Boulder, Colorado
alternatingcurrentarts.com

ISBN-10: 1-946580-02-3
ISBN-13: 978-1-946580-02-3
First Edition: March 2018

For **Matt** —
You would share your last jellybean,
and you would somersault in sand with me.

Advance Praise

"If you can't cuddle up with a good friend and trade life stories, the next best thing is cuddling up with Blankenbiller's charming *Eats of Eden*. From buying your first bra and attending the dinner anniversary of the Titanic's sinking to joining Weight Watchers (again) to navigating the peaks and valleys of a writer's life, Blankenbiller parses these relatable, tender, human moments with candor, humor, heart—and food. A bon vivant who finds ultimate joy in cooking and eating, Blankenbiller takes us on a culinary tour of her life— recipes included!—with delicious, and nourishing, results."

—Sarah Sweeney,
author of *Tell Me if You're Lying*

"Reading *Eats of Eden* is like having a delicious, leisurely lunch with a smart and insightful friend. Blankenbiller is sharp and self-aware in these essays about food, writing, and being a person, and each one is a distinct pleasure on its own. The collection—complete with recipes —comes together like a satisfying and well-balanced meal."

—Sarah Einstein,
AWP Prize in Creative Nonfiction award-winning author of *Mot*

"Blankenbiller has packaged longing, self-doubt, body image, and love for others and food into fun and fulfilling narrative recipes for living an authentic life. *Eats of Eden* demonstrates the ways food can bring people together (or tear them apart), how pursuing one's dreams is never futile, and that the best meals—and moments— come from creative practice. This 'foodoir' is a funny and reassuring read for anyone who has ever felt like a front-line cook in a world of gourmet chefs."

—Melissa Grunow,
author of *Realizing River City* and *I Don't Belong Here*

"*Eats of Eden* is truly a delicious treat! Blankenbiller is a confident essay writer, making it look easy as she lets us into her hungry heart in this bright, satisfying collection. She waxes on food and being a writer and wrestles with rejection, ambition, and cheese-lust. Peppered with recipes, pop culture, sugar-sweetness, and plenty of nostalgia, this book is a unique, honest, funny, glittery, high-energy explosion of a sparkly cupcake—easily and greedily devoured."

—Leesa Cross-Smith,
author of *Whiskey & Ribbons* and *Every Kiss a War*

"A writer's life can be ridiculous, between the self-sabotage, the hours spent moving commas and carefully crafting our public images, never mind the risks we take to create moments of deep luminous beauty only for the world to ignore them. Blankenbiller writes a triumphant, existential comedy of errors about finding her way as a creative person, making readers laugh one moment and nod the next. I love when books can be this fun and vulnerable. She laughs without hiding behind the humor. She also includes recipes, because she knows salvation lies in food and friends. Take a risk. Bake a strata. Read *Eats of Eden*."

—Aaron Gilbreath,
author of *Everything We Don't Know* and *This Is: Essays on Jazz*

"Wise, funny, sharply observed, and eminently readable, Blankenbiller's *Eats of Eden* is literary comfort food. The stories at the heart of these essays—and the recipes that follow—offer the nourishing warmth of companionship and intimacy."

—Steve Edwards,
author of *Breaking into the Backcountry*

"*Eats of Eden* starts with a generous helping of humor and adds dashes of writerly anxiety. Focused around the food and the recipes that feed the soul and the body, Blankenbiller mines her memories for evocative details and snapshots. Come for the stories, and stay for the cooking!"

—Sonya Huber,
author of *Pain Woman Takes Your Keys
and Other Essays from a Nervous System*

"A feast of the senses and the writerly sensibilities, Blankenbiller's foodoir cuts to the heart of the things that elude us—success, ex-friends, the perfect lemon meringue pie. A debut to savor."

—Kendra Fortmeyer,
author of *Hole in the Middle*

"*Eats of Eden* is a sensitive, generous, and laugh-out-loud funny collection that I want to return to again and again. This book is a must-read for creative women with big appetites—for life, for success, and for excellent cheese."

—Kelly Davio,
author of *It's Just Nerves: Notes on a Disability*

"Blankenbiller's enthusiasm and energy and voice and personality comes through on every page, sweeping you up and carrying you along for the ride, like a best friend dragging you into line after line after line after line at Disneyland, all but making you love it all and feel like a kid again. She made me care about cooking (which I don't, at all) as much as I care about writing (which is a lot). I even read every recipe! (Though will never make any of them.)"

—Aaron Burch,
author of *Stephen King's 'The Body'* and *Backswing*,
and editor of *Hobart*

"This book is pure comfort food, warm and filling. Peppered with confessions of desire for literary stardom, each of these essays feels as light and crisp as croissants fresh from the oven. Blankenbiller shares her recipes here for not only tasty dinners but authentic, often hilarious, living as she candidly charts her own uncertain path to becoming a writer. I had to resist devouring them all in one sitting."

—Melissa Wiley,
author of *Antlers in Space and Other Common Phenomena*

"Reading Blankenbiller's delightful memoir, *Eats of Eden*, is time spent listening to a good friend tell smart, heartfelt stories over plates of delicious food she's spent all day cooking just for you. And yes, she'll share the recipes."

—Cari Luna,
author of *The Revolution of Every Day*

"Is there anything more important than feeling good, eating well, and living passionately? Blankenbiller's essays would suggest there is not, and I would suggest that with *Eats of Eden*, there may be no one writing more urgently, humorously, or touchingly about these topics than Blankenbiller herself."

—Ben Tanzer,
author of *Be Cool: A Memoir (Sort Of)*, *Sex and Death*, and *Orphans*

"At turns hilarious and heartbreaking, but always genuine, Blankenbiller's *Eats of Eden* will leave you satiated. An enthralling narrative and a remarkable meal: if there's more you want from a book, you're just being greedy. This is the real deal."

—Andrew Brininstool,
author of *Crude Sketches Done in Quick Succession*

"Lush, rich, and delicious, these essays are as tasty as the recipe she delivers: Blankenbiller dishes not only fun but depth and honesty. She shows us that literature is not meant to fly above taste but delve into it. What a satisfying read."

—Rene Denfeld,
bestselling author of *The Child Finder* and *The Enchanted*

Essays   *Menu*   Recipes

Cucumber Risotto by the Sea

The Colony House in Rockport Beach, Oregon, was erected at the top of a hill, a swelling beachside drift carved from the coast over a millennia, now covered in long straw grasses and shell fragments. I parked my Prius V (The V stands for "Very much bigger than the kind you're thinking of, thanks.") at the base of the hill and stared up at the vacant chateau. I was the first to arrive. I'm always the first to arrive. I like to settle myself into a place, pick the perfect seat, watch something come together instead of wander into a minefield of variables.

I popped open the hatchback, reusable shopping bags and overnight totes slumping toward me, their contents shifted around Highway 101's sea-tracing curves. The trunk was at capacity for a long Valentine's Day weekend, Tetris-stacked with a full-sized Samsonite suitcase, carry-on bag, laptop case, two Whole Foods grocery bags full of boots, a Crock-Pot and cooler bag of soup ingredients, three coats, and a hatbox carrying a Mary Poppins-channeling vintage hat. I packed like a girl in Taylor Swift's entourage, bound for a weekend of meticulous Instagram shoots. Not like an unestablished artist heading to a DIY-writing retreat.

The house was a vertical hike up the hill to a porch accessible only by the Lombard Street of sea-salt-pummeled stairs. I loaded myself in the pack-mule stylings familiar to all of us overpreppers, with four bags swung over my shoulders, a roller-bag in each hand, and a purse crooked in my elbow. The house key was in my coat pocket, picked up from my friend, Susan, last weekend. Everything about the Colony House was analog: brass keys sent in the mail, their handwritten reservation book, a story contest sign-up sheet tacked to the kitchen bulletin board, the map of the house Susan drew for me on the back of an envelope, revealing the entrance secret of coming in through the basement.

"You can't come in through the front door. It only opens from the inside," she warned. "I spent half an hour circling around with that mistake."

The basement door, like the front and back entrances, was a solid timber slab. As I stood on its frayed wicker mat, sanded down to thread by a thousand gritty beach shoes, the door felt two stories tall. It must have come from a tree bigger than life, like the redwoods under which I posed on camping trips as a child, anxious to hurry up and get on to the gift shop. The best part of any experience was the novelty you could bring home and show off. The knob was a heavy wooden knot too big for my hand—what you'd imagine concealing Paul Bunyan's vault. It was after wrestling with this beast of an entry that the Colony House forever became to me the Sasquatch House.

The door opened to an antique gap-toothed staircase shadowing the flotsam of a hundred-year dwelling — ancient paint cans, a rancid mop, balding brooms. I could feel the ghosts of unfinished restoration projects mingling with the immortal scent of stale ammonia and paint chips so old and leaden, I practically got cancer just standing in their same zip code. To the right was the first bedroom, with windowless, rust-red streaked walls and a sanitarium-style iron frame twin bed that evoked all the charm and comforts of a recently unearthed suburban basement kidnap chamber.

I can't be here by myself, a voice weaned on psychological thrillers insisted within. First to arrive, first to die.

"Don't let the basement freak you out," Susan had warned. "It's a bad precursor to the rest of the house."

Despite my horror-movie trauma, I took full advantage of First Dibs prerogative and kept lugging my bags past Room Option One. Sorry, whoever has a misbehaving GPS.

I heaved the load up the small flight of stairs to a lofted cabin tucked with touches of macramé and poetry anthologies. Caved-in sofas, with velvet patterns too soft and worn to decipher, clustered around a hearth, leaving just enough room for a dining table crafted from the other half of the front door redwood. Strong enough to dance a publication victory lap atop, to survive that eventual west coast 'big one' earthquake beneath—elemental furniture that was less fixture than outcropping of the house itself, built to carry and endure whatever joy or frustration a person arrived here dragging alongside.

I'm supposed to make *something here.*

Leaving the basement door cracked, I staggered back and forth from my car three more times for every last boulder of luggage. The shoes I wouldn't end up looking at again until I picked them up to head back home. An armful of inspirational tomes I'd forget to peruse. A dry-cleaned dress for a party that was neither planned nor ended up happening. On the last trek to the car, hot and winded, I retrieved my black Smith-Corona typewriter case. I'd received it as a Christmas present a few weeks before, a treasure my husband, Matt, discovered in our neighborhood antique shop. The case was still packed with every Don Draper-era certification and tag it was originally sold with, including a manual listing the local repair dealer in southwest Portland, long vanished in the decades' tides. The bulldozed location now housed an architectural firm, a necessary fixture for a city intent on 're-imagining' and 'high-density demanding' itself out of an identity. Impractical, heavy structures like the Colony House did not survive in Portland. It was a city ambivalent to its history and obsessed with dictating the future. A place I was feeling less and less a part of, since returning from an 18-month stint in Tucson. We'd gone to accommodate Matt's job transfer, then moved back to our Oregon house in November, a month before that antique typewriter gift was unwrapped, meant to realign my tangled-up direction.

"It's for good writing luck this year," Matt explained.

I had to pivot forward in 2015, out of a year of creative shipwrecks and a home in upheaval, into a new idea just cresting into my heart. My memoir, a book I'd tried for five years to launch, was finally archived in an external hard drive where it could live out its days not gelling and not being what the market wanted, freeing me to ponder fresh starts. Over the past year of withdrawing from consideration and breaking up with my agent, a distant possibility kept hinting from the periphery. A novel rooted in my nonfiction, a postmortem of a decimated friendship that I was finally garnering enough distance to stare down. The time we'd been estranged was beginning to outpace the years we'd been together. I could run my fingers over the scab left over, begin to puzzle out the many tentacles of 'why' that led me here.

When I sent Susan my deposit for the Colony House, I imagined sitting on a terrace above the Pacific tides, just up the coast from where I'd earned my MFA a few years before. I'd circle my craft back to its basic elements on my Real Legitimate Author™ type-writer, rotary keys thumping tape and ink, pummeling words onto real paper. No switching over to Google: *how to spell 'bougainvillea,'* and falling down a research hole where, three hours later, I'm on YouTube watching director's cut scenes from *The Devil Wears Prada*.

I tugged the case's handle toward me. Twenty-five pounds of portable printing press battering against my calves, my dream of This Perfect Writing Trip beating me with each step. Who needs a 5-pound laptop when you can be photogenic?

"You … are … ridiculous," I muttered under my breath. I'd hauled this thing here to look like I was Serious, to take an Instagram with fresh pages and black coffee in an earthenware mug. I'd take a walk into town where cell service flickered back, and the social media world would see that I was working very hard, that I hadn't failed at my dream, that the best was yet to come. If I could make it look right, I could make it true.

I stuffed all my props and expectation into the second-best bedroom's far corner (I left the suite with water-facing bay windows up for grabs because I'm not a total selfish diva … all the time), burying its second twin bed in a luggage mountain. I set my laptop on the desk and my typewriter suitcase at my feet. I listened for the sound of mighty doors opening.

Car by car, the grand lodge filled. Susan and fellow MFA grad, Lisa, the elvin-faced poet, split the Queen Suite facing the ocean. Erin, a Portland writer who wrote an essay (that still catches in my throat to this day) about crows and their predilection for giving gifts, didn't argue with the basement.

"I actually get a lot done when I can't see outside," she said.

We fit as a perfect quartet. Our vague writing retreat structure consisted of sequestering ourselves to a nook in the house, writing all day, and meeting down at the slab table for dinner. I volunteered to cook first, the calendar scheduling equivalent of running early, with a Moroccan Chickpea Stew I felt would appeal to the Portland artist palette. Before locking myself into the upstairs room, I emptied everything in my ingredient bag into the transported Crock-Pot: San Marzano tomatoes, vegetable broth, and enough dried fruit to raise an eyebrow. But sometimes you get one of those cookbooks that has been so damn good to you in the past, you forget to listen to your sensibilities. It becomes the GPS that hurls you off a cliff.

I cranked the pot up to High and retreated back to my quarters, confident that I'd win the Potluck Crown. Susan was perched atop the sea, revising an essay. Lisa claimed the light-drenched mudroom for rearranging her poetry collection. Erin had story edits from *The Sun*. My goals were hazier.

1. Get to the house.
2. Figure out what to do now.

My Book, the memoir I'd been working on in one form or another for almost ten years, was a coming-of-age memoir in essays. It spanned from college to mid-marriage, netting all of my twenties. No one, it turned out, wanted to read about a middle-class white girl's pursuit of perfection in all things. I didn't even want to read it by the end of its prolonged, stumbling death. Like anything that gets tossed around and hoped upon and rejected enough times, you lose the will to keep hammering at it in attempts to get it right. The allure of working on something new becomes gravitational.

A rainstorm was rolling off the sea. The wind battered pellets into my window, blurring my view of the spindly pines that survived the coastline edge as I surveyed the course ahead of me. Maybe I could pull out the best essays from the memoir and submit them throughout the year, create that writer platform upon which the stuff of dreams is built. More followers, more blog posts, more credits, more appearances.

"It's too bad she isn't famous," a Big Five editor had responded to the book's submission.

I agreed. It was too bad.

I didn't have the energy even to look at the title page of my shelved book, much less to dissect its insides and harvest the tenderest morsels.

Avoiding the task at hand, I tapped into my phone instead and pressed the Twitter bluebird. I had a fraction of a service bar and one tweet, a deliciously snarky literati's review of the *Fifty Shades of Grey* movie, made its way through. I tried reading the linked story, but the page loaded for infinity. Frustrated, I tossed the phone back onto the desk.

I mentally thumbed through the New Essay File in my mind, the Rolodex of topics I considered Important and Worthy, that had to be written and submitted to places that may or may not give any shits. I'd tried to rein the essays into paragraphs and structures, but they spun out of my control. I couldn't contain a succinct thought from start to finish. The roots were snarled together, and the more desperately I clawed at the soil, the deeper they seemed to run.

I wanted a new story. Something that wasn't just me and my mess.

My foot nudged the black typewriter suitcase. My good-luck charm. The reset button.

I sat the stalling laptop on the bed and unlocked the typewriter from the base. When I was in middle school, I filled spiral notebooks with novel attempts, which were mash-ups of my favorite movie of the moment and our history class unit. There was a Revolutionary War saga slashing Benedict Arnold with *Chocolat*; a *Titanic* time-travel saga brimming with more facts I read outside of Cameron's 90s masterpiece. The sentences were not particularly great, but they looked beautiful, indented into the paper in sprawling cursive. I loved the physicality of handwriting, moving along the opalescent blue lines, feeling the impressions of what I'd last accomplished bleed ghost etchings onto the next page. The ink and wear made the notebook thicker and heavier as I moved through. The spiral books were evidence of a time when I wrote instinctually, without expectation or disappointment. When I created because I *had* to, not out of obligation.

The typewriter home keys felt like the ivory piano I played as a child—back before I ruled out music as a thing I'd ever be good at—cool and light and tethered to something mighty and unseen. Fresh paper spooled like a horizon. I knew what I wanted to start; I'd just been at a loss on how to begin.

Probably a first sentence.

I sat straight in the chair, like an ergonomic work-safety poster, and hammered out the first words: "The helicopters were always a bad sign."

The pristine blank page was suddenly a disaster.

Errant spaces gave the words knocked-out smiles. The 'A' key stuck and left ghosts where a vowel was supposed to be. I'd pounded with the same tempo and force I used every day on a keyboard, spitting out over a hundred words per minute. The typewriter keys couldn't keep up. They got stuck and tangled before they could accurately strike the paper. The brute force made the letters leap ahead of themselves.

I removed the messy page and balled it up, a most therapeutic alternative to any iteration of Delete key. I tried the same sentence again, slower, more precisely. It wouldn't get me through Peggy Olson's pre-Sterling Cooper secretary school, but it was largely legible. Through dialing back the pace, forcing myself to think about each word as its permanence tattooed on pulp, something miraculous happened. I focused. For the first time in recent memory, I forgot what time it was or where I was or what I wanted to do after I got this writing thing out of the way.

I was enjoying myself so much I almost forgot about the Moroccan Chickpea Stew, which would have been a blessed omission. It was terrible. I mean, candy gross. The syrupy dried fruit didn't want anything to do with the tomatoes, which still tasted like their cans. The Greek yogurt topping did nothing but glop it up even more, like when you are stupid enough to order Taco Bell when you're sober, and you end up biting into solid pockets of what you only hope is sour cream.

"Lunch!" I called up to the rafters, then scurried back into my room before anyone would be politely obligated to tell me it was good. I took an afternoon break and drove out to the Tillamook Cheese Factory to wash my mouth out with extra sharp cheddar.

That night, we reconvened on the dining table slab with a potluck spread of wine bottles, Susan's dinner setting on the stove. She pressed a warm, leathery card deck into my palm, an invitation to shuffle. "If you want a reading," she said.

Of course I did! Essayists are way too self-obsessed ever to pass up fortunetelling. I slid the cards between one another, forming and re-forming its familiar stack.

"Turn out the first card, whenever you feel like it's right."

I tried to focus on important things, like manifesting myself at the Powell's book podium, or my name in Association of Writers & Writing Programs Featured Presenter typeface underneath a wistful, half-smiling, black-and-white headshot. I let one card slip out like a loose Jenga piece and flipped it onto the lacquered wood.

"Oh, the ant!" she exclaimed, greeting the red insect clinging to a green spring leaf. "The ant knows how to do the work. They're born knowing what they have to do. It's an instinct; it's compulsive. It's not a question of what you need to do, because you know that. You've always known that. Right now you have to accept The Thick of It, that you're going to have to go through the process and the time to manifest what you want."

"I'm always an ant," I laughed, topping off my glass with an even-keeled Willamette Valley pinot donated by Erin. "Never a queen bee."

"But you know this guy always gets there," she pointed out. "Even when there's a roadblock or half the colony gets wiped out by Roundup. He finds his way through. It's only a matter of Doing the Things so they're ready when the rest of the world is."

Lisa, reappearing from a moonlit smoke break, called from

the kitchen, "I think your risotto's ready."

Leaving ant on the table, we crowded around the stove, spooning up some of the strangest, most perfect risotto I've ever had. The creamy rice was punctuated by sweet, salt-kissed salmon flakes, and something none of us could place.

"Cucumbers," Susan revealed. "I don't know how anyone came up with it or why it works."

But it did. In the least obvious way anyone could have foreseen or planned, salmon and cucumber risotto was outstanding. Despite my overpacking and early arrival, I didn't win best dinner. My nasty soup went in the garbage, the same place so many of my best ideas and big breaks had given up the ghost.

We lingered at the table, old plastic donated plates crusting over with our last flecks of risotto. We brought what we'd made out from our nests: Susan's essay, Lisa's poems, Erin's story, and my first chapter of a novel I'd spent months too scared to start. After all, I was an essayist. How could I transcend the genre to which I'd pledged my loyalty, the one printed on my Master of Fine Arts degree, which was non-transferrable?

"The helicopters were always a bad sign," I read from my smudgy page. The table laughed at the main character's quirks, her passive-aggressive road rage. They gasped at the right places and gave me the permission we don't always know we need.

"You need to be writing that," Susan said.

I had hauled a sizable chunk of my earthly possessions into this coast cabin, but these six words were all I needed to leave with. Too bad I still had to schlep all that shit back down the hill.

This is Susan's recipe for Cucumber Salmon Risotto, which I hesitate to recreate again because the dish she served us, out of a pan used to serve hundreds of writer covens before ours, was so exhaustively perfect. The warm bowls of creamy rice, tender salmon, and the almost imperceptible textural *je ne sais quoi* of the cucumbers rejuvenated selves we had spent the day wringing dry. I can retrace my steps all I want, but I'll never have that moment again: the gushing with new friends about the strange inspiration of an old, sturdy, poetry-haunted beach house animated by four women plotting the next turn of their writing lives.

But you weren't there. So recreate away.

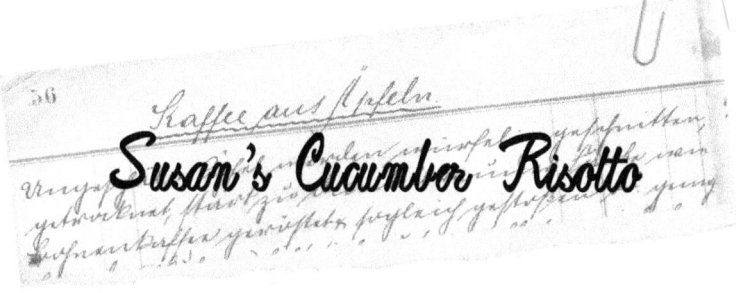

Susan's Cucumber Risotto

- o   2 tablespoons butter or olive oil
- o   1 bunch green onions, chopped
- o   ½ cucumber, peeled, seeded, and chopped
- o   1 ¾ cups Arborio rice
- o   3 ¾ cups chicken broth
- o   ⅔ cup dry white wine[*]
- o   1 pound salmon fillet, boned, skinned, and diced
- o   3 tablespoons chopped fresh tarragon
- o   Salt and pepper to taste

Heat the butter or oil in a large saucepan and add the green onions and cucumber. Sauté for 2-3 minutes, until they just begin to soften.

Add the rice and sauté to coat in oil/butter for 1 minute. It will get golden and toasty, which was the secret to why Rice-A-Roni was edible. Do you know how many boxes of Rice-A-Roni I went through in my first apartment? Enough to cause a crisis in the Great Salt Lake's reserves. I didn't even use the stovetop directions like a civilized human. I made it *in the microwave*. We all have a few filthy culinary secrets.

Add the wine and stir constantly for 1 minute, scraping up bits of onion and cucumber that may be clinging to the bottom of the pan. Add the broth and bring to a boil. Reduce heat to a simmer and let cook for 10 minutes, stirring occasionally. Add the salmon and tarragon. Cook for an additional 5 minutes.

Turn off the heat. Season with salt and pepper, and let stand for 5 minutes before serving.

---

[*] I always use chardonnay for such purposes.

Accidental Fire

*T*he pings started early in the morning. Chimes from down the hall, doorbells to nowhere.

"What the hell is up with your phone?" Matt wanted to know. I left the living room to check on my wailing Samsung.

I swiped the lock screen, and a familiar avatar filled the first tile. "Holy shit," I said.

Matt, in our house where every such utterance was easily heard, peeked his head around the corner. "Is everything okay?"

"Cheryl Strayed tweeted my essay."

"Seriously?"

Was I serious? There she was, Patron Saint of Portland Literary Arts captioned by: *Loved this essay by @tabithablanken.* Likes and retweets mushrooming up my wall.

"She read it?" Matt clarified.

"I think so."

Cheryl wasn't just any famous aspiring memoirist/hiker/ heroine played by Reese Witherspoon. She was my favorite writer, my hero, just like I wrote on my MySpace profile in 2006:

Tabitha Jensen (myspace.com/yummycheezu)
20 Years Old
Now!
Heroes: Fiona Apple. My mom and dad. Cheryl Strayed.

Before Oprah had Cheryl's phone number, or a word of *Wild* existed, my college sophomore English professor assigned us reading from *Best American Essays 2003:* a selection titled, "The Love of My Life," originally published in *The Sun,* about a young woman flailing through her grief and using her body to exonerate the agony of losing her mother to aggressive, relentless cancer. I don't know what actually drew me in to read that particular assignment. I was a charlatan English major who could whip up a frothy, meatless but authoritative-sounding paper from nothing but *Spark Notes* and a couple tangents about existentialism. These were the essential skills that delivered me into my day-job life: corporate copywriting.

But I did read "The Love of My Life." I read it, alone in my Concordia University double dorm room, nestled into the couch bed, which was extra furniture issued by the college for a roommate I did not have. I covered the second extra-long, twin-sized bed in old comforters and hand-me-down pillows. It was set to the bottom rung. No loft. Easy access.

My first two years of college were a mess of mistaking validation for liberation, of using terrible templates as road maps for whom I wanted to be (Samantha from *Sex and the City!* End-of-*Grease* Sandy!). All of high school I'd spent as the best-friend sidekick, the Model United Nations representative, the girl who never had to flex any of her D.A.R.E.-program anti-drug moves because no one offered me a thing. But it was all good, I told myself. Because there was a time and a place for everything. And that was college. If I could make it there, I could experience all the things 90s movies promised.

Except for one tiny problem.

I didn't end up at a kegger college. Or a hookup college. Or even a serious-academics-but-hard-weekend liberal arts college. I was, thanks to some good scholarships and my spectacular lack of foresight into my needs, at a miniature private Christian college. I was in the middle of the two poles: partying jocks on a free ride for soccer skills, or Christian Education and Seminary majors pairing off like penguins for life in the church.

I was lonely. But even worse, I was desperate. I reeked of it. As the first weeks of school cemented into permanent best friendships and prayer circles, I didn't fall into place. So I did what any well-adjusted, self-fulfilled person would do: I grabbed the closest stock-personality trope — sexy bad girl — and padded it into armor. I was trying so hard to be fun and sexy, I was more puppet than human being. I had to get a job? Lingerie salesgirl! I needed wall décor? Elvgren vintage pinups! I wanted a little Christmas tree? Cover it in corset ornaments! You don't like me, little Christian college? Well fuck that, I hated you first.

The thing was, this wasn't my college dream. This wasn't what I wanted college to be, whom I wanted to be. I wanted to be a full person with new clusters of friends and the cozy nook of a boyfriend who wasn't mine forever, but long enough to leave a moment of a memory. I wanted movie binges and all the sex I didn't have in high school. I wanted to meet my future bridesmaids. I wanted the milestone of a breakup. I wanted to love enough to be lost. But I didn't know how to get there.

Like some kind of Match.com spider's lair, I spun the anonymous men of Portland up to my Lutheran university corner. The men I saw were older. Much older. I think the top of the range was 50 to my 19. I met that senior at Milo's City Café on Broadway, one of the only brunch places in Portland before they became as ubiquitous as Starbuckses, back when boysenberry compote was really freaking fancy. I remember he was wearing a floppy khaki baseball hat embroidered with a largemouth bass. It was like sad Dockers upcycling.

"I'm really into Pink Floyd right now," I said, my breath spiced with clove cigarette. "I've been listening to his CD non-stop."

"I saw them live in the 70s," he said.

"Wow, really? I didn't even know if he was still alive or not!"

"You do know they were a whole band, right?"

That was all we said to one another before digging into our pancakes in shame and then parting ways for eternity.

Most of the men were in their thirties. There was Dave, the stand-up comedian who claimed that Carrot Top stole his bits; Nathaniel, who sang with the Portland Opera Chorus and ended his breakup email with, "Just in case you were still planning to come to the show next weekend, I had to give your comp ticket to my mom's friend"; and Oliver, the Cirque du Soleil acrobat.

Each relationship, to stretch the word, followed the same storyline. We'd see each other four or five times over a month. We'd eat out at chain restaurants, the choice dictated by coupons. I'd humblebrag about selling lingerie for minimum wage. We'd have sex next to dorm walls with the structural integrity of phyllo dough. That's when things would get weird. Red flags crept from the corners, like the fact that we could never go to a bar, or that I'd have to hide in the car when they went into Safeway to buy wine. They'd start to notice how I was biologically young enough to be their daughter. When they got past all the artifice of being hot and wild and young, the truth behind my living 900-number-ad act glared. I was just a girl. A needy, ridiculous, empty girl. So they ran.

The disappearance of these men from my life only made me chase harder. I started trolling chat rooms for random hookups. I'd go visit my then-best friend Claire at Evergreen State College in Olympia, whose doomed friendship with me would eventually inspire my novel, and I would drink until someone agreed to come to bed with me.

It was after just such a weekend that my lit class was assigned reading from *The Best American Essays 2003*. Up north at Evergreen, I screwed a grad student who'd just broken up with his girlfriend. Their dissolution was a devastating blow to everyone in Claire's circle, as they were the most super-serious couple on the heavily forested campus.

"They had a handfasting ceremony and everything," she explained.

Claire and her boyfriend, Micah, were outside most of the night, smoking cigarettes and joints from weed they were trying to grow on the garden patio, too impatient to let the leaves actually dry. The man (Dave? Scott? Tom? Your guess is as good as mine.) kept nestling closer to me on the couch as I continued to empty tumbler after tumbler of orange juice and vodka.

"You would feel so much better after my day," he said.

I liked to be needed. "I can't sleep with you," I said.

"Why?"

"Because I only met you today, and I don't sleep with men the same day I meet them!" It was a random, untested, and ungrounded principle, like something Carrie Bradshaw or Cher Horowitz would irrationally stick to in order to advance a plot point.

But his hand was already far beyond my bra, and I didn't know the next time I'd have a guy on board. Days? Weeks? "Hey, look at the clock!"

"Huh?"

"It's after midnight! I didn't meet you today anymore!"

Too early and without saying goodbye, I rolled out of the spare-room bed we'd hijacked. I drove three hours back to Portland with Modest Mouse blaring in my minivan, trying to untangle what was wrong. Casual sex was supposed to make me feel powerful. It was supposed to set me free from the smalltown nothingness of my youth. It always had before. I didn't need someone to love me forever, but these men didn't even *like* me.

I knew, even wasted, even 19 and stupid, that I wasn't special to the man. I was merely there. The biggest reason I bolted so early wasn't to get a jump on nonexistent Sunday morning Olympia-to-Portland traffic; it was upper-hand rejection. I knew he wasn't going to beg Micah for my number or dig around for my email. And compared to the assholes standing me up and letting me down on the Match.com trial I kept renewing, he was a stand-up gentleman. At least he wasn't kicking me out of his house in the morning without coffee or time to find my missing bra because he didn't want to be late for spin class.

My tears fell onto the minivan's Hello Kitty steering wheel cover, mixing with the grime from my learning-to-drive, sweaty high school palms. I was so tired. Tired of being lonely, of pretending I didn't care how people treated me, of being a make-believe hard-ass. *What if this never ended?* I wondered. *What, then?* Modest Mouse, my favorite band, remained preciously upbeat, even in their album of dirges.

Good News for People Who Love Bad News was so clearly a collection about demise and the afterlife, it could have been just as easily titled *Modest Mouse and the Existential Fear of Death*. If song titles like, "The Good Times Are Killing Me," "Dig Your Grave," and "Satin in a Coffin," weren't clear enough, there's the subtle lyrics like:

Your body may be gone, I'm gonna carry you in.
In my head, in my heart, in my soul.
And maybe we'll get lucky and we'll both live again.
Well, I don't know. I don't know. I don't know. Don't think so.

But I didn't actually listen. And I didn't read. I drifted, the manufactured melancholy feeling like the appropriate chords for my listless days. I was too distracted weaving chaos as an alternative to nothing; I didn't realize that I was grieving my slipping self. My loneliness was poisoning me.

Back in my dorm room, on a quiet school night, I propped myself up with my generous couch-bed pillow stash. I'd spent the summer before collecting pillows from garage sales and clearance racks, going for Beyoncé's Destiny's Child-era *MTV Cribs* genie bed effect. It was much more comfortable for reading than for screwing random people.

I did not deny, Strayed wrote. *I did not get angry. I didn't bargain, become depressed, or accept. I fucked. I sucked. Not my husband, but people I hardly knew, and in that I found a glimmer of relief.*

"The Love of My Life" swallowed me whole. It was not the dry, lifeless classical canon my white male professors built their syllabi around. *The Scarlet Letter, Lord of the Flies, Macbeth*. For the first time since declaring English as my major (mostly because of a lack of any other decent contenders), I was captivated. I was opened. I read it through twice, lingering on the last paragraph for an hour: *Healing is a small and ordinary and very burnt thing. And it's one thing and one thing only: it's doing what you have to do.*

I didn't know yet what I had to do. It was a suggestion calling out to a version of myself not yet formed, an apparition of the future shouting at me from the other side of a chasm. Her essay didn't prescribe a way to fix my life. It did not answer a question. It clarified the gnarl inside of me. *I thought about how I was never again going to sleep with anyone who had a title instead of a name*, she wrote. *I was sick of it. Sick of fucking, of wanting to fuck the wrong people and not wanting to fuck the right ones.*

I folded myself up as tight as my limbs would compress. I wept into my knees. I cried until my eyes were too chapped and dry for tears, but the emotion kept ebbing back up in heaves from my stomach. I was exhausted, but I wasn't alone. My agony had been felt by someone else, someone who was able to distill it down into its purest, most potent form. When I did not know how to speak, her voice had all the words.

I woke up the next morning on top of *The Best American Essays 2003* with a throbbing post-hysterical-sobbing hangover. My head hurt. I was dizzy. The muscles in my arm were sore from twisting into a broken pretzel for hours. But I also felt cleared, like the day after Christmas, when you unhook the wreath and tear down the lights and wrap all the precious glass balls in tissue. Nothing but walls and bare shelves and indents in the carpet where a gigantic tree was blocking the living room. There was a clarity bridging that fracture between who I was and who I was going to be: a single strand I could scarcely see but knew was there, entwined between my fingers, tugging toward a destiny I spent years avoiding head-on. I knew that morning that if I was able to become a writer, I needed to make people feel the way that essay made me feel.

I needed to repay the debt to this brilliant, incredible stranger. She'd saved my life. She was, in my heart and MySpace page, my hero.

After class on the day our *Best American* readings were due, I tried to explain to my professor, one of the only women who taught me during my conservative college education, how much her assignment meant to me.

"I've never read anything that felt this true," I said. I grew up in a book house—my mom read to me until I was practically in high school, and even after I crossed that threshold, I'd lurk outside my little brother's bedroom and listen to her read Harry Potter in her even Enya-song of a voice. I earned my first rejection at age ten, when I slipped a homemade picture book into a manila envelope postmarked to Scholastic, the address for which I found inside *Clifford the Big Red Dog*. The book was returned with a form letter explaining that they didn't accept unsolicited manuscripts, and that Tacoma, Washington, was running short on literary agents willing to represent second graders.

"You should tell her how much her essay meant to you," my wise instructor told me. "You know she lives in Portland, right?"

I did not know Cheryl Strayed lived in Portland. I had no idea she could have been sitting next to me on the MAX train at any moment, her pulsating genius camouflaged in mere mortal form.

"Writers like to be told that their work matters," she pressed, and, as if hearing the panic in my pulse, she added, "I promise."

That night back in my dorm room, I wrote my fan letter—in the old Hotmail interface that defaulted to Courier font. A few days later, a reply manifested in my inbox, warmly thanking me for writing and cheering our class' inclusion of *The Best American Essays* work. Probably three sentences, but sometimes that's all it takes to change a world.

In the next decade of my life, I put a face to the name (when I ambushed her at Powell's Books during her debut novel *Torch's* release in 2007, and word-vomited all over the signing table: "You emailed me in college, and you're my hero on MySpace!"). I saw her at a conference on the Oregon Coast and a house salon on Portland's Belmont Street. I skirted the edge of her widening shadow, watching from the margins as she catapulted from Local Author I Loved, to Household Name Played by Reese Witherspoon.

The girl I was hiding on the couch-bed could only dream that someday her favorite writer would read the words she, herself, had strung together. Now, not only had Cheryl read my essay about joining Weight Watchers for the third time, she'd found it worthy of recommending to her thousands of followers.

I can't believe this is real life! I emailed my best friends alongside a screenshot.

You need to query this, my friend, Sharon, wrote back almost instantly. *I think this is your book.*

Her immediate confidence caught in my throat. The essay had been my first pinky toe back in nonfiction for several months since the beach house retreat. I'd built myself a tall, luxurious fort out of the explanation, "I'm working on a novel." I switched to fiction to explore a story that was unresolved in my real life: the friendship with Claire I had from middle school to college that ended in a giant blowout fight. One phone call, and the closest relationship, my best friend for so many years, was gone. I tried coming at the story from all kinds of memoir angles, but it was a bottle-rocket. I aimed it one direction and off it went, veering aside to set a house on fire, or worse, never leaving my hand, then exploding and making a royal mess of my palm. Putting it into fiction was supposed to be my chance to stand back a safe distance to examine a breakup I would never resolve in my real life.

And best of all, this book like nothing I'd attempted before. Like nothing I'd already failed at.

Sharon's confidence was an itch tapping into the most anxious, impulsive nerves of my soul: the pathological fear of missing out. My head swelled with a hodgepodge of platitudes.

Strike while the iron's hot!

Opportunity is not a lengthy visitor!

Take a leap and grow your wings on the way down!

The inspirational bookmark phrases pinpricked my resolve to focus in one direction, or in this particular case, to repeat a catastrophic failure. Wouldn't it look really great to approach those fancy New Yorkers while my work was maybe being whispered about? And what if I just queried a couple of them, a few dream shots, for practice?

The more my phone pinged, the firmer the notion set. This was my big break. Let it pass or dive on board—that was up to me.

"I need to write the best query letter of all time," my inner Kanye West announced.

"Is your novel done already?" asked Matt.

I'd barely been back from the coast for a month, and the last 30 days weren't exactly a NaNoWriMo-style bender. "No. I think this essay's supposed to be a book."

"I thought you were giving up on memoir."

"I never said I was 'giving up.'" This was why I didn't talk about writing projects at home. My technical engineer husband's mind divided and conquered in flow charts and formulas. My tangents and switchbacks shorted his circuits. We had an open marriage—I fucked around with art, and he knew better than to ask questions.

"Well, then. Awesome!" He sat on the couch and watched the screen where a roomful of chefs opened baskets of sadistic garbage ingredients.

"You're okay with dinner late?"

He lifted a bottle of Ninkasi Total Domination IPA. *Don't worry about me. The fridge is full of beer*, it meant.

The first time I went after an agent, high on post-MFA

graduate endorphins ("Everyone's going to want me! I was the COMMENCEMENT SPEAKER!"), I carpet-bombed Manhattan. This time I was after a select four, each representing one of my favorite writers who'd published the style of book I imagined sharing my Amazon 'Customers Who Bought This Item Also Bought' reel.

"Can you read this?" I called to Matt from my office. This was unheard of. Not since my nerves over grad school applications had I asked for a second eye.

Matt scrolled through the page, pausing to laugh at me halfway through. "Be sure to take note of how much Cheryl Strayed likes my essay," he paraphrased.

"You have to namedrop!" I said. "Do you know how many of these they get a day?"

"I'm kidding. You have no reason not to be proud of yourself," he said in his quiet, I'm-sorry-I-know-this-is-the-most-important-thing-to-you voice. "Besides, you waited until paragraph three to bring it up."

"See? I'm a classy broad like that."

"Who are you sending it to?"

"Just four this time, to see if it actually has a shot."

"Well, then. I say go."

I sat down, brought the page back up to the top. Read it again three times.

"Have you sent it yet?" Matt called from the living room.

I double-checked the email address. Okay, quadruple-checked. Melissa Fredericks of Fredericks & McCullough. I'd read interviews she'd done with independent presses, earning the gritty Brooklyn pedigree I adored so hard from afar. She was repping Twitter stars and musicians, and most importantly, another writer who'd published her own body image battle stories. She was my first recipient, my number one choice.

"It can take, like, three months to hear back from anyone," I announced to everything and nothing in the living room.

"So you can just enjoy what you accomplished today, then," Matt replied.

I should have been breaking into the best wine we owned in our mini-fridge cellar, giving extravagant toasts about how, if only that little slutty Lutheran school girl could see me now, with our hero taking 20 minutes between texting Reese Witherspoon and Oprah to read my story. I should've dug out my glitter-crusted stilettos from the closet and paraded around our cul-de-sac, telling the inevitable smalltown cops that, "I've had the best Twitter day of my life!"

I should have rooted down into this single perfect moment and cried and sang and screamed for joy. And I did—for a minute or two.

Until my gaze wandered back to my quiet, blank phone. I double-checked the outbox. Sent.

Ping, my heart nudged. *Please. Ping.*

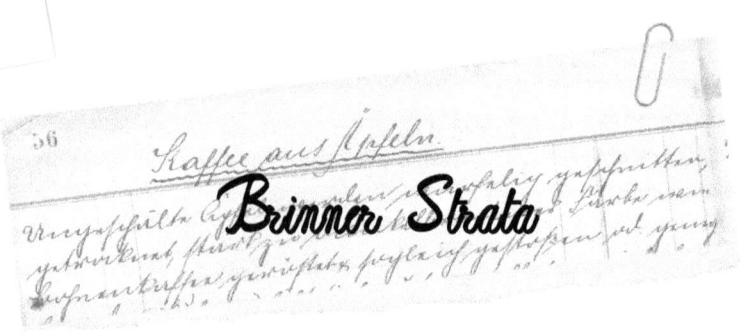

Brunch Strata

*M*y home is what you might call 'borderline nowhere.' Hubbard is technically a town about 30 miles south of Portland, but if you ask anyone in the city if they know where it is, you will get blank stares and uncomfortable pauses. The suburbs are Portlandia Chernobyl, an uninhabitable wasteland of chain restaurants and gluten-laced cupcakes.

Unfortunately, Hubbard doesn't even have the benefit of a Buffalo Wild Wings or P. F. Chang's to bring it down. Our fair city has two gas stations, two stoplights, a tavern that reeks so bad of half a century's worth of fryer oil that I can't ride my bike past it without gagging, and a church that keeps re-purchasing an ABORTION: A LIFETIME OF REGRET banner, no matter how many times someone spraypaints a mustache on the stock photo of the teen hanging her head in eternal shame.

There is no takeout in Hubbard. Pizza Hut in the town over will swing by with boxes of beautiful, salty grease, but there is no pad thai, no bánh mì sandwiches, not even a grocery store to pick up an abhorrent crate of Stouffer's frozen lasagna.

So when I have a night where inspiration is pecking at me, or I'm a week behind in writing emails, or I promised I'd have that review sent over by a very generous Pacific-time end-of-day, it's nice to have a few recipes that are low-maintenance and flexible. Panini and other grilled sandwiches are good for this, as are random burritos and enchiladas. But when it comes to a dish that takes a few scant minutes of prep, soaks up whatever is lurking around the refrigerator, and cooks long enough for me to get a few paragraphs in before serving, there's nothing like a breakfast-for-dinner strata. In fact, as I type, an eggy bread pudding is plumping up in my oven.

- o   2 cups 2% or whole milk
- o   6 eggs
- o   4 pieces of bacon, cooked and sliced
- o   4-oz log of goat cheese (or ½ cup feta cheese)
- o   4 cups stale bread
- o   1 large leek, thoroughly cleaned and sliced

- o   2 chicken sausages, sliced*
- o   2 cups shredded Dubliner, Cougar Gold, Extra Sharp Cheddar, or whatever other hard, sharp cheese you prefer
- o   ½ cup Peppadew peppers, quartered
- o   ⅓ cup sliced fresh herbs (basil, flat-leaf parsley, and whatever else is still alive in your garden)
- o   ⅓ cup shredded Pecorino Romano
- o   Olive oil
- o   Vegetable oil
- o   Salt and pepper

Preheat oven to 350° F. Toss the stale bread in a tablespoon of olive oil with salt and pepper to taste, then spread on a baking sheet. Bake for 15 minutes, until bread has become crouton-like. Remove from oven and cool slightly. Reduce temperature in oven to 325° F.

If you're in a real hurry to tear into a project, you could use store-bought croutons instead of making your own. But are you even going to get done picking the right writing music playlist in 15 minutes? I think not. Unless you know the answer to "What should I write to?" is always "A Max Richter soundtrack, preferably *The Leftovers*." Then by all means, crouton on.

Add a tablespoon of vegetable oil to a cast iron skillet. Heat on medium-high then add the leeks and sauté until soft and browning, 5 to 7 minutes. You can add in any other vegetables you may want to include that need a little precooking, like mushrooms, onions, broccoli, rainbow chard, what have you. Remove the vegetables from the skillet.

In a large mixing bowl, whisk the eggs, milk, salt, and pepper until well combined. Stir in the toasted bread and all remaining ingredients except for the Pecorino Romano. If you're using a cast iron skillet, pour the entirety of the strata into the skillet. Otherwise, pour all ingredients into a Pyrex dish oiled with a dash of olive oil. Sprinkle with Pecorino Romano cheese and place on a baking sheet (to catch eggy cheese oozes), then bake for 20 minutes. Go get a few sentences in. STAY OFF TWITTER! There is nothing in your feed but existential terror and sadness.

After 20 minutes, turn the strata 180 degrees. While wearing oven mitts, preferably. Bake for another 30-40 minutes until the strata is vigorously bubbling and the cheese and top bread chunks are browning. Allow to cool for 10 minutes before slicing and serving with your favorite hot sauce. Go ahead, take a bowl into your office with you. Shut the door. Lock it. Blast "Last Days" by Max Richter until the outside world disappears.

---

* Alternatively, you can use ham, leftover cooked bulk sausage, cubed steak, or hearty sautéed mushrooms.

No One Throws Dinner Parties Anymore

*D*ressing up for dinner is one of my most treasured life rituals. Stripping away whatever it was you spent the day in, whether yoga pants and a sweatshirt for running errands or a tidy skirt and blouse from the office. Shedding that skin for an alternate life in a dress that doesn't get a lot of play outside of its dry cleaning bag cocoon. A Clark Kent spin from workaday routine.

There's a reawakening that happens when you get ready at twilight, when you're fully conscious and caffeinated. The extra time you take to make sure your hair curls the right direction and your eyeliner ticks out in a neat tapered line. The consideration of which nylons and shoes work best together, examined with all the lights on, eyes open. Without the out-the-door shove from the shower and toothpaste, the smell of perfume and pressed foundation powder lingers. You emerge as a reconsidered self. You feel bound for something special.

It's when you reach your destination and the atmosphere crackles with warmth and a tinge of anticipation, as if this place has been waiting for your arrival, a force of personable service that makes it possible to believe that this table, this menu, this restaurant exists for this shiniest version of yourself. As the Ritz-Carlton in a Tucson resort fortress made me feel on my 30th birthday, seating us at the kitchen's entrance with a pair of menus titled, "Happy 30th Birthday, Tabitha!" waiting for us. Or L'Auberge in Sedona with one of my best friends, where we were led to a table in the shade of the only creek I ever saw in Arizona. A sight for eyes so sore, I almost smudged my mascara. The manufactured banks of Disneyland's Blue Bayou, waving as boatloads of tourists meander out to the high seas underneath a constellation of Chinese garden party lanterns.

And then, if it is the most welcoming, ethereal place, and your waiter—who seems to get you so well that you want to slip him your number, just to hang out and be the best friends you were always destined to be—comes back from the kitchen and bar and pâtisserie with plates of transcendent, maybe-I-should-die-right-now-so-nothing-else-touches-my-tasebuds-again   edible poetry, well. Everything around you lilts into a higher state of being. A casual conversation becomes the most illuminating exchange you've had with another human. The name of the wine you're drinking must be carefully noted, so you can track it down and stock up by the caseful. The check seems inconsequential, even if you need to take out the 'emergency' credit card to cover it confidently, because how can you pass up a night like this one?

A night feeling fed.

A night feeling seen.

A night cared for.

You often get fragments of perfection. A masterfully designed space overlooking the city, with a staff so put-up, you feel the need to apologize for intruding into their precious space. I've been to an otherworldly restaurant carved into the side of a canyon, with the sweetest waitress you could cast, where I was served food that looked ready for its *Bon Appétit* closeup. Microgreens arranged by tweezers, gastrique painted by pipette. It tasted like magazine paper.

The place, the service, the food, yourself. Either they culminate, or they don't. Less can be nice, but all is ecstasy.

My first truly memorable dinner out was in 8th grade. That was 1999, if you're counting. Tamagotchis hung from our keychains, the Spice Girls were a plucky new upstart, and I saw *Titanic* 13 times in the theater. And in the few waking hours I wasn't absorbing James Cameron's disaster porn (or making my own by killing that poor Tamagotchi), I was obsessing over all things related to the British oceanliner. I watched movies featuring the heartbreaking leads, including *Quills* with Kate Winslet, where Geoffrey Rush plays the Marquis de Sade and smears poop all over his walls. I checked out every book in the library and any volumes our smalltown branch could import from Tacoma. Old tomes encased in textured blues and reds, only thin gold lettering along the spines serving for titles, pages smelling like a church basement book sale. I memorized the dates and times like they were secret admission requirements to a date with Leonardo DiCaprio:

April 10th, 1912: The *Titanic* sets sail from Southampton!

April 14th, 1912: The crew receives a series of iceberg warnings, all willfully discarded!

April 15th, 1912: The *Titanic* radios for help that never arrives!

I was a walking encyclopedia on the lives of Maggie "Molly" Brown, John Jacob Astor, and Isidor Straus. I could point out each of the film's instances of historical accuracy (the automobile in the cargo hold) and deviation (the incorrect welding techniques used on the reproduction ship's propellers).

When I ran out of source material (After all, there's only so much you can learn about a ship that sailed for five days, if you can even count that last day), I clawed for anything tangential. *Entertainment Weekly* featurettes, J. Peterman's Kate Winslet-inspired costume collection, and on one particular library afternoon, the *Last Dinner on the Titanic* cookbook.

"That seems awfully morbid," my mom commented, while I hunched in the minivan front seat, reading the hundred steps to make consommé. This was my mom's response to all my Titanic absorption. Writing fan fiction novellas about a bunch of dead people you wish you were around to meet is awfully morbid, Tabitha. Making a homemade room number placard for your bedroom in honor of a cabin that's at the bottom of the Atlantic Ocean is awfully morbid, Tabitha. Wanting to eat the last meals of ill-fated steerage immigrants is awfully morbid, Tabitha.

In between the book's menus arranged by passenger class were entertainment tips to help bring the pomp and privilege of Victorian travel to your living room. Or at least, someone's living room. One that is lightyears away from my tax bracket.

Do not try to prepare the menu by yourself. Enlist a minimum of one sous-chef and a dishwasher to help you through the day and night.

Unless there's a trumpet player in your immediate circle, announce dinner with the ringing of a gong.

Follow the common Victorian and Edwardian custom of dividing the gentlemen and the ladies, the former repairing to a room or porch you've designated as the smoking room for cigars and port, the latter to your reception room for coffee.

Reading the book now makes me want to launch into a tweet-storm, culminated with video as I pitch the copy into our patio chimenea. The patio that is not, I'm afraid, exclusively reserved for the men and their cigars. But at 14, I was foaming at the mouth with the pretentious possibilities.

"Can I throw a dinner party?" I asked. Maybe we could rent some reproduction first-class china, get a string quartet to play. My dad could wear a tie and play the waiter.

Mom snorted in that pure, involuntary way that only escapes when your flesh and blood says something uproariously stupid. "Who has dinner parties anymore?" she asked. "Who would come over?"

All the people I've still yet to meet in life who want to design period costumes and nosh on aspic. The same nonexistent clique that stages elaborate mystery dinners and steampunk squads. I knew my mom was right. I let *Last Dinner on the Titanic* slip through the library return slot, to be discovered by fancy people in dramatic circles.

A few weeks later, a postcard arrived from the Four Seasons Hotel in downtown Seattle. They were teaming up with their Fifth Avenue Theater neighbor to bring Washingtonians dinner and a show—specifically, *Titanic: The Musical, complete with* recreation of the first class' last dinner to be served in the hotel's opulent Georgian Room, a turn-of-the-century time capsule tucked into the city's heart.

I rallied Natalie, my closest (and frankly, only) friend into a lobbying campaign. She lived up the hill from my backyard, and we shared a talent for thinking too big for our hometown, a condition exacerbated by our shared love of watching *Daria*. We were theater kids bound for a football high school—she a future lawyer, me a someday-writer, both of us dreaming of being sent away to a stuffy boarding school in downtown Seattle that could better understand us. In the next few years, I'd establish myself in the small arty, aspirational cliques of AP classmates and band kids. Natalie would assimilate into The Beautiful People and join the cheer squad and wouldn't speak to me again until we were long past grown up.

But when our eighth-grade selves pored over the postcard invitation in her basement, musing over what a 'spring pea portage' could be, we were united by our mission: a jailbreak. A pre-adult, pre-boyfriend date with our fabulous selves. We craved a taste of the lives we were so sure we could start if only we could get out of the deadend logging town with a main street that's still recognizable from its original 1800s settler portrait.

Pestering two sets of parents was much more effective than the lone-wolf strategy. Playing off our parents' sympathy that we really only had each other, and the fact that they probably wouldn't have to pay for prom dresses down the line, eroded their no-way defenses like so many glaciers. "But Natalie said she could go!" "Don't make Tabitha go alone!"

"This is a fancier dinner than I've been taken out for in years," my mom complained after booking our Four Seasons reservation over the phone.

"You don't even like *Titanic*," I reminded her.

"That doesn't mean I don't like lobster at the Four Seasons," she said. I wanted to remind her how awfully morbid the whole affair would be, but she held the tickets, the car keys, and the costume jewelry I so wanted to wear.

At 14, I didn't have a wardrobe. I had half a closet crammed with snow pants, fleece pullovers, and Daisy Kingdom Easter dresses from the years I still believed in a bunny leaving me baskets. Full disclosure: I didn't falter in my belief in Santa Claus, the Easter Bunny, and the Tooth Fairy until I was 12 and my parents sat me down with the truth. I watched a lot of Christmas movies trumping the power of believing, okay?

I didn't have occasions for fashion and no inherent sense of style. I loved clothes when I was a kid—I spent hours tearing through my Dress-Up Box (basically my mom's Goodwill donation bag), always hoping I'd find some new, secret dress or hat at the bottom. I dumped out my Barbies just to dress them up and admire the tiny, dainty details of their princess gowns and plastic heels. I wore my Snow White Halloween costume so much my mom had to steal it in the night just to sneak it into the washing machine. But that was before I was 11 and got my first fashion police citation.

Just like any other afternoon, I'd bridged the crosswalk to start my walk home from school. Mom was waiting for me in our minivan in the adjacent parking lot, which was strange. She wouldn't chauffeur me the few short blocks home unless I had a dentist appointment scheduled or it was pouring rain. I took the passenger seat, and asked what was up.

"I thought we could go shopping together," she said, turning onto the main road that led to Sea-Tac Mall. This was our last year living in northeast Tacoma, right on the border with Federal Way, a suburb bursting at the seams with cheap apartments, clapped-together houses, and gaudy strip malls.

"For what?" Our big back-to-school shopping trip at the Nordstrom Anniversary Sale had already come and gone. I'd picked out bubble gum-colored tennis shoes (chosen because I thought the box was cool), a deafening sunflower print vest, stiff new jeans that cleared my belly button—what else did I need?

Mom bit her lip and drew in a short breath, a nervous tic I rarely saw. I was an especially easy-going kid, the one who rarely needed a talking-to. I ran through my day: the hour in the computer lab coaxing a wagon toward Oregon, the scheming I'd done with my friends to stage a school play. Where had I stirred up trouble? The Aerostar, still so new we weren't allowed to eat snacks in it, now felt like a trap. How cunning, snatching me up from my walk—no running ahead or pretending I couldn't hear her now.

"I got a call from your teacher today," she admitted. "Ms. Bye said she heard some of the boys teasing you at school," Mom said slowly, picking each word with a kind of precision I imagine parents employ when they're desperate to avoid deep scarring, future therapy sessions, or family memoir.

I shook my head. No, I told her, no one had said anything to me. It was all routine on the playground: looked at the swings line, decided against waiting. Watched nimble girls skate across the monkey bars with an ease I knew I lacked with my arm strength, and then sat down by the tree with my little circle of girlfriends to compare notes on our American Girls dolls. There was no boy heckling to be had.

"She said she overheard them in the hallway," she explained. "They were talking about how, um, your ... well." Each syllable was a stumble, the blow impossible to cushion. "They could see through your shirt. To your chest." Mom turned to look at me, avoiding anything below my jawline. "Ms. Bye wants me to get you a bra."

The humiliation of her words scorched me from the inside out. I felt a betrayal I couldn't articulate, but that flustered and burned itself permanently in my mind. I hated that my teacher, a plump woman with cat-eye glasses whom I'd mistaken for an ally, had pinned the problem on me. In her eyes, I was the issue, not the creepy boys. Their moms weren't getting phone calls. Just me and my out-of-control prepubescent C-cups. And how stupid was I, I thought, letting the guys get the drop on me? My breasts were right there, hanging in the mirror since summer. If I weren't such an idiot, I would have marched up to Mom myself and asked for a bra. It was like knocking out a tooth and never bothering to visit the dentist. No self-pride. I sank back into my seat and felt like a revolting, oblivious fool.

Mom tried her best to remedy the mood and cheer me up. She took me into Victoria's Secret, with its lovely pink walls and satin tables, and offered to buy me any bra in the store. I couldn't play along with celebrating my chest with satin prints and lace inlays. The vivid raspberry and turquoise Very Sexy Push-Ups were exactly the lovely little treasures I'd dreamed of growing up and collecting as an alternate, unseen wardrobe, an extra layer of beautiful, but I was too busy pitying myself to notice. All the other girls in my class were still girls—little girls, girls who could run around the playground and smack a dodgeball and pirouette down a hopscotch without their bodies betraying them. I wondered what exactly the boys had said. Was I ugly, frumpy, gross? And which dirty, rotten bastards of the bunch had turned against me?

A salesgirl heartily recommended an unpadded Angels bra in white with scalloped petals up the band, and I tried it on without once looking in the mirror. I could get the snappy bands to meet below my shoulder blades; that was good enough for me. I answered all of Mom's questions with the easiest answers to push us out of the mall as fast as possible. Yes, it fit. No, I didn't want another color. Yes, we can get it and *go*. I wanted to make my whole body disappear, never to be the topic of lewd conversation that riled school administrators again. The salesgirl took extra time at the cashier to wrap the bra with the logo sticker seal; a coquettish *VS* in gold foil. She tucked extra pink paper at the top to look like an enticing bridal shower gift.

"I've never helped someone get her very first bra before," she said with a sweet-natured giggle. "So exciting!"

Twenty minutes later, all the poufy packaging was in the kitchen trash, soaking up banana ooze and cold tomato soup.

That day marked my new obsession with ginormous T-shirts. The more shapeless, the better. I picked Adidas as my brand of choice (The logo offered more coverage than the Nike swoosh.) and selected the tees two sizes too big from the racks.

I remember picking out one of my signature shirts at JCPenney after Christmas. Mom and I were returning a knit fuchsia sweater with teddy bears playing piano intricately portrayed in the cut-rate, itchy wool—the kind of gift you receive at age 13 that makes you realize your grandmother doesn't know you at all. I had a $15 in-store credit at my bidding. I went straight for the place somewhere between swimsuits and running sneakers that can only be described as Unisex Activewear. I saw what I wanted hanging on the wall. Labeled "shirt," it more closely resembled a tunic. A black, long-sleeved, knee-length tee with a big white ADIDAS that would mask any chest that might be burgeoning. I bought it that day and wore it to tatters, loving its extra bonus feature: full ass coverage, as well. I wasn't sure how I felt about my flat butt, but it was best kept under wraps until I figured it out.

It wasn't that I 'liked' this look. I simply didn't see any other option. I wanted to be feminine and detailed, like Reese Witherspoon with her *Pleasantville* midcentury sweaters, or Nicole Kidman's *Moulin Rouge!* sequined corsets. But these bland, shapeless clothes were the only way I knew to be unseen by the hostile students around me who could sniff out insecurity like sharks. Fashion statements would be heard and blow my cover. I couldn't be whom I wanted to be when I was too busy surviving.

By the time I started planning the Titanic affair, I still didn't have my ass figured out. I still don't, really. What are you supposed to do with a flat German butt? It's as one-dimensional as a pounded schnitzel cutlet.

But ~~even Rihanna~~ anyone but Rihanna would be a joke wearing durable casuals into the Four Seasons' opulent Edwardian dining salon. My sights shifted to my mom's closet, filled with a lifetime's worth of workwear, wedding dresses, and funeral frocks. Already at 14 I was too broad-shouldered and chest-heavy to fit into my favorites, the Jessica McClintock 1970s pioneer dress (which looked like Laura Ingalls Wilder's on the cover of *Little Town on the Prairie*) or the silk kimono-style smoking jacket. My fashionista newlywed mother was an eternally-out-of-my-reach size six. I was a much better match to modern-day (late 90s) Mom and her beaded Nordstrom cocktail dress. You know the one. It's made by Adrianna Papell? You tried it on once but went with the Betsey Johnson babydoll instead. Knee-length, paisley seeded-bead swirls, a little cap-sleeve action on the side?

Mom's navy version, with a costume jewelry cubic zirconia choker my hoarder Great Aunt Eva left behind amongst 50 years of *Ideals Magazine*, was the closest approximation I could cobble together to Kate Winslet's wardrobe. A Heart of the Ocean homage, if you will.

I don't have a picture from that night. It was, after all, 1999, and our family Fuji camera was high on the coat closet shelf, strapped into its leather case like a straightjacket. I wouldn't get my own point-and-shoot until my next birthday. There's no evidence of Natalie and me hugging at the Four Seasons entrance, framed by two-story stone columns and floor-to-ceiling Palladian windows that look out onto the whole wide, shifting, humming world of the greatest city on Earth. We didn't take selfies with our *Titanic: The Musical* playbills. As Old Rose would say, that night "exists now, only in my memory."

It's been 17 years—I've had thousands of meals since. I've cycled through sizes and styles, and my old friendship with Natalie is more of a footnote than a story now. I remember how secluded and otherworldly The Georgian felt. I can't imagine that we were the only people in the restaurant before the touring cast sang some extremely forgettable showtunes atop a bloated sinking ship set. But the plush booths were deep and shaded by towering potted palm fronds, an old-school kickback in a restaurant white-linened beyond the pale with crystal chandeliers and baroque carpet. I remember how our tuxedoed waiter didn't let on that we were wide-eyed girls in dresses borrowed from our mothers, dropped off at the door by my dad while he hid in the hotel lounge nursing sticker-shock cocktails, our Claire's Accessories purses containing exactly the *prix fixe* cost of our dinner in cash.

"Are you ladies going to be seeing the show this evening, as well?" the waiter asked us like we were true grown-ups with a metropolis full of options.

"We are!" I said, batting my mascara-less eyelashes.

"This evening we're starting out with the spring pea portage," he said on his return with two gold-scrolled bone china bowls of green soup so smooth it was like cupped velvet.

"SOUP!" We both exclaimed as soon as he'd disappeared behind the palm.

I remember the dismay in my mother's face when I told her there was something black and gnarled and disgusting topping my whipped potatoes, nestled against a beef tenderloin glistening with reduction sauce. "I flicked it into my napkin," I said.

"You flicked a black truffle into your napkin?!"

"That wasn't a burned piece of potato?"

"I think you left half the cost of that dinner in the Four Seasons laundry hamper," she said.

After the fourth course, the waiter checked in to make sure we were ready for dessert. "I know the menu lists Oranges en Surprise, but we made a little something special tonight." April 14th, 1999. The 87-year anniversary of the iceberg collision. The kitchen was as reverent as my heart. The Georgian, they got me.

He returned with two plated white-chocolate mousse clouds, suspending a blue sugar shard of sea above the china. Sailing in the frozen water was a dark chocolate Titanic with its tip sunk in a whipped cream iceberg. It was awfully morbid. Deliciously, deliriously tacky. Stupid, fleeting, perfect joy.

"It's so incredible, I feel bad eating it," Natalie said as we sat, spoons aloft, breath cut short.

Wincing, we plunged our spoons into the blue sugar, and with a *crack*, the illusion folded in on itself. A mirage, just as every incredible dinner out is—this is not your kitchen or your home. You can't live in formal dresses. The national theater packs up the troupe and shuttles off to the next tour stop. I think that night I understood: You don't go out because decadence is a permanent state. You go out because you need to elevate a moment. A celebration, a relationship, a transition, a stationary Thursday that would otherwise be forgotten with all the other stationary Thursdays. That night at the Four Seasons was my moment perched between imagining what I might be and setting out to become it. The unintentional clarity that this fusion of pomp and whimsy is my life's bliss. This is how I feel beautiful. This is how I am fed.

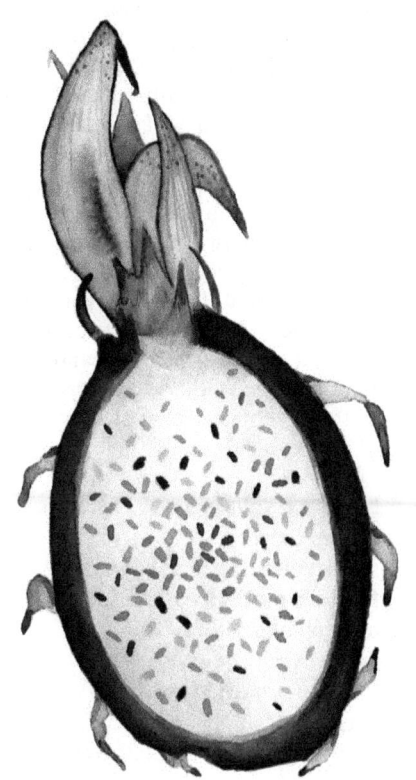

Steerage Split Pea

*A*ll being a smart-ass and live-tweeting my reread of *Last Dinner on the Titanic* aside, I have to recommend any lover of food and gonzo historical periods to give it a read. Although out-of-print, copies are readily available online and in libraries. You might not need the tips on hiring a sous chef or picking a string quartet for a fussy dinner party I can't picture anyone scheduling or attending, but the insight into the lives of actual passengers overlooked in the grandiose nature of the famous disaster is incredible, and important. One of the things you'll notice in reading the contrasting menus of first class, second class, and steerage passengers is how much more appealing the humble peasant food remains. The Rose DeWitt Bukater menus haven't aged well. They are remarkably complicated and utilize many ingredients that have fallen out of rotation and favor, like mutton, tongue, herring, and squab.

The third-class menu, however, reads like a delicious new gastropub's happy hour menu. Roast beef. Curry and rice. No spring pea portage, just Pea Soup. In lieu of an immaculate purée that requires the love and attention one must provide to a newborn unicorn foal, I'm giving you my steerage-friendly recipe for split pea soup. This is an inexpensive, low-maintenance meal for nights that need fewer toasts and more rib-sticking. But I'd also put it up as one of the best things I ever make. And that's the loveliest thing about ye olde steerage food: classic, warm, and true.

- o   1 bag dried split peas
- o   1 onion, diced
- o   3 stalks celery, sliced
- o   3 large carrots, sliced
- o   6 cups chicken stock
- o   2 bay leaves
- o   ½ tablespoon dried thyme
- o   1 teaspoon salt
- o   1 ham bone from a leftover baked ham with a good

amount of ham still clinging to it*, or 2 ham hocks with 2 cups additional sliced ham

Combine all ingredients in a Crock-Pot, and allow to soak overnight in the fridge (This gives the peas time to rehydrate). Remove and cook in the Crock-Pot on low for 8 or more hours, after which time the soup will become thick and silky. Remove the ham bone or hocks, along with the bay leaves, before serving. Add salt and pepper to taste. I like this best topped with a dollop of sour cream and a handful of croutons.

---

* This is why we buy and bake hams periodically throughout the year.

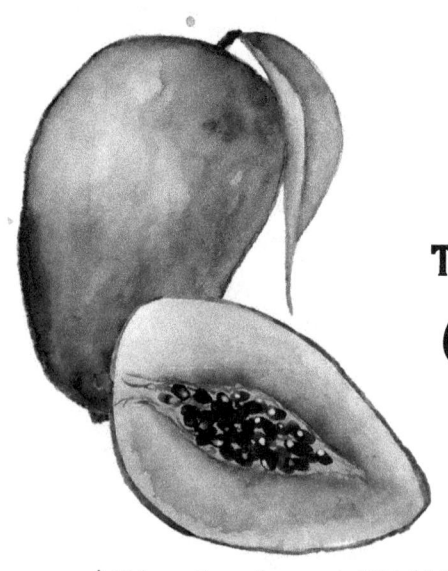

The *Celibate Celebration*

"I'll have the red snapper," I told the Oswego Grill waitress.

"And on the side?" the waitress, nondescript in black slacks and jacket, asked. Our local steakhouse was old-school, with dark woods and deep booths. A cave of meat and martinis.

"Brussels sprouts," I said, praying that she received the telepathic message from my heart: *fully loaded baked potato*. Message failed to send, but she wrote down my order on the pad then turned to Matt.

"We're going to start with the jalapeño onion petals," his opus began. "And what did you say the soup of the day was?"

"Clam chowder."

"How big is a cup?"

The waitress made a shot glass with her hands.

"Hmmm, I'll do a bowl of the chowder, then. And the prime rib with the fully loaded baked potato."

She smiled and took her notepad back into the darkness.

Matt tipped his head at me, disappointment sour on his lips. "I thought we were out celebrating," he said.

"We are. I got a mango-tini." I raised the sugar-laced glass.

"You can treat yourself every once in a while, you know."

"I like the red snapper," I insisted. And I did. Matt hates fish, so I only get moist, flaky fillets when we're picking our own plates off a menu. Oswego Grill envelops their snapper in the lightest spring-is-just-around-the-corner jacket of crushed hazelnuts, grown in the gently rolling orchards stretching between our farm country house and the suburban restaurant. Granted, I liked it even better with a fistful of their fresh garlic butter-brushed sourdough bread and a heap of nutty rice pilaf to make the crust sing. And three more martinis. And half of Matt's onion rings. But I was trying to be good. I'd worked on so much sacrifice, I couldn't let my hungry, thinning self slide backward.

"Don't you have Flex Points?" he asked.

This had been our dynamic for a decade, ever since our first meal together at Chevy's Fresh Mexican, when I ate half my grilled fajitas, and he scarfed a whole burrito combo. For Matt, the menu is an open invitation, its possibilities only limited by his preference and pocketbook. Want enchiladas? Go for it! Why not get the surf AND the turf? Why NOT double the meat? Why WOULDN'T you want a pile of calamari before a platter of chicken parmigiana?

Meanwhile, I ride the carousel between resisting what I really want (ALL THE THINGS) and giving in to the devil in the opposite seat. My body gave testament to the strength of my current will.

My eyes fluttered closed for a breath. We had left the cats behind and dressed ourselves up for dinner at the best place we knew that didn't involve schlepping all the way into Portland to celebrate a success built on my fat-girl essay, the story I wrote for *The Rumpus* about joining Weight Watchers for the third time. Ever since my senior year of high school, I lived in the perpetual cycle of gaining and losing the same 40 pounds. My latest struggle began while living in Tucson. I was miserable in the desert with no family in the same time zone and my closest friend a day's drive away in Phoenix. I hated my day job of editing technical manuals for copper mines. I loathed the pack of poodles in the house next door that howled relentlessly both day and night.

But I loved the food.

Light, crisp *chile rellenos* you had to devour the moment they arrived at your table, lest they lose their ethereal crunch. The legendary In-N-Out Animal-Style Double Double, the restaurant's palm tree gateway beckoning from the stoplight corners. Tamales an old woman sold outside the Safeway in Oro Valley where I spent my week fighting with engineers over proper comma placement. Pita Jungle's Curry Chicken Salad in a creamy spiced dressing studded with plump, juicy grapes, and topped with fried onion strings. The shockingly good Indian buffet minutes from my office with as many pakoras and tikka masala scoops as one lunch hour could carry.

The food was my bright spot and my comfort. I ate some of the best meals of my life in Arizona while I plummeted into worse and worse shape.

"You do realize that those onion rings would be a week's

worth of Weight Watcher points," I tried to explain.

"Yeah, if you eat the whole plate. Is one bite really going to hurt you?"

Not the first one, maybe, but it was never just one. Soon it was bite after bite after bite.

The waitress returned with the plate of jalapeño onion petals stacked like an Egyptian pyramid. Each gigantic Walla Walla petal was dusted in *cotija* cheese and parsley. I picked the smallest onion slice from the top and set it on my plate to cool. One, out of nine. I watched as a platter of fries was delivered to a man in the booth across from us, a man who surely wouldn't count how many he dipped into ketchup. He wouldn't be trying to guess how many tablespoons of ketchup he'd squirted onto his plate. I was surrounded by a world that wasn't counting, but was always watching. Noticing when a body went up or down, tightened or swelled. In the three months since restarting Weight Watchers, I'd lost eight pounds. The website gave me a silver star and stock praise: *Keep up what you're doing, Tabitha!* I paid 50 dollars a month to be coddled like a preschooler.

Which, apparently, is my love language. It was just enough to start nudging myself back into my clothes. The dresses I adored, collected over years of stalking my favorite stores' clearance racks: vintage pinup reproductions from Las Vegas' Tatyana Boutique—wiggle dresses and circle skirts spotted on burlesque queen Dita Von Teese and my *The Girls Next Door* favorite Holly Madison. Quirky cat prints and flared faux-fur coats from ModCloth. The two things I adore most, food and fashion: like loving meth and a good night's sleep.

I dipped my fork into the spicy ranch dressing, coating the tongs in illicit creamy goodness. *Weight Watchers Tip: Don't dunk! Dip your fork in dressings, and you'll use much less and guarantee full flavor in every bite!* I cut the petal into three pieces, stretching what I could easily devour in one ravenous mouthful.

Like my first round on Weight Watchers, this one began with a photograph. Back in 2002, my mom developed a roll of film from our summer vacation in Arizona. I Vanna White'ed in front of the Grand Canyon sign and struck a showgirl pose at the Paris Las Vegas. But the girl in the four-by-six prints was unrecognizable from the self image I carried with me: puffy, hunched, my new tanktop bulging above my shorts.

That couldn't be me.

I wasn't the fat girl. Not in my head. I was the girl who wanted to bring poodle skirts back, who loved the opaque shimmer of a pearl on a downy cardigan. I thought the world saw my flair for details and moviestar camera poses. But my body—it hulked in the way.

This re-registration was spurred by an Instagram my friend posted from an annual writer's conference. I was seated at a white linen convention center table with a plastic pitcher of water and microphone stand—a spot I'd always dreamed of being. It was my first time outside of the audience. I felt ethereal, arrived, effervescent. It wasn't until I saw the notification on my phone that I remembered what I looked like. A walrus in a tiny folding chair.

I'm so proud of my friend! the caption read. And I knew she was, that she wasn't trying to immortalize my broad shoulders hunching down. Up. Around. But that was all I could see, all I remembered now.

"Come on, you've got to help me out here," Matt said, dunking his fifth onion petal into the spicy ranch sauce. "I've got clam chowder on the way. I can't do this on my own."

"You ordered them."

"I thought you'd want them, too!"

What was this world like, where 'want' and 'should not' signed a peace treaty in Geneva? I hadn't had this freedom since the summers between middle school grades, when I would ride my bike up and down the hill behind our house past my friend Natalie's to shave off the hours. I worked all summer until I could get up the super-steep grade, trading the agony in my calves to weightlessly plummet back down, diving into a wind so fresh and high it was even worth the entire layer of skin the pavement scraped off my leg the one time I finally biffed it.

I'd come home and raid the fridge for a pint of milk. Chips and ranch. Slices of Tillamook cheddar cheese. All the salty, creamy goodness I could find.

Then school started, and I stopped going outside. But the fridge was still there. Still stuffed.

"How are you doing over here?" the waitress entered stage right, taking stock of our onion pile. "Still working on those petals?"

"I don't think we're going to finish them," Matt moped.

"I can wrap them up in tinfoil for you," she said. "They reheat super-well in the oven. Just put it on broil for a few minutes unwrapped. As long as you don't put them anywhere near the microwave."

"That would be wonderful, thanks," I said ten octaves higher than normal.

The young woman glanced around our carnage—my half-finished ten dollar sugar booze bomb, the trail of onion crumbs leading back to Matt's appetizer plate, the bourbon film left skimming the bottom of his glass. My rigid posture in Spanx and dress stitches slowly, glacially moving back within my reach, Matt's least-rumpled button-up office shirt. We were a rained-out birthday party.

"Are we celebrating anything special tonight?" she asked.

I paused for half a breath. I loved the Chevy's birthday sombrero, the Red Robin circle of claps. 'Tell them it's my birthday!' I'd make my parent promise when we went out to dinner as a family. Instead, I said, "I just found out that someone wants to sell a book I'm writing."

"You wrote a *book?*" The wide-eyed reaction of a person who's never undergone the crushing process of writing, editing, querying, selling, publishing, and promoting a book. So hopeful! So optimistic!

"Well. I am writing it," I said. A week after writing the Best Damn Query Letter Ever and sending it off with Hotmail carrier pigeons to the big city, the recipe for chicken gyros I was reading on my phone was interrupted by a single new email *ping.*

Tabitha, thanks for reaching out. I'm intrigued by your project— body image issues are a vital topic right now. Can you tell me more about your plans for the book? Let's talk.

"What's it about?"

"It's kind of a coming-of-age memoir, but not really a memoir in the traditional sense … more like an essay collection," I Hannah-Horvath-in-*Girls* rambled.

"Congratulations! That's so exciting," the waitress said.

I felt my unsullied destiny unfurling before her eyes: the Barnes & Noble shelf, the lines of admirers clutching copies to their chests as they waited in line for my Sharpie pen blessing, the Oprah Book Club sticker, the movie rights and Jennifer Lawrence casting. Pure, limitless dream.

"I'll be back with that chowder in a minute, okay?"

Matt looked at me like I'd just lied my way into a return at Macy's. "You haven't sold your book yet," he reminded me.

"I didn't say that I sold my book. I said someone was *interested* in selling my book. Which she *is*. Besides," I said, tossing the rest of the martini back, "didn't you say we were celebrating?"

"We were celebrating an agent email, not a book deal." We'd been through this before, after all. He'd witnessed my pacing around the living room, my screams when my inbox was false-triggered by Bed, Bath & Beyond. He'd seen my hopes rise to the heavens like a literary Tower of Babylon, only to rot a slow, sarlacc-monster death.

"Clam chowder?" the waiter asked, and Matt raised his hand. "Can I get you another mango-tini?"

"Actually, I'll have an Old-Fashioned," I said. I tore a hunk of garlic butter sourdough off the loaf and sank it into the forbidden heavy cream depths of the soup.

My red snapper was everything that my Puget Sound saltwater veins missed about seafood. Delicate, buttery, punctuated with the light crisp of the hazelnuts, like a savory Almond Roca bar. I tried to stretch it out, to cut the fillet into microscopic bites, to enjoy the treat as long as possible.

It was gone before Matt finished fiddling with his steak knife.

I sat impatiently and watched Matt eat after devouring my own sensible little portion. I inhaled my side salads while he slowly picked through steak fries. I shoveled the strict portions in while he took his time through a smorgasbord of options.

I tried to calculate the number of points on the full plate across from me. Real sour cream hiding a geyser of butter, flecks of sharp aged cheddar cheese: the small, innocuous building blocks that bomb dress sizes out of possibility.

"Bite?" he offered.

I can say no, but I usually don't. "Thanks," I murmured, when a luscious pink sliver of steak appeared next to my Brussels sprouts. The meat was decadent and heavy, coating my mouth in a film of what I couldn't have. I longed for one last bite of snapper to bring my palette back. I remembered the talk at my last Weight Watchers meeting, where a woman who lost 15 pounds in the 70s warned us against all food-based joys. "Beware the BLTs!" she said from the front of the class. "Bites, licks, and tastes! All of those little points you ignore add up!"

God, how I hated meetings. I sat in the back and folded my arms like the angry kid in the last row of the school bus, waiting for the moment I could take my victory sticker and go.

In my last two forays down the Weight Watchers path of righteousness, I endured their slander of festivity.

"Can you even guess how many points are in a typical Thanksgiving dinner?" our leader asked us last November. Her easel board propped up a poster with a stock-photo turkey day plate. The point values were covered with Post-Its like the world's most depressing round of Guess Who. Gravy will kill you. Pie will ruin everything. Is any mashed potato as good as your goal weight?

Food is not celebration, the talking points insisted. Find new ways to reward yourself that don't involve calories!

This was my doctrine snag, the place where the foundation cracked, my evidence against God. Birthdays were for cake. Achievements were measured in toasts. The love I shared with my husband was solidified in hundreds of nights over a thousand plates. Food and joy were intrinsically tied to my being—the connection between heart and body and memory. I could eat well on the day-to-day; I could pass on office donuts, even learn to drink black coffee for a smaller size. But I could never separate food and love.

From a few booths down, a glittering sparkler caught my eye. Our waitress bounded down the dark walkway carrying an ice cream sundae that can only be described as Vince Lombardi Trophy-esque. A vase of ice cream layered with fudge and pineapple and strawberry sauces, sprouting an entire banana. "We're just really excited for you!" she said, setting the frozen monument in place of the snapper. She slid an envelope across the table, which I opened as soon as she'd disappeared back around the corner.

Congratulations on your book! the card read, signed by the entire staff. I had a whole extra set of people not to let down.

"You scammed a sundae!" said Matt.

"I told them someone was *interested* in selling my book!"

"Scammer."

Vanilla. Fudge. Whipped cream. There was enough dessert to feed five watchers of weight for three days. A goblet of celebration. It was that disgusting side angle in a picture that gave me Ursula the Sea Witch face, the dress zipper quitting at my rib cage, the automatic monthly withdrawals from my bank account every month for the privilege of deprivation. The glass brimmed with everything I guilted and bargained and scammed myself into thinking I did not deserve, even on a day that was special, was different, may never come again. I could kill that part of me that turned meals into joys. I could snuff my heart out.

Or I could celebrate myself.

I ate every last bite.

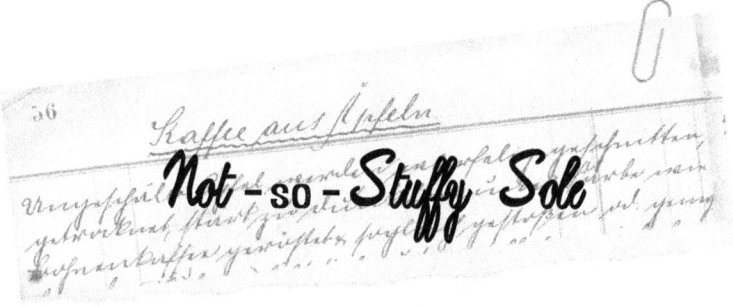

Not - so - Stuffy Sole

*H*ere was the plan: I was going to sweet-talk the Oswego Grill into giving me the hazelnut snapper recipe because I was a regular and a fan and, hey, remember how excited they were about that book? Granted, this may be a different book. Details.

After going back and forth with the owner's assistant, however (I had no idea restaurant owners had personal assistants), it became very clear that either (a.) she was not interested in relaying writer messages or (b.) he was not interested in sharing hazelnut snapper with the essay-cookbook-memoir fans of the world.

But dry your tears. Because I have another outstanding white fish recipe for you. This is my mom's recipe for stuffed sole, and she gave it to me without even asking when the rights reverted back to her. She'd make it while I was growing up, usually served with baked potatoes, and if we were really lucky, she'd shred some Tillamook cheddar for topping, and damn, who needs a stuffy steakhouse when you have that in your life?

Presented here in its originally emailed form:

I'm reminded of the "recipe" of Grandma Kroll's for fruit torte where she told me to "bake until done" when I try to think of how to make the sole you like. It was one of those dishes I think was originally from a magazine but evolved into just whatever I had on hand to top the fish fillets with. You guys always liked it, though, of course who doesn't like cheese?

Usually I'd start with 4 sole fillets. Try to get some that are somewhat large as it will be easier to fill and roll them.

Mix a cup of fresh soft breadcrumbs, ¼ cup of sharp cheddar, 2 tablespoons of cream cheese, 2 sliced green onions, ½ teaspoon salt, 1 tablespoon parsley. After mixing together, gently fold in ⅓ cup of crab or shrimp. If shrimp are large, you may need to cut them into desired pieces.

Spread this mixture over fillets and roll like a cinnamon roll. Place in a baking dish with the seam side down. Sprinkle with fresh lemon juice, ¼ cup additional shredded cheddar, and small amount of chopped fresh parsley. Bake at 350° F until done (probably about 20-25 minutes tops) [smiley face emoji].

—*Tabitha's Mom*

(I think she also sprinkled them with paprika because I distinctly remember red flecks, but let's not get into a debate of the fallibility of memory and the illusion of truth in memoir.)

Pot Pie for Sale

*W*hen dinner is okay, we are quiet. We eat it and are content, because it's food, sustenance. Grilled chicken, veggie burgers, stir-fry over rice. These are the easy, healthy, serviceable standards. But every few weeks or so, when time and a decent idea is on my side, there is something truly memorable for dinner. This is when we are rapturous.

This was our reaction to Cheddar Biscuit-Topped Chicken. It's a love child of chicken pot pie and chicken and dumplings, freeing the creamy filling from the confines of oppressive crust and upgrading to pillowy cheddar biscuits. Every bite is savory ecstasy. We ate what was on our plates and went back for more. In Matt's case, he returned to the skillet four times.

"You could sell this," he proclaimed.

I half-laughed, half-shrugged. "Yeah. Probably. Should I put out a tip jar?"

"No, seriously," he pressed. "You should be doing this. You need a restaurant. Screw this whole writing thing."

I think this is a thing that non-writerly loved ones do; when they see your suffering, your frustration, your crippling disappointments, they want to fix the problems. They don't understand the intricacies of the writing process that you spent all that MFA time and money honing—the ability to surf the waves of rejection, ride the swells of a hot streak, to keep from drowning in the grind and jealousy. It's too tough to explain how we learn and unlearn this struggle every single day. So they make suggestions. Well-meaning suggestions. Suggestions that make you want to jump off a bridge.

This suggestion didn't make me angry, though. Not like the

notions that I write something happier, more commercial, less personal, with zombies. This comment knocked me back almost seven years when I brushed against the other dream. I was 24, just married, just laid off. It was 2008. I received my pink slip a few weeks before the banks shuttered and the market crashed.

I sat around my apartment with nowhere to be while Matt worked overtime to pad our budget. I refreshed Craigslist job postings with little success. The rare company that was hiring received hundreds of applications, no matter how menial and entry-level the work. If I was lucky, I got invited to a giant interview cattle call, where dozens of interviewee clones speed-dated the HR department. The women in the lobbies with résumé portfolios had 10, 20, 30 years of hard office time over me. Being offered an Administrative Assistant position at Prestige Tile felt like landing a starring role on Broadway.

While my prospects to restart a career I never liked in the first place regressed, my heart wandered to what I'd always wanted to do. My second-story apartment window overlooked an empty commercial space, part of a 'master-planned community' that had yet to materialize from more than the watercolor conceptual renderings hanging in the leasing office as empty vows. Glass and concrete canvas meant for shops and cafés to make a little 'village' in this new suburb. It was a master plan with terrible timing. One day on a whim, I called the number on the For Lease sign.

"The developers are anxious to get a restaurant into one of those spaces," the agent twisted my arm. "They'd definitely be willing to work with you on rent."

I met her a few days later at the empty glass box. She was small and neat in a red Macy's dress suit. I was in Unemployed Formalwear: a Sailor Moon T-shirt and recently washed jeans. She unlocked the door, and we stepped in, though there was nothing to see. Exposed ceilings, power cords, dust on the floor, a lingering Home Depot smell of fresh building innards.

"You can get kitchen equipment pretty cheap nowadays. So many places are closing and throwing their stuff up on Craigslist."

I tried to imagine my deli case stacked with ceramic mixing bowls of pea salad and curry-scented chicken, but all I could see was poured concrete and exposed wire. The blank space was too vast. I'd never been behind a counter, let alone inside a commercial kitchen. Then again, the possibility of being invited into an office every day with my name in the directory felt just as far off.

The next week, I was at the Portland Culinary Institute as a student prospect, waiting in the lobby for a tour. Next to the couches and coffee table stacked with *Bon Appétit* was a glass case displaying the students' knife roll kits. They gleamed in the halcyon nest, delicate paring knife next to bone-slicing cleaver. An entire package of purpose. To carry these tools was to have someplace to be, a reason to exist. Pardon me. I have prep work to do.

I peeked into classrooms full of people in white hats and aprons, tasting marinara that lilted on the tongue like poetry. One girl stopped me in the hallway with a platter of glittering cupcakes.

"Would you like to try one?" she asked. "We just had a whole class on this new edible glitter."

This was tangible, and shimmering. I could almost glimpse a hazy future for myself flickering into focus, starched uniforms, feasting on stars.

I brought home the application packet. I Googled job prospects and average salaries. Read anecdotes of grueling hours and lost holidays. The investment was huge and the return small. Success was rare and, in the aftermath of my failure, I was hardly feeling like an exception to the rule. The real estate agent stopped leaving me messages as I turned this uncertainty over in my palm, talking myself out of a leap. We could lose everything on a failed restaurant, and we didn't have much to begin with. Maybe I should just keep looking for a job. Maybe I can do this later.

Nine months after losing my job, I found another one. It was a job working for men who expected me to wrap their wives' Christmas presents for them and to book their family vacations with company air miles, and who refused to promote me because it would mean I was less 'available for them.' The position was an awful, deadending, tyrannical one that made me quickly realize I had to find something, anything, else to do with my life. When I looked at going back to school a few years later, my sights turned to an MFA. I could take my lifetime of writing seriously, maybe even become a professor (I thought, naïvely, at the time). The prospects seemed small but more stable, the risk more calculated. I felt more certain that I had a book inside of me than a successful restaurant.

There are a finite number of dreams one person can chase down in a lifetime. Most of the time, I'm sure in my footing. Book, teaching, great literary conversation. Immortality. I've come far from that girl who was stuck in her apartment with no direction, who had to take one worst-case scenario to get out of another. Far from the girl who applied for an MFA when she'd hardly typed a creative paragraph since her undergrad classes. Far even from the wide-eyed, heartful, exhaustively earnest commencement speaker with *Bird by Bird* printed on her heart. Since graduating I'd learned how much harder the dream was, a dream I'd understood was a long shot. Rejection is something they tell you about in school. Burnout is not. There's still so much I want to do, so many places where I feel I've fallen short. I keep a running tally of the goals I question my ability to achieve. It's on these days that I look down at my plate and wonder just how much someone would pay for a bite. I dream of trading my Submittable queue for a menu. I wish, just maybe, I'd followed the glittery cupcakes.

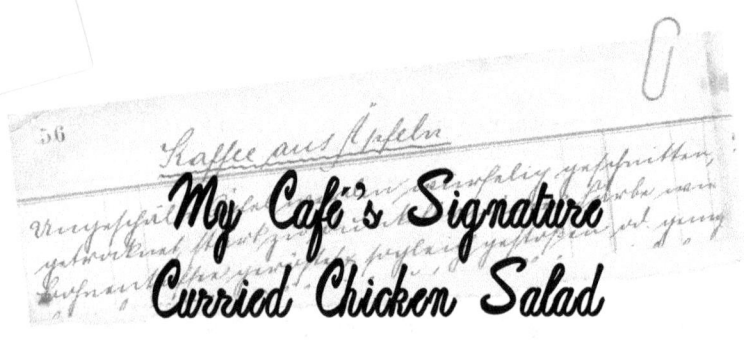

My Café's Signature Curried Chicken Salad

never settled on a name for my theoretical café, although I remember Mimolette (my favorite name for a cheese) and Mehitabel (my eldest cat) as contenders. I did know what my signature dish would be, however—the one that people could pick up during office lunch breaks or in plastic catering tubs to take back home to the neighboring apartments: chicken salad with a generous amount of curry. This old-fashioned chicken salad recipe is reminiscent of English high tea, and my mom made it for my bridal shower. I asked for the recipe, and this is the version that evolved in the subsequent nine (!) years.

I remember the original recipe suggested serving the salad rolled into leaves of iceberg lettuce, as P. F. Chang's serves you addictive scoops of ground chicken and peppers. In the years since, I've normally scooped it into tortillas with fresh spinach as a wrap, or the occasional sandwich.

Oh, who am I kidding. I usually scoop this straight from the mixing bowl with a spoon while I stand at the counter watching *South Park*. Most times I don't bother dirtying a spoon when I have perfectly good fingers.

- o 2 cups rotisserie chicken, cooled and shredded
- o 2 stalks celery, chopped
- o 3 green onions, diced
- o ½ cup salted cashews
- o ⅓ cup flat-leaf parsley, finely chopped
- o ¾ cup plain Greek yogurt
- o 1 tablespoon Dijon mustard
- o 1 tablespoon honey
- o ¼ teaspoon ground ginger
- o 1 tablespoon curry powder
- o 1 teaspoon cumin
- o ½ teaspoon cayenne pepper
- o Vegetable oil
- o Salt and pepper to taste

- o 1 heaping cup stemmed grapes, halved[*]
- o ¾ cup mayonnaise[**]
- o The juice from half a lemon[***]

In a cast iron skillet (or nonstick pan) lightly greased with vegetable oil, cook the cashews over medium heat until they begin to toast and get a teensy bit brown, stirring on the regular. This should only take a minute or two: keep close watch, because these flip from perfectly toasty and delicious, to burned in all of seven seconds. When ready, immediately remove from heat and allow to cool.

Scoop the yogurt, mayonnaise, Dijon mustard, honey, curry powder, ginger, cumin, cayenne pepper, and lemon juice into a Mason jar. Tightly fit the jar with the two-part seal-and-ring lid, and shake until emulsified. You could also make the dressing by whisking all ingredients together, but I've found that the jar method is the least frustrating and most successful every time.

Add chicken, celery, green onions, reserved cashews, grapes, and parsley to a large mixing bowl. Toss with the dressing. Season with salt and pepper to taste. Serve on your carb delivery device of choice.

---

[*] If it's the dead of winter and all the fruit is a depressed and weary traveler, or I don't have any on hand, I substitute ⅓ cup Craisins.

[**] Feel free to use a light variety—I usually do.

[***] Matt doesn't like lemon juice, so I don't get to use this much, but it makes such a vibrant difference—hopefully you don't live with such a wanker.

Crater Lake Blackout

I left for Crater Lake right before the Fourth of July, a few days after sending my book proposal to the agent. I pressed Send the week prior, technically a holiday week — and the email was heading to New York, where they seem to stretch those holidays, right? I mean, you can't even submit books to editors during the summertime. Come June, Manhattan empties out into a husk of boarded-up brownstones and abandoned hot dog carts, the publishing world transplanted from skyscrapers to Hampton cottages pasted with seashell-apothecary jar arrangements and 'Life's a Beach' stenciled plaques.

This is what I told myself for four days as I swiped my thumb down the middle of my phone over and over, watching the refresh circle spin, the time update. Zero messages.

Four days, of course, is nothing. I know. Four days is barely enough time to read a fresh email, let alone open up its precious attachments, the Microsoft Word documents I'd been tenderly plotting and avoiding and, on a couple of hot streaks, worshipping. And yet.

Where was my "Got it—thanks!" Did they not have Wi-Fi on the Jitney bus? Did my email, weighted with attachments, get dumped into her junk folder? How long did I have to wait before I sent my obnoxious "Just checking in!" missive, the mosquito of electronic communication?

At our campsite, along the rim of America's deepest lake, my publishing career was Schrodinger's Cat. My anxiety was not founded or confirmed; it was irrelevant. My email wouldn't chime until we were about 80 miles outside of the park. It was almost as if I'd planned it this way, this escape into an untouchable lagoon, distracting myself for the weeks trailing up to deadline. Which camping chair is the highest rated? What will I be most hungry for days from now in the middle of nowhere? I bought a new Dutch oven for this trip, and a tripod stand to hang over the fire, like the one Alton Brown uses on *Good Eats* when he pretends he's hours away from a southern California film studio.

In reality, I had to make this reservation a full year out, as the summer camping spots fill within days of opening up their calendars. Camping in an iconic state park is too Pinteresting and affordable to allow for spontaneity. Every so often, serendipity is on my over-planning side. I planted an escape hatch in my summer with no idea what I'd be running from.

Before we left, I tried to work around the technological destination of Crater Lake. "I need to make my laptop work in the woods," I texted Matt. I could run into town on the way back from the Oregon Vortex, or scam a Wi-Fi password from the park lodge. I could snatch my answer out of the cloud and press forward, write whatever she needed, staying up until dawn in the dimming firelight and churning out half a book.

Matt returned home with a big adapter box that plugged into the cigarette lighter and had a fan that sounded like a turbine engine. "Won't your truck battery run out if I use that all night?"

"Maybe don't write until sunrise. Maybe enjoy your vacation."

After an hour of double-clicking on the LODGE_GUEST one-bar network and batting mosquitoes away from my screen, I folded up the laptop. I set up the kitchen station on our picnic table with our scratched pans and the travel-sized bottle of dishwasher soap. I read the Ranger Talk schedule. I showed our visiting German site-neighbors how to make a s'more.

And then I'd be at the gift shop running my hands over Pendleton blankets and remember that maybe my whole life was answered in a message, and I felt that tilt-a-whirl vertigo of what and if and how, and a twinge of guilt that I had the audacity to live when I should be obsessively worrying.

I couldn't forget. Not completely. But I could pretend to. It's much easier to fake being chill about fate and the universe when your refresh button isn't working.

This is what camping is, after all. A long weekend of make-believe. Pretending that you are outdoorsy, that your fire-making skills would see you through the apocalypse, that citronella candles work, that you could never tire of living underneath a swath of canvas. That your answers—or lack thereof—lay dormant on the other side.

Dutch Oven of
Writer-Purgatory Woe

A.K.A. Campfire Chicken & Biscuits

- o   2 cups cooked chicken, torn apart[*]
- o   1 tablespoon of leftover bacon grease[**]
- o   1 bag frozen mixed veggies
- o   2 cups milk
- o   1 onion, diced
- o   1 can cream of mushroom soup
- o   1 can cream of chicken soup
- o   1 tablespoon of favorite herby spice, like Herbes de Provence
- o   Salt and pepper to taste
- o   1 tube of super-pressurized Grands buttermilk biscuits[***]

Build a fire, or instruct your long-suffering partner to do so, the one who has spent this trip hearing you gnaw through whether the sample chapter you sent was as 'zingy' as you thought it was a week ago. As he rips apart the *Crater Lake Summer Newsletter* bulletin to use as kindling, start to tear up, and when he asks why, go on a tangent about how someone worked *really hard* to write that.

Heat the bacon grease (or oil) over medium-high camp stove heat in the Dutch oven pan that's so new you're still eating Chinese factory fumes from the surface. You wanted to buy the Made-in-America brand, but you're still waiting on your last essay feature's check to arrive, so the cheapest Amazon special wins.

Add the onion and sauté until golden brown. Turn off the heat, then stir together the chicken, veggies, soups, milk, herbs, salt, and pepper. Remove from the camp stove and place the lid on top. It is now ready to hang on the cooking tripod over the

---

[*] while staring vacantly ahead.

[**] or vegetable oil, if you haven't been stockpiling breakfast scraps.

[***] that make you scream when they pop open because your nerves have HAD IT.

roaring fire.

It only takes about half an hour to get the mixture boiling. In the meantime, feel very bad for being such a jerk about the newsletter. Partner will plead with you to just, please, don't cry again.

Remove the lid and place the biscuits on top. Now, wait until they're golden brown. Wait an hour, then check and notice that, yes, they are still puffy and white. Wait another half hour, check again. Same deal. Start reading the random book you've agreed to review and become enraged that such repetitive, poorly paced drivel gets this huge marketing blitz from a Big Five. Contemplate converting your high school *Legend of Zelda* fan fiction into a trilogy.

Wait 20 minutes more and then say screw it and remove oven from fire. You can't wait another second for these bullshit biscuits and their lack of browning cooperation. Scoop two heaping portions onto paper plates and dive in. Discover that the biscuits haven't goldened but have puffed and cooked perfectly inside, like dumplings.

It's like chicken pot pie under the stars, and it's good enough to forget everything, even the schlocky metaphor of good things coming in their own time and way.

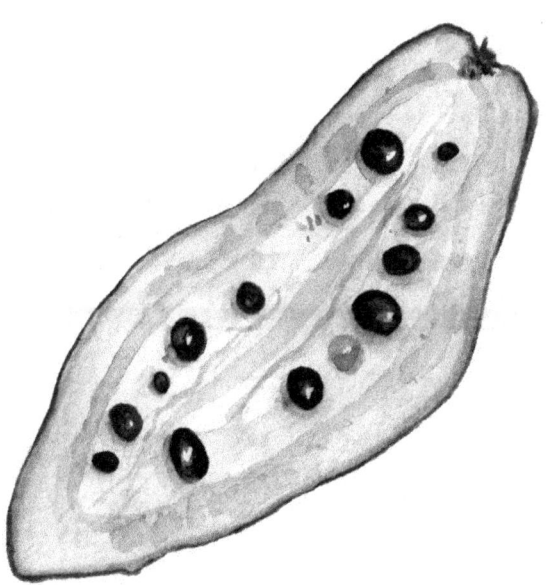

Tequila for Dinner

*T*here may be people out there who are graceful in accepting bad news.

I imagine these individuals could be labeled as #mindful. They are accomplished at yoga and at nurturing packets of seeds into flourishing brambles and vines. When people speak of the transcendent power of mistakes and the holy evidence that rejections prove dedication, it is their even, measured voices that articulate what most only begrudgingly realize.

I am not one of these people.

When we turned out of Crater Lake National Park onto the main freeway, my phone lit and buzzed and popped with new messages. Nordstrom Rack wanted me to know that the Spanx Event of the Year was happening. Weight Watchers didn't want me to feel discouraged (or hungry!) at all these summer barbecues. Twitter was so confused—*Girl, where have you* been? But amidst the chorus of notifications, my (maybe? hopefully?) agent's name did not appear. She was a black hole of silence in a clutter of routine correspondence.

No news is good news, I knew I was supposed to think. I ran through the reasons I should not freak out as Matt's truck snaked the pine-shaded forest backroads of rural Oregon. A list of possible explanations raced through my head:

Why would she reach out to you if she wasn't interested in your book?

Why would she ask you to write a book proposal if she didn't want to sell it?

She's a literary agent, not a volunteer taking up charity cases. Why would she waste both your time and hers if this weren't real?

I knew what I would tell any friend in this same situation to yank her back from the brink. *Don't forget that you're talented! Don't lose your perspective! Remember how long even the tiniest thing takes in this game!* I'd embed a relevant GIF—Kermit waving his arms, or a Stephen Colbert high-five. I would sign the message 'Sincerely,' and I would believe it all to be true.

It's only when I turn the lines in on myself that formerly foundational certainty dissolves into platitude. The bedrock cracks and the torrent of doubt floods me with worry.

What if I didn't articulate what I wanted to say?
What if I don't actually have anything to say?
What if she sees through me?
What if she changes her mind?

I would fall into a fog, staring at my office computer screen or at the opposite couch in the living room, my mind a spiral of Pacific-to-Eastern-time conversions and horoscope snippets and the maw of a gigantic idea: *your dreams will never come true.*

A few days later, her name appeared with the ultimate in email subjects: "RE: Book Proposal." I held my breath through the miniscule sentences:

Tabitha, so sorry for the delay. I'll get back to you by the end of the week. Great stuff, though.

GREAT STUFF, THOUGH. Sixteen letters I clung to, an invisible talisman I rubbed raw. I copied the lines to my best friends and parents, the update they'd all been too scared to ask me about. They wrote me back a chorus of encouragement: *This is so exciting! See, you were so worried for nothing!*

And I floated on it. For a day. Then two. Even three, as the week ground to an end.

New York is always late. Hasn't Rent *taught you anything? That city does not have its shit together.*

If she's this busy for her other writers, imagine how hard she'll work for you!

GREAT STUFF, THOUGH!

The next Tuesday I was waiting for onions and garlic to sauté down to caramelized mush while Matt was on the couch with the cats watching the previous night's *@Midnight*. I was scrolling through The Pioneer Woman's blog on my phone, seeking the next step in her spicy chipotle beef recipe.

PING. The Agent's name rolled at the top of my screen with a new email message:

Tabitha, again my apologies at taking so long to respond. I'm afraid I'm not sure how I'd sell this book, and I'm going to have to take a pass. Women's memoir is such a tough, saturated market right now, and

I'm not sure that this narrative has what it takes to stand out in any significant way from the glut. I'm sorry that we won't get the chance to work together on this, but I wish you much luck on this and future projects.

"Is that burning garlic?" Matt asked.

My ears rang. I scarce heard him from six feet away.

I don't know how long I stood there, staring down at the paragraph that hardly took up the four-inch Galaxy Note display that had suddenly ruined my life.

"It's browned," I corrected, quietly scraping the charred bits into the garbage. My zombie self retrieved a fresh onion from the fridge and two more garlic cloves from the cabinet. I didn't say anything as the beef cooked or the polenta gurgled. I let the TV play on as I set dinner plates down and ushered Matt over, letting Chris Hardwick and his comedian panel serve as surrogate conversation.

I only distractedly agreed with the fact that dinner was delicious and Ree Drummond really knows her shit, even if the way she pronounces potatoes 'pa-tay-das' is the most irritating Food Network colloquialism this side of 'the train to Flavortown.'

Only when we were in bed, and Matt was seconds away from sleeping, did I address my devastation. "I got an email from my agent."

"When?"

"When I was making dinner."

"Oh." He didn't turn over to face me, less an act of disinterest than simple self-preservation. My rollercoaster of a personality was bad enough; the added variable of writing strife made me an emotional roulette wheel. "So. It wasn't a good email."

"No," I said. It was all I could say. Matt fell asleep, and I broke.

There are two times when working in a corporate office is unbearable: when I've received sensational news, and when I've received the worst possible news. In each case the ordinary things I'm supposed to care about—Excel spreadsheet formulas, shipment notifications, project assignments—feel spectacularly irrelevant. What do spreadsheets matter when my real true life is taking off/falling apart?

The day after the rejection, the gray cubicle walls seemed to press inward like the Death Star's garbage compactor, crushing me slowly, me helpless to stop it. This job didn't feel like a means to an end, but a wall, mounting evidence on the futility of my ambition. The hours would not stop tallying in my mind: 40 a week, 2,080 a year. I grew older and the company remained the same, as indifferent to my contributions as if I weren't even there. I could feel the life siphoning out of me. All my hopes were going to die in this chair. Everything ended here, in a monochrome suburban office complex.

I needed a walk.

I was pacing the thin grass strip between the office parking lot and the street when Matt called. This was surprising; we aren't checker-inners. We texted each other facts and phoned only in emergencies.

"How're you holding up?" he asked. This was also suspicious. Matt was usually too cautious to check in on my emotional state, fearing he'd catch me at the wrong nanosecond.

"I haven't cried yet," I said proudly.

"Please don't."

"I won't." I didn't feel sad, just doomed.

"So, I was thinking. How would you like to go out for some drinks after work?"

Of all the freaky alien-speak coming through my speaker, this was perhaps the most uncharacteristic of all. The Blankenbillers did NOT go out on weeknights. Not for movies, not to pick up milk, and definitely not to rack up a bar tab. Not since six years before, when we signed our mortgage papers as a legally binding marriage into Adulting. We ate what was at the house. We watched what was on the DVR. Beer was in the garage, wine in the fridge, liquor in the cabinet. Anything different would have to wait for the weekend.

"Are you sure?" I asked.

"Yeah, I mean, you probably shouldn't get fall-down drunk since we do have to work tomorrow, but we can still drink away some of it, right?"

Please, god, yes. I needed tequila down to my marrow.

We met at a new Mexican restaurant a few miles from my office. It was one of the super cheffy, industrial chrome eateries encroaching on the chain restaurant suburban turf, giving those of us who don't want to drive all the way into Portland a blessed outlet for our pretension. It was the first time since moving back from Arizona that we were paying someone else to serve us tacos, avoiding our old Oregon stop for sloppy enchilada plates that we knew—after our first Tucson bite of Poco, and Mom's roasted New Mexican chile platter—to be a paltry false god.

One of our makeshift hobbies in that unfamiliar city was trying to learn as much about southwest cuisine as we could. We bought Rick Bayless' highest-rated, James Beard-winning cookbook and worked through the tamales, homemade refried beans, and from-scratch mole. We bought a mortar and pestle and smashed the smoothest avocados we'd ever met. Our pantry filled with cornhusks and dried chiles. I tried making scratch tortillas and ended up with oblong pita bread, but it was still better than any Mexican cuisine served up in the well-meaning, far-removed north.

But this place had a magnificent patio and artisanal margaritas, and so it won the honor of sorrow-drowner. We snagged the last table outside in the July sun, now waning behind Lake Oswego's greenspace. I'd never seen the actual lake itself; it was a private reservoir accessible only to those owning some of Portland's lushest, most expensive waterfront mansions. This was the closest we proles ever got—overpaying for fancy food behind a buffer of tempered forest.

There was still one hour of happiness left, and the pairs around us lingered over ramekins of cementing *queso*.

"I'm getting *queso*," I told Matt. And guacamole. And entrees. Weight Watchers could eat a dick.

The perfect beach resort warmth, a rare and sacred Oregon treat, pushed the small Wednesday night crew past capacity. When a waiter finally reached our island, he was panting and begging his tip back in apologies.

"So we're going to start with two shots of Patron," I began, "and *queso*. And guacamole. And a jalapeño-cilantro margarita."

"Johnny Walker on the rocks," finished Matt.

"Doing it right," the waiter approved. He was fresh California import with dark curls you could still shake the sand out of. Beautiful, and immediately hustled away from us, back to the small blondes at the neighbor table with their skin fake-baked to a burnt pizza-crust caramel.

The 15-dollar shot slid down my throat without a spark, hardly needing the lemon wedge I shoved between my teeth. I was gun-shy from college nights with further-than-bottom-shelf, hole-dug-in-the-liquor-store-floor vodka masked with orange juice.

Matt choked on his.

"How can you drink bourbon without blinking, but tequila kicks your ass?" I asked. I'd tried his very best whiskeys, watered down in cold sips, but they made me feel like my whole body was made of heartburn.

"Apples and oranges," he managed through a cough. He drew on the amber liquid lifeline.

I stared at the rim of my savory margarita, caked in pepper-flecked rock salt. I always forgot to ask for no salt. It seemed like such a given—don't mainline my beverage in sodium.

"So," Matt began tentatively.

"So."

"What are you going to do?"

"I don't think I want to write a memoir anymore," I told him. I hadn't vocalized this to anyone else. It wasn't a safe thing to say to my writing friends.

"It's probably not so easy to write that kind of book when your parents weren't trapeze artists killed in a plane crash or something," he said.

It's not the subject! I wanted to shriek at him. *A good writer can tell any story well!*

We wrote this in our MFA notebooks, were told to underline and star the affirmation. No one ever gives you the caveat in an inspirational craft talk.

"I think the agent had a point," I said. "Maybe I didn't have a whole book of a story. Maybe I just had an essay."

I'd been so in love with what my piece could be, I didn't take the time to consider what it couldn't do. The fact was I said what I had to say, succinctly, in 77,000 words too few. I manufactured a flimsy plot about self-actualization, hoping a few brilliant pages could ferry it through. I recast any scent of flaws I picked up as a lack of confidence. I thought I knew better than to leapfrog into a project without vision, and yet. Everything I'd wanted seemed so close. If I only reached just a bit more, maybe ... but no. Nobody wants your loosely chronological coming-of-age memoir. That was supposed to be the lesson the first time around.

"And you're not Lena Dunham," he reminded me.

Last time I checked, no. I was not. I gulped as much margarita as I could through the straw, before the vile salt could melt into it. I wondered what it was like, that notoriety cache. The proving of yourself complete, the unfettered access, the ability to chase whatever pursuit you wished. *I want the cover of* Vogue. *I want a book deal. I want to make out with Adam Driver because, you know, the script says we have to.*

"Do you have it out with any other agents?"

"There were three others," I said. They hadn't responded, and still haven't, as of this writing. "But I think there's something else I'd rather try instead."

"Yeah?"

"Remember when I went to the beach house in February? I kind of started working on a novel."

I didn't tell him that there was a whole first chapter saved on my desktop. That was too much accountability. I wasn't a fiction writer. Not since college when I wrote "Taco Tuesdays," a short story narrated by a stripper with a heart of gold about the Forrest Gump-type regular who came in for the taco special and was murdered by a Hell's Angel for smiling too much. It's what a workshop would label 'problematic.'

"You should write more stories like 'Taco Tuesday,'" my mom liked to suggest whenever a particularly depressing, excavating personal essay of mine hit the interwebs. Did I really have to go back and bring up how mean the girls in sixth grade had been to me? What good did that do for anyone? I, however, wasn't convinced I could write something that wasn't true.

Matt, on the other hand, wasn't so sure. "I've been telling you that!" he said. "I've been telling you to try fiction forever!" Whenever I lamented a fan fiction writer's six-figure advance or James Patterson's book-writing sweatshop, Matt's eyebrows ticked up to the crown of his head. *Maybe you should get in on that.* "What's it about?"

I needed more tequila. The waiter had vanished. Our collection of empty glassware grew. "It's about these two girls who were best friends in high school and college, and had a huge falling out. Then ten years later, they're thrown together again when one of them shows up as the new employee at the other's office. They have to reconcile their past relationship in order to move forward."

"'Reconcile their past to move forward?' Who wants to read that?"

I slammed back the last puddle of melted margarita. A few years ago this comment would have wounded me beyond repair. *No one will want this!* But now, I'd already gotten that answer. The worst-case was the scenario. And I was still here, wanting to work. I could put the criticism into context. By now I'd turned his disinterest into a mandate. My husband, the engineer, the man who'd only read two titles in the ten years I'd known him: *The Lord of the Rings* and the *Sin City* boxed graphic novel collection. He'd seen my hurt and wanted to ward it off at the pass, even if he didn't have the first clue how.

But at this point, I was getting used to face-planting. It was becoming less greatest-fear and more natural-state-of-being.

I tossed my hair back and tilted my gaze to the side, as if he were too boring even to stare at anymore. "I'm never discussing synopses with you again," I vowed to the open air. "You know nothing of literature."

"I guess that's true," he admitted.

I might not, either. But with enough liquid courage, I was at least willing to dive. Again.

Kaffee aus Äpfeln

True Mole

*A*s with good writing, there is true mole and there is all other mole. Do not waste your time settling for not-so-great mole out of a bag or from a jar with a stylized sun-sketch label. Or ordering it from restaurants that are also serving happy hour *queso* boats. *Queso* is delicious. But *queso* is not true. An experience as transcendent—and tradition as sacred—as the making of mole deserves time, love, and attention.

This recipe is based on a version of Rick Bayless' from one of my favorite cookbooks, *Rick Bayless's Mexican Kitchen*. You can tell it's beloved by all of the wrinkled, water-damaged, and chipotle-splattered pages my copy holds. I like to think that Rick would be willing to subtitle it *How to Survive in Tucson When You Are Lonely and Starving in Every Way,* just for me.

- o   8 chicken thighs, bone-in, skins removed[*]
- o   2 dried ancho chiles
- o   Vegetable oil
- o   1 small onion, diced
- o   2 garlic cloves
- o   4 small tomatoes
- o   1 cup dry roasted peanuts
- o   ⅓ cup panko breadcrumbs
- o   2 canned chipotle chiles in adobo
- o   ⅛ teaspoon allspice
- o   ½ teaspoon cinnamon
- o   1 tablespoon dark chocolate powder
- o   3 ½ cups chicken broth
- o   ½ cup pinot noir
- o   1 tablespoon cider vinegar
- o   2 bay leaves
- o   1 tablespoon sugar
- o   Salt and pepper to taste
- o   Serving stuffs: warm corn tortillas, sour cream, pico de gallo, cotija cheese

---

[*] because in braising recipes like this, bones are precious, and skin is flappy and gross.

In a large Dutch oven (like a Le Creuset), warm 1 tablespoon of vegetable oil over medium-high heat. Season the chicken thighs with salt and pepper, then add to the pan in batches. You're not trying to cook the chicken thighs completely, just sear them. Allow them to get a nice crust on each side, about 3-5 minutes per side. Add more oil if necessary (if they're sticking badly or if there's any burning), but try not to mess with them too much; the less they move and the more room each thigh has, the more irresistible crunchiness will happen. This is texture. This is everything.

Remove the thighs and refrigerate until we move on to their next step.

Warm a cast iron skillet on the stovetop (no oil necessary) on medium-high. Add the dried ancho chiles and toast until little tufts of steam billow out when you press down lightly with a spatula, about 1-2 minutes each side. Don't let that steam turn to smoke, though. That's bad.

Remove the chiles and place in a bowl of warm water for 30 minutes to rehydrate. Stir occasionally. When they are finished, remove the chiles, and discard the water.

Add a tablespoon of vegetable oil to the Dutch oven. Add the onion and garlic cloves and sauté, stirring frequently, until browned, about 10 minutes. Remove and place in a blender or food processor.

Place the tomatoes on a foil-lined baking sheet and broil until blackened, 5-8 minutes on each side.

Remove and allow to cool until you can safely handle them. The skins should easily slide off. Remove skins, and then place the tomatoes in the blender along with the peanuts, panko, chipotle, soaked ancho chiles, allspice, cinnamon, chocolate, and 1 ½ cups of the chicken broth. Blend until smooth. Press through a medium strainer into a bowl to catch any seeds or skin.

Heat 1 tablespoon of oil (again) in the Dutch oven on medium-high. When the oil is hot, add the mole purée base. Stir constantly until it thickens and darkens a bit, about 5 minutes. Stir in the remaining 2 cups of chicken broth, wine, vinegar, bay leaves, and reserved chicken thighs. Drop heat to medium, partially cover, and simmer for 45-60 minutes, stirring regularly. It can go longer, too, if you're busy with other things or simply want your house to keep smelling like mole. When ready to serve, remove the chicken thighs and bay leaves from the pot, discarding the leaves. Allow chicken to cool slightly. Shred the chicken from the bones (This will not be a chore), then add back into the sauce and stir. Sample the sauce, and add salt and pepper to your liking.

Serve with accoutrement to make your own little tacos, like your favorite salsa, cotija or feta cheese, sour cream, hot sauce, what have you. Rice, beans, and Juanita's tortilla chips are also acceptable.

Happy New Year

Cross my heart and hope to basic, I love fall. Fall is when the plumping and excess of summer dry up and crisp, leaving nothing but a dust that scatters in breezes so brisk they stun a weary warm-worn heart back to life. Most people begin the New Year on January 1st, but my fresh starts tend to cluster around the Autumnal Equinox. Maybe it's the years of anticipated first days of school, or my October birthday or September wedding anniversary, but it's the season I've always started new, including with infinitely better jobs. Fall was the time I applied for, and was accepted into, grad school. Last year, it was when my husband Matt and I were able to move back into our Oregon house after a long and complicated struggle to leave Tucson. Write all the pumpkin spice-hating thinkpieces you see fit. You will never convince me that this isn't the best time of the year.

Fall of 2015, to celebrate this most beloved of seasons, Matt and I met friends at Oktoberfest in Portland's Oaks Park. I didn't have time to wrangle a dirndl in time, but I wore a gargantuan fascinator I made a few years back, complete with faux dahlias, a stuffed owl, and a hot-glue gun gone mad.

"You must really love fall," the woman at Admissions keenly observed.

Five steins, half a bratwurst, and a drunken rollercoaster ride into the night later, my friend and I ended up in the Tarot card booth. A young woman shuffling a deck over a requisite purple tablecloth asked if there was anything in particular on my mind.

"I am a writer!" I proclaimed. "Tell me about writer things."

The first card she flicked in front of me was The Tower inverted, followed by an inverted Death. It was a carnival-tent horror movie cliché, and the woman immediately told me to calm down.

"This has nothing to do with physical harm," she assured me. "This is about the end of something in your life, destruction of what's holding you back, and a sign to move forward."

But I was already grinning. And no, it wasn't just the beer. It was the unequivocal evidence of what I already knew: my old book was dead. The one that had been through two agents and 10 years, more versions than I could store on a hard drive, the one I didn't want to look at—let alone write—any longer. After my devastating rejection in the summer, I was tentatively putting my energy back into what I had labeled on my computer desktop as *Emily and Julia*, the novel I'd started at the Sasquatch House. I was afraid to take it seriously; it was too fun. I was smiling too much when I wrote and reread it. It required my heart and my work, but when I sat down with it, the task felt effortless. This wasn't painful enough to seem legitimate. Not enough burning tower and grim reaper.

The next card, an inverted Nine of Cups. "Everything you desire will come true if you stay the course," she said.

Again, I already knew. I had always known. It was what kept me opening documents and hitting the Submit button at journals, even when the universe offered nothing but contrary evidence that it needed any more opinions. I hustled straight from the fortuneteller to the rollercoaster line, just to keep the high going. I wanted to live in the buzz of knowing I was doing the right work, that I was still The Ant.

The next day, as our hangovers subsided, Matt and I booked a room in Washington State's Bavarian town of Leavenworth for Oktoberfest 2016. One year from that day we'd be packing into my car to embark on an even bigger celebration of fall.

"A year," my husband marveled when we received a coveted hotel room's confirmation number. "You can do a lot in a year, you know."

I laughed. "Like write a book?"

In that off-handed instant, I knew exactly what we'd be toasting to when the pumpkins spiced in 2016: a completed novel draft ready for next steps, ready to take off. I divided the number of words I'd need by 365: 180 words a day. A hefty paragraph. A rambunctious email. Something concrete and achievable even on my most tired, inebriated, and otherwise shitty days. At last, in all the time since this book's concept occurred to me, its creation felt real.

More-Writing-Time Butternut Squash Soup

- 2 medium-sized butternut squash, peeled and cut into chunks
- 2 tablespoons olive oil
- 2 tablespoons vegetable oil
- ½ teaspoon cumin
- ¼ teaspoon paprika
- 1 dense and tart apple[*], peeled, cored and chunked
- 1 onion, diced
- 1 teaspoon dried sage
- 2 ½ cups chicken broth
- 2 ½ cups water
- ½ cup heavy cream
- Salt and pepper to taste

Preheat oven to 425° F. Toss the butternut squash cubes in the olive oil, then sprinkle with the cumin, paprika, salt, and pepper. Spread on a baking sheet lined with tinfoil. Roast for 25-30 minutes, until softened and irresistible to eating straight off the tray. While they're roasting, go and write your hefty paragraph. NO, do NOT turn on *House Hunters!* This is prime novel-progress time. But definitely take a few bites of that insanely good roasted butternut squash, because you need to be living your best life. Loudly proclaim your penchant for perfect spice combinations. It's part of the whole Queen of Fall deal.

Add the vegetable oil to a Dutch oven on medium-high heat. If anyone gives you crap for having two kinds of oil in this recipe, tell them it's because vegetable oil has a much higher smoke point that won't break down and destroy your delicate soup when you're sautéing. Roll your eyes for good measure. Sauté the onion, apple, and sage seasoned with salt and pepper for 4 minutes, until it begins to soften. Dump in the chicken broth, water, and butternut squash, bring to a boil, then drop the heat to

---

[*] such as Granny Smith.

low and cover. Let it sit there for however long you need. Want to finish this chapter? Do it. Read a craft book for inspiration? Whatever! The soup is fine. Forget about it.

But when you're so hungry you lose the story, remove the soup from the heat and stir in the heavy cream. Get out your immersion blender and purée the soup until it's chunk-free. If you don't have an immersion blender, log onto Amazon Prime and get one in an hour. The soup will wait. Or, if you don't want to support the evil corporate overlords that I hypocritically pledge my debit card devotion to, you can purée it in batches via regular blender, too. Serve with croutons and your favorite bread. Inhale. Resume chasing dream.

Procrastibaker

I marvel at the concept of writing full-time. Although in the last few years I've leaped over hurdles to defining myself as a writer (When a Lyft driver asks what I do, I now tell him I'm a writer without hesitation or apology), I have not made a transition into a life that is day job-free. I work full-time in a corporate capacity. I am assigned a cubicle. I manipulate spreadsheets and PowerPoint slides. I'm really handy with the Adobe Illustrator pen tool. It's not an awful job, and it's not a bad company. But it is eight hours of my weekdays behind a desk that is not dedicated to my own, personal work. And it's not teaching, which, despite the numerous pitfalls I understand and sympathize with, recognizes summer as something outside of just another quarter, and where publishing is integral to success.

Writing time is time I have to carve out with a chisel and an unrepentant heart. Things like relationships and yoga get the swift ax. I push off all errands that stop me from getting home as soon as I can, although, preserving these swaths of time is only a fragment of the challenge. Keeping it sacred for its intention is a second battle, a psychological thriller waged in the shadows. After work, I thrash against my best intentions:

ME: But I wanna watch *Empire!*

ME: You can watch *Empire* after you've written your 180 words.

ME: But then I'm going to miss all the live-tweeting!

ME: You're not even supposed to be ON Twitter right now.

ME: The whole point of the Golden Age of Television is live-tweeting!

ME: GO WRITE. It will literally take you 20 minutes if you

shut up and do it.

ME: Can't I just stay up later?

ME: YOU ARE A DISGRACE TO YOUR CRAFT AND A DISHONOR TO YOUR FAMILY!

It's not that I don't enjoy writing. The process feels cathartic and worthwhile. I love a fresh new document. I love hitting Save and Close on something now complete. If this game had any sense of logic, I'd be spending as much time at my writing desk as possible. A win-win scenario, if you will.

But then I have a weekend like I did a few Sundays back, when I'd dodged plans and had no commitments. The laundry was done. The fridge was stocked. The house was (kind of) clean. My beloved Seattle Sounders were on a bye week. I had a day that could be spent ceaselessly writing, without interruption.

"I think I'm going to make cookies," I said.

Not just one batch of cookies. Nah, with the miracle that is the KitchenAid Stand Mixer, a single batch of cookies would only take half an hour. I propped my Kindle up in the kitchen with tabs open for cranberry-oatmeal chocolate chip cookies, Linzer cookies, banana bread, pumpkin bars, and a humungous vat of gumbo (because we needed to eat dinner, too).

There is a quiet in baking that's tough to replicate in anything else. Time churns at an exponential speed while you're measuring, mixing, and switching sheets and pans out of the oven at the demand of the microwave timer. I slip into a kind of meditation where 'what is triple three-quarters of a teaspoon' is all that exists in the universe. When the world is whittled down to its narrowest lens, there is no room for anything else. All of the questions that felt inescapable all week (Will anybody care about these characters? Is this boring? Am I flushing another year of my life away on a project that won't go anywhere?) are lost in one singular concern: What is next?

Eggs.

Vanilla.

Oven.

Switch.

The same few steps over and over, the ingredients or technique tweaked slightly, yielding more possibilities than you can try in a lifetime. All the junk I keep stocked in the pantry—the flour, four kinds of sugar, mad scientist vials of extract—stirred to life. From inedible bags on the counter to divine Instagrammed bites. Seeing nothing become something wonderful in a single afternoon is good for the nerves. It reminds you of what's possible.

When the light had expired and the gumbo was thick, there were mountains of baked goods waiting on the table. Everything turned out the way it was supposed to. The banana bread stayed moist; the cranberry-oatmeal-chocolate mounds became my favorite new cookie. I didn't get lost or distracted; I surrendered to the process. The time and the work. The equation that I continue to doubt, but if I actually follow, never falters.

The next morning, I pack all the goodies up in Ziploc bags for freezers and friends. I double-check my novel math. Three hundred forty-three days. At pace for 61,740 more words.

Another weekday arrives, with the commute and the hours in the not-writing-desk and the gumbo leftovers for lunch and the drive back and a new dinner and new dishes and a few hours to breathe. It's so easy to get lost in every other thing. I could clean the bathroom or watch all the Netflix I deserve.

Such little time. So much work.

I bring a cookie and a cup of tea into my own office. I start another line.

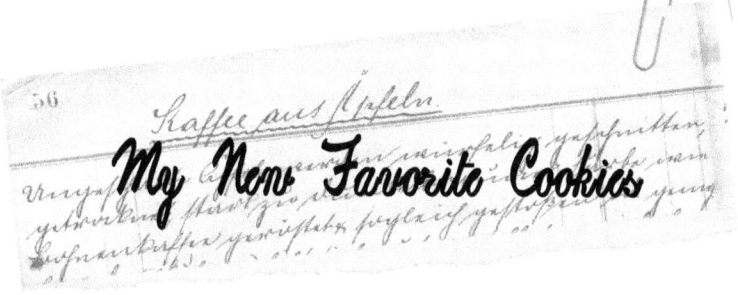

My New Favorite Cookies

*A*dapted from a recipe from Ocean Spray. Who knew corporate-mandated recipes were actually good?

- ○ ⅔ cup butter
- ○ ⅔ cup brown sugar, packed
- ○ 2 large eggs
- ○ 1 ½ cups old-fashioned oats[*]
- ○ 1 ½ cups flour
- ○ 1 teaspoon baking soda
- ○ 1 teaspoon vanilla
- ○ 1 cup dried cranberries[**]
- ○ 1 cup chocolate chips, or your favorite dark chocolate bar, cut into small chunks[***]

Preheat oven to 375° F. In a small mixing bowl, combine the oats, flour, baking soda, and salt. Set aside while you deal with more pressing matters.

Use a KitchenAid mixer to beat butter and sugar until fluffy. If you don't have such a mixer, you can use a spoon, and it will be much better for your arms. Either the surprisingly difficult manual labor or the hypnotic spin of the KitchenAid batter paddle will lull you into a magical state where you are not thinking of all the cool Brooklyn-based journals you've yet to land a story in. How do they have room for all those cool-kid journals in Brooklyn, anyway? How big and literary is that neighborhood? Is it just one giant, abandoned library?

Add the eggs, just until they're incorporated into the butter/sugar cloud. Add vanilla until it's just stirred in. Add the flour mixture in several additions, allowing it to mix fully into the batter before adding more. You won't be able to check and see all

---

[*] No millennial oats allowed.

[**] You know what's better than dried cranberries, though? Dried cherries. Use those if you can.

[***] OR, in my case, leftover Hershey's bars from all the summer s'mores I never made.

the Twitter calls for submissions you're not responding to because your hands are full of bowls, and the only thing that matters in this moment is making sure you don't overmix. It's okay. Less cool stuff is happening than you'd think.

Form into 1-inch round balls, and place on a greased cookie sheet about 2 inches apart from each other. Bake for 9-12 minutes, depending on how hot your oven runs. You'll want to keep watch the whole time and definitely not go off and check if anyone's visited your website today.

Cool on wire racks. Use as a bribe to get yourself to finish whatever it is you're putting off today.

Teriyaki Meatballs Reborn

*T*here's a story I wrote eight years ago that my mom still won't stop talking about.

Notice I said *story*, not essay.

"You should write more stories like 'Taco Tuesday,'" she'll say, harkening back to ye olde undergrad days at Concordia University when I was an English major who had to take four courses in Dead White Man Lit for every one creative writing credit. As much as I loved the writing classes as sunbreaks in between analysis of *The Scarlet Letter* and *The Turn of the Screw*, I wasn't a good writer. I wasn't even trying to 'be' a writer, a career I lumped in with Astronaut and Hello Kitty Merchandise Tester on my unreachability scale. I wanted to be in marketing. In my imagination, any company marketing department was a cluster of cubicles full of inflatable palm trees and Nerf gun wars, where creatives with financial responsibilities sat around all day thinking up pun-filled slogans and funny commercial ideas.

I did not realize, as I discovered one Bachelor of Arts too late, that it would be a lifetime of pasting talking points into PowerPoint slides that the higher-ups can't figure out how to use, stale blog entries written in 'the corporate voice,' and cropping product photos into Amazon.com page dimensions. But I digress.

When my mother wants me to write more stories like "Taco Tuesday," what she's saying is that she wants fewer essays about how much I threw up in middle school, or how desperate I was to fuck strangers in college, or how depressed I became when we moved to Arizona. She wants to dial back any mentions of her, or my dad, or my siblings, or anyone we've ever mutually known, by a solid 97 percent.

"Taco Tuesday" did not feature me, my parents, my relatives, or ninth-grade teachers I crushed on. Just like my *Legend of Zelda* and *Pirates of the Caribbean* fan fiction didn't represent anyone in our world (aside from visitors on the screen I could plagiarize instead), and neither did my Benedict Arnold historical spy novel that I thought, in 8th grade, was such an accomplished opus, it deserved a prequel.

These are the stories I use as my perennial examples of why I don't write fiction, since they were the last fictions I wrote for nearly a decade. After my short-story class, I moved on to a course introducing the new new journalism, where I discovered Susan Orlean and Thomas Wolfe and never looked back at the garbage pile of stripper tacos, softcore *Legend of Zelda* videogame erotica, or historical epics about teenage girls who became spies for George Washington. I buried where I came from.

"I'm an essayist," I mantra'd. I didn't write fiction. I was terrible at it.

I didn't move out into my first apartment knowing how to cook. I went on a few culinary adventures in my dorm room, none with any notable success. The most foolproof dish was Campbell's Chunky Gumbo microwaved and served over gummy grains I made in a bargain rice cooker. Mostly there were disasters. I had a dorm-contraband hot plate next to my TV/VCR combo deluxe 13-inch entertainment center, and a few days before Christmas break, I took the plate full of boiled pasta noodles into the community bathroom to drain, which I thought I could do without a colander by holding the lid at the right angle. Except that I am exceptionally uncoordinated and let the plate slip. All the noodles slipped down the drain, and I quietly retreated, unseen, and tried to forget the incident until, two weeks later, I noticed a Roto-Rooter truck parked outside the dorm. That was the end of Elizabeth Dorm Hall pasta nights.

I loved food in college, just as I always had growing up, but I was stuck in foodie purgatory. In the small, restricted space of a dorm room, I couldn't get any better at cooking. With a bank account fed only with a trickle of part-time minimum wages from my Frederick's of Hollywood underwear salesgirl job, I could scrape together enough for the occasional splurge, like a half-sandwich from the fancy New Seasons grocery deli with house-smoked turkey and avocado and aioli, but most of my meals were from the cafeteria—and one must temper her expectations when relying on a college cafeteria.

The Concordia University Cafeteria of 2003, however, was beyond bad. It was comically bad. Sold-the-food-contract-to-the-lowest-bidder- and-the-corporation-had-to-get-creative-with-how-they-could-deliver-on-the-bottom-line bad. The place dredged Eggos through imitation eggs and flour and called it Waffle French Toast for dinner.

One afternoon, while waiting outside for the cafeteria to open (my customary nightly ritual in this perpetually bored and hungry time), I found myself browsing a pop-up book fair. Like the ones from elementary school, but with less Boxcar Children and more Vonnegut. After picking up Barbara Ehrenreich's *Nickel and Dimed*, I noticed a pink gingham-covered binder stacked on an endcap. *The Better Homes and Gardens New Cookbook*, the same basic cooking bible that my mother had. And most likely, her mother, as well—the first version having been published in 1930.

The book was boulderesque. Over a thousand recipes for everything from jam-print Christmas cookies to peanut sauce Thai noodles. I held it to my chest like an infant, cradling the weight of what my future could be. *This could be* my *cookbook*, I thought, squinting out through the fog into what I'd become after securing my four-year English degree. I could see the Seattle apartment I'd always imagined with a loft floorplan and panoramic windows, like Aleksandr Petrovsky's playboy artist penthouse in season six of *Sex and the City*. I'd battle my way home through a swarm of calls and emails because I would be very important and very necessary to somebody. Doing what and for whom, I had no vague clue, but those were periphery details. Much like Carrie Bradshaw and her holy inner circle, what I did for work was largely irrelevant (save for a few window-dressing episodes set in a gallery or PR office) against what I did after work: cocktails, best friends, shoes that cost more than any balance I'd ever carried in my bank account. I'd be the best Girlfriend in every sense of the word: the girl who was constantly getting texts from her closest confidants, and the sexy goddess who could lace her own corset, deep-throat a banana, AND make a frittata. I'd be good for everyone.

Like my inventory of thigh-high stockings, *The Better Homes and Gardens New Cookbook* was a prop—a hoarded souvenir from the future that I could only dream of using. I squirreled it away as if I were building a spell that could skip over all the fumbling, graceless becoming and deliver me as this glorious full version of self, living a purposeful, fulfilling life without the plight of earning it.

I have tried to explain my friendship with Claire in a dozen iterations of the same essay. It was one of the first stories I tried to tell in graduate school, the piece passed around the table at my first workshop.

"You have a great ear for dialogue," someone praised.

The lines were scraped from my first writings on the subject drafted during my last year at Concordia, sentences lifted straight from my college LiveJournal. I tried to keep them true, but they've been copied down and rewritten so many times, I now know each of the character's inked scripts better than I remember the actual night.

"I like the details," said someone else. Ian's Jesus Christ cast-off sandals. His Dandy Warhols T-shirt. Claire's pixie posters and the clove cigarettes we shared that tasted like cinnamon.

"But I don't fully understand the relationship between them."

"And what about the ending? I really didn't get the ending."

There is no ending to Claire and Tabitha. There was an explosion and a crater, and I have fumbled in our darkness ever since.

We were best friends from middle through high school—ubiquitous, each the other's mascot. "Where's Tabitha?" anyone might ask. Claire would know the answer, and vice versa forever. Weekends were spent on each other's floors, eating foods stocked in either house's cupboards (her mom and dad becoming my second set of parents). We registered for the same classes and sat in the same circles of friends, our Venn diagram of talents bringing disparate cliques together. I brought in the Model United Nations and the Honors English Class; she brought Drama and Band.

After walking each other down the graduation aisle, we forked along the I-5 corridor. Claire enrolled at Evergreen State College in Olympia, a leftist greenhouse best known for not giving grades and cultivating Nirvana and Macklemore. I crossed the state line into Portland for Concordia, a Lutheran university I picked for dubious reasons like 'Portland seems cool,' and 'I got a scholarship because my family used to go to church' and 'They were nice and sent me a free T-shirt.' In my aimless college search, they were the first, simplest answer.

It's here where the story begins to fracture. If you could find Claire and ask her what happened to us in college, I don't know what she'd say. You only have my version, which is that she drifted away from me, into this lush world of organic-vegetarian cafeteria produce and midnight screenings of *Priscilla, Queen of the Desert* and polyamorous roommates who embarked on naked vision quests in the woods between campus apartments. I'd explain that I did everything possible to remain relevant and loved by the best friend I ever had. And my plan worked, up until the moment I stopped faking.

The night I met Matt for our first date was the end of drinking until I couldn't close my eyes because I'd die of dizziness. It was the end of trying to sleep with people not because I was attracted to them or even wanted to be anywhere near them, but because I had a quota to meet to be considered still sexy and free. It was the end of me seeking to renew my visa into Claire's bohemian universe. I no longer had to try to be loved, because I'd found someone who would love me without my begging, or even trying.

It was not, I thought, the end of my best friendship. I brought Matt over to Claire's apartment on a summer night a month after we'd met, the first and only time they were in a room together. We shot vodka while *Family Guy* reruns droned in the background. Matt and I slept in the spare bedroom and left early, careful not to wake Claire and Ian in the master. I think I left a cute note on the fridge saying something like: *Thanks for the couple's date!* But that could just be wishful thinking.

If I'd known it was the last time I would see her, I'd have shaken her awake, screaming as we catapulted into the abyss. *I love you! I always did! How can you forget that?*

She stopped calling and emailing. I got worried, then hurt, then annoyed, then furious. Rumors crept in from the molding crevices of our mutual friends.

"She didn't like Matt," one told me matter-of-factly over the phone, with all the sensitivity of pointing out I had spinach wedged in my teeth. When I asked why, she just said, "You'll have to ask her that yourself."

A difficult proposition, as every transmission I sent ended up in a void. It wasn't until the next January that Claire answered my phone call. I was fresh off work at Frederick's of Hollywood, where I'd performed my nightly ritual of vacuuming the cheetah-print carpet. The store vacuum was an old toothless junk-pile with a cord; I would've done a more effective job shuffling my feet in circles around the floor for 20 minutes. But a new one would come out of our location's bottom line, and our manager wasn't in the mood for a District Supervisor lecture on upselling with perfume and marabou slippers. The loud, useless vacuum did drown out the store's Muzak station of Christina Aguilera covers, and the loops around the thong tables and corset racks lulled me into a white noise Zen state outside of Lloyd Center Mall, to whatever was gnawing hardest at my heart.

That night I thought of all the shitty boyfriends I'd put up with that Claire had brought around over the years—the boys she leapfrogged from in a state of perpetual taken-dom from the day we met in 8th grade on through that very night, as I hung back, always single and available, content to play any role as long as I were allowed to stay. The smart friend. The hilarious friend. The slutty friend. The blacked-out-in-the-bathtub friend. Claire's boyfriends were a palette of asshole shades, from the one who told me he wouldn't set me up with his friend because he didn't feel the guy should have to 'settle,' to the one who was too cool and punk rock to learn my name. They were all the worst, but she was the best. As with most things at the time, I didn't know any better.

How dare she throw us away, I thought, flinging myself into each vacuum thrust, the beltless mouth mawing each syllable. *How. Dare. She.*

By the time the manager closed out the cash register and locked the gate, I was shaking. I would have whipped my Ford Aerostar to the right of the parking lot and hell-run all the way up to Olympia if it meant closing out this account once and for all.

But I didn't need to. For the first time in over six months, Claire took my call.

You might wonder what happened on the phone that night. I know I do. I wish I could submit some kind of special request form to the NSA for a hall pass. I'd find a wall of file cabinets from January 2006 and flip to my maiden name, past the call recordings between Matt and me, and Mom and me, and find that one conversation that snapped Claire and me in two. I'd listen to the lines I've been replaying in my memory for a decade, getting scratchier and distorted and further away with each repeat and rewind like the mixtape cassettes I used to make.

I'd read the transcript of us sniping back and forth, as Claire admitted she didn't like my boyfriend, and I accused her of abandonment. I'd grow angry at the impotence of it all: the pettiness of two girls scarce old enough to drink balling up the longest relationship that either of them ever had. I'd see the click from my end when I had finally had enough of Claire's accusations of—what, exactly? Her anger is tangled around my own, and as the years pass, I lose the ability to recall her claim, or her voice, or her face.

And I know that even if I had that definitive master track transcript, I still wouldn't know why she disowned me for life. All the replays in the world will never let me into her heart for that. She had her reasons for letting me go. My reasons for caring won't square with them, and the more I try to reconcile what I won't know with what little I do, the further I get from either of us. We are a puzzle missing half of its pieces.

So the essay stumbles off a cliff. I trip up on the unraveling truth. I lose myself in woods without light. After a dozen failed attempts to excavate Claire and me, I realize that I'll need another way in. A way that isn't constructed from fact.

The Better Homes and Gardens New Cookbook made it out of my Concordia dorm along with the other random housewares that had caught my eye before I had a house: Japanese rice bowls, half a dozen pairs of chopsticks, a Hello Kitty alarm clock.

"This has every recipe in history," I told Matt, giving it a place of honor behind the toaster in our first kitchen.

That starter kitchen was the size of my current closet and was an overworked, under-upgraded, one-eyed teddy bear of a space. The linoleum curled on every edge like pages in an ancient tome, collecting grime and rice grains between its teeth. The stove was baked brown from decades of boiled-over Kraft Macaroni & Cheese. Mold crept in and thrived around the drafty windows, knitting a second, fuzzy frame.

That being said, it was an entirely appropriate kitchen for a terrible cook. And I was a truly appalling cook. It wasn't that I lacked passion. My desire to be excellent kept me trying and fooled me into thinking I was making more progress than I actually was. I couldn't afford good ingredients or halfway-decent tools. My cabinets were stocked with anything my mom had decided she didn't want, like a set of old Pfaltzgraff dishes and Calphalon pans. Gifting them down to me was the perfect excuse for her own upgrade. I stole steak knives from McMenamins Kennedy School restaurant where we'd order burgers, until my dad visited one weekend and found the bent, stubbly things in my drawer.

"Are these your only steak knives?" he asked, running the dull, serrated edge along the thick callus of his hand. "I don't think this would scratch butter." Before he left for home, a modest set of Macy's replacements appeared on the counter.

I picked steak cuts and ground beef out of the discount basket at Fred Meyer and Safeway, plastic packages with fluorescent orange REDUCED stickers slapped like warnings.

"I don't know if I trust this stuff," Matt said.

"Why? They can't sell it if it's bad."

"But it smells bad," he pointed out.

"Bah. No, it doesn't."

"Now it doesn't! You covered it in seasoning salt."

"It's fine."

We spent the night trading places on our apartment's sole toilet.

But I kept trying. I'd take the pink-checkered cookbook down into our living room where Food Network played on endless loop. It was 2005, before the channel turned into living culinary clickbait with *Chopped*, *Cutthroat Kitchen*, and *Diners, Drive-Ins and Dives*. I flittered in and out of the kitchen to the soundtrack of Alton Brown making a dehydrator out of air filters and box fans, Ina Garten extolling the virtues of using 'the good maple syrup, not that disaster they sell in a bottle shaped like a *Gone with the Wind* character,' Giada De Laurentiis overpronouncing mOOntzaRelLA. These were the sages I beamed into my novice life. I learned that pasta water had to be salted and that vegetables can't cook properly in a crowded pan ratcheted up to HIGH. Open the oven door when you broil! Keep it shut while you bake!

"Help me pick out something for dinner," I told Matt, nudging the cookbook toward him.

He eyed it with suspicion, as if it were a stray dog, uninvited and costly.

"What sounds good?" I asked.

"I don't know. Not Asian."

Which was odd, I thought, because he always wanted to go out for Asian. Thai! Teriyaki! Hell, even the sack of Chinese deli boxes you could bring home from Safeway to feed us for under $10!

"We've had a lot of it lately," he claimed, until the next day when we splurged on takeout.

It may have been because I was a substandard cook in general, but when it came to anything from Japan, Taiwan,

Thailand, or Vietnam, I was downright appalling. Not only was I crowding my pans, I was adding sauce before adding the ingredients to the heat, instead of waiting until moments before they were pulled from the stove. The innate hoisin sauce and teriyaki sugars charred in the extreme heat, giving the meal a distinct creosote flavor. I made pad thai from box kits they've since discontinued from Trader Joe's. My standby specialty from the *Better Homes* cookbook was a spicy peanut noodle with globs of Skippy's and canned pineapple tidbits.

But I could make anything, I believed. I had the instructions right there. I kept flipping through and trying.

"Oh, teriyaki meatballs!" I said one night. My mom used to make them with a jar of Chicken Tonight, the 90s premade sauce that may have been made from pure high fructose corn syrup but held up that thick, buoyant consistency that I loved, tossed with deep-fried pork bits at the Americanized Chinese restaurants around Seattle with their pagoda doors and video lottery lounges.

"Are you sure you want to try that?" Matt asked. "It seems kinda tricky to get right, you know? Like maybe it's a secret recipe you need special equipment for?"

"It'll be fine." I waved him off. "Look. It calls for cornstarch. Cornstarch makes everything work." A token of Rachael Ray wisdom. She did love to steer me asunder.

I stood on the creaky kitchen floor a long time that night, whisking a teaspoon of cornstarch in a pinch bowl with equal parts water, then another, trying to elevate the ginger-spiked meatballs out of the brothy sauce in which they puddled. No matter how much miracle thickener I drizzled into the pan, it remained thin and textureless.

The texture might be off, but maybe it tastes fabulous, I assured myself.

I spooned rivers of sauce onto the beds of rice, which slipped right through the grains to the bottom of the plate, soaking into the frozen egg rolls I'd toasted in the oven. The flavor wasn't bad. It wasn't anything. I'd succeeded only in making the meatballs, canned pineapple, and green pepper chunks kind of wet.

We both spooned the food into our mouths politely without comment, focusing the conversation instead on how we were never going to make a special crawfish incubator tank out of a cooler, no matter what Alton Brown said. That night, after Matt went to bed, I quietly took the *Better Homes and Gardens* book out from behind the toaster. I can't remember if I tucked it right into the garbage can under the sink or went the civilized route of disposing it in my Goodwill-bound bag—along with the collage boots I bought on clearance at Frederick's simply because they were $8.00—but I do know that I haven't seen it since.

I never did get The Claire Essay out. I wrote and rewrote the narrative from graduate school, including it as part of my doomed memoir manuscript. I sent it out to literary journals on its own and fielded a brief rejection from each one. As my writing progressed, Claire kept creeping into the periphery, appearing in a flashback here, mentioned as a high school best friend there. I finally folded our friendship's story up in the drawer with other ill-fated work, too frustrated to keep hacking at it.

"Sometimes a story isn't going to work out," I'd once heard in graduate school. This was the sign of a mature writer, one of my advisors claimed—knowing when to walk away.

Even though I gave up on ever getting my friendship essay right, I couldn't shake it out of my head. It lingered. The years that are now an expanse larger than our friendship was, an insurmountable chasm that will continue to grow for the rest of our lives. As much as I like to think I'm strong enough to forget her, as rarely as I allow myself to speak her name, as hard as I try not to speak of her out loud, I still remember her birthday. When I watch our favorite turn-of-the-millennium movies, I can smell her bedroom and the Bath & Body Works spray. I remember her commentary on *Sailor Moon* and *Kill Bill;* I can pin the points where she laughed at anime gags and bitched about how annoying Daryl Hannah's voice was. I haven't rid myself of her. She's only suppressed.

It wasn't long after our blow-up that she began appearing as fiction.

A reoccurring dream. I find myself in line at Starbucks or a teriyaki shop. She turns around and we're face-to-face for the first time in whatever time it's been. We laugh—it's absurd! We both want to know, what exactly were we fighting about all this time? What even happened?

"I'm sorry," I say. Every time. I apologize for being angry and swinging the hammer. I've wanted to fix it. I've tried. I didn't know how.

"Don't worry about it." She waves me off. "We've already wasted too much time." Through her benevolence we are delivered. We plan to meet later. Maybe share the coffee. Leave together. I wake up before we get to the counter.

I used to curse myself any time this dream appeared. *Why do you still care so fucking much?* I chided my pathetic subconscious. *She isn't thinking about you.*

Grief of any stripe is not something you get over. It becomes a part of you: a new appendage you learn to maneuver with eventual grace. You still stumble. You still trip on the memories and the thick, insatiable want. Claire would haunt me, I learned. That was the way my heart was wired. I couldn't love another person that fiercely and expel her ghost. She may have been blessed with a talent for cleaving people out of her life. We were not the same.

I remember a senior-year afternoon, in the wake of being offered a New York college scholarship. We loitered on the swingset in my neighborhood's park overlooking a drainage pond rebranded as prime Pacific Northwest scenery. The idea that we could be spending what I imagined to be the four most important years of our lives on opposite coasts was seeping into my bones, and a sniffle kicked off a howling batch of tears. Claire kicked her feet in the wood chips, bringing her lithe body to a halt and scenting the air with wet cedar. She hugged me until I had nothing left, only mute heaves of breath on her shoulder.

"This had to happen someday," she said. "We can't be friends forever."

I looked beyond the cotton of her shoulder, the faux island crammed with pines, the houses our parents mortgaged fatefully close, the city limits I vowed to bolt from, staring into the face of the question that girl and this woman cannot answer: *but why not?*

The reconciliation dream became less frequent. I became less angry. My impatience with myself folded into a curiosity. What would happen if I did see her again? Would I recognize her now, over a decade later? When I try to draw her face in my memory, I'm splattering with thick strokes and daubs. Can I imagine her voice any longer, or am I thinking of an actress who could pass for her, like Kirsten Dunst?

One day, a few weeks before I packed my car too full for Rockaway Beach and the Sasquatch House writing weekend, I was talking to my mom on the phone.

"I can't be sure," she said, "but I think I saw Claire last weekend."

I felt as if I'd just finished sprinting a mile, heart pounding, breath caught in my throat. "Where?" I asked.

"In West Seattle on Alki. When me and Dad were waiting in line at that Thai place. We had a Groupon that was about to expire."

Our last remaining mutual friend had dropped that name over a beer. *She's living on Alki now. I think she was supposed to get married? But then she didn't? I don't know; we don't talk much.* I didn't push.

"She was with a guy. He looked like a hipster. Wearing a leather jacket and skinny jeans."

"That sounds about right." At least, if her type hadn't changed since high school. "Did she ... recognize you? Or say anything?"

"She didn't say anything, but she had to have seen us," Mom said. "Maybe it wasn't her."

"No, it had to be her." It had to be. This was the only thread between us in a decade. Thin and frayed and once-removed. "What a bitch. She couldn't even say hi to you?" What I wouldn't trade to see her parents once again, the honorary relatives I'd lost in our divorce. *I love you. I grew up. Are you proud?* I imagined her mother working at the library as she had all the years I'd known her, shelving books in the B section.

Would she know my married name?

Would she recognize the platinum-blond woman grinning up at her from the back cover as that round-faced, redheaded girl who practically lived in her house?

I didn't ask any further questions. I kept my desperation under lock and key.

I have a tendency to charge when I should tiptoe. I chase mirages. I believe in myself before I've proven a thing.

When I am too young or inexperienced or ill-equipped and I miss the mark, I get discouraged. I think, *If I can't get it now, I never will.* This idea that life can circle back on itself closer to what my heart's been after, that inspiration and ability and energy ebb and flow in their own seasons—this is new. I'm only just brushing my fingers against this idea that failing once isn't failing forever.

The idea that there may be another way is a revolution.

In the fall of 2015, almost a decade after Claire's and my breakup, I was in Costco on my lunch hour. It was a trip for picking up essentials—the humungous loaf of Tillamook cheese, garlic compound butter, jalapeño yogurt dip. I was on high alert for checkered tablecloths and blue-aproned silver-hairs marking the free sample tables. The promise of half a Bagel Bite or taquito was enough of a reason to pick up supplies at Costco over Fred Meyer or Safeway or Target. They weren't sharing.

Today was extra special in the realm of promotional bites. From across the warehouse the Aidells canopy tent towered, sheltering Crock-Pots full of meatballs and sausages. Sausages are, after all, my favorite form of protein, with meatballs nipping at their heels.

"Chicken pineapple teriyaki meatballs," a woman announced as she held a toothpick offering out to me. Light, salty, with just the faintest touch of tart-sweet balance. "Wonderful over rice," she promised.

Wonderful over rice and surrounded by a thick, bright sauce playing the same notes. With chunks of grilled pineapple, onion, and sweet bell pepper. These little meatballs were born to swim in sweet and sour sauce. I could see it ten thousand dinner plates ago, the molten red atop my childhood bed of rice, the Chicken Tonight my mother so brazenly used with beef. A dish I hadn't reattempted for a decade, now a craving with only one cure.

I placed a two-pack in my cart.

That night I did not announce what was for dinner. I worked over the skillet quietly, tasting relentlessly, in and out of the fridge for more 'something' five times over. I was getting tired of biffing it in front of a crowd—the same reason I hadn't let a soul read the first 100 pages of *Emily and Julia*. In the kitchen there was always my garbage can; on my laptop, the Trash bin.

To the highest-rated AllRecipes instructions, I added Dijon mustard (It seemed too sweet). I added sweet chili sauce (It needed to be sweeter but also spicier and maybe goopier, too). I kept my industrial-strength Clear-Jel thickener at the ready in case of soup. I made backup plans in my mind (There's a bag of chicken strips in the freezer that can come to the rescue in 27 minutes). I brainstormed other ways I could use the Asian-themed meatballs: skewered with Yoshida's teriyaki dipping sauce, perhaps, or halved in fried rice. Safe, finesse-less dishes that were too banal to violate the Asian foods ban.

But as I kept stirring, my spoon circles met with slightly more resistance. A path carved in the sauce as I swept. It was *thickening,* suspending the vegetable and pineapple slivers in its silky, gelatinous slurry. Was this the joy that kept Jell-O molds and aspics so inescapably popular for all those years? Happiness congealed from magic only you can coax into being. I ran my finger along the ring of the skillet, coating the tip in a glop of sauce.

It tasted like the sweet and sour of my youth: wildly inauthentic, more comfort than I knew I needed.

This is not to say that I have transcended onto some Masaharu Morimoto plane of culinary existence. It is not to say that I won't catch the last half of *Ghost World* on HBO and remember seeing it at an arthouse Tacoma theater with Claire. I love too hard and I make a mess. I was never going to come out of this as the cool girl who could brush off a heartbreak—my hands are clumsy. I'm sure my lumpy sushi rolls would be banned on Okinawa, and my sweet-and-sour meatball win is as American as nailing a double bacon cheeseburger. But sometimes one ringing success can drown out a thousand other disasters. It can make you try what you've roped off from yourself as too abstract or too hard or too painful. It is the simple permission your heart grants to try again. Set yourself at it once more. This could be the time you nail it.

Try Again (and Again) Teriyaki Meatballs

*T*his is my recipe with all my taste-adjustment additions, which I keyed into my phone as soon as I could before I forgot them forever. I obviously used chicken meatballs from Costco, but I've included my favorite scratch meatball recipe here if you want to be way less lazy than I am. Just be warned, you're missing out on some bomb-ass free samples.

For the Meatballs
- ¾ pound ground beef[*]
- ¾ pound ground pork
- ½ cup panko breadcrumbs
- 2 tablespoons heavy cream
- 1 egg
- 1 teaspoon soy sauce
- ¼ teaspoon ground ginger
- ½ teaspoon garlic powder

For the Sweet and Sour Sauce
- 1 white onion, sliced
- 1 red bell pepper, sliced
- 1 green bell pepper, sliced
- 1 cup packed brown sugar
- 3 tablespoons cornstarch[**]
- 3 cups water
- ½ cup rice vinegar
- ⅓ cup, plus 1 tablespoon soy sauce
- ½ cup ketchup
- 1 tablespoon Dijon mustard
- 1 teaspoon Worcestershire sauce
- 2 teaspoons sweet Thai chili sauce
- Cooking oil[***]

---

[*] not the leanest kind; you need some fat, so 80/20 would be my recommendation.

[**] I use Clear-Jel because I'm paranoid, but if you feel that you have superior jelling skills, by all means, go ahead.

[***] I use vegetable oil.

For the meatballs, gently combine the beef and pork with your hands to get it going a bit before adding all other ingredients and mixing until combined. A spoon will not work with this. You've got to get all up in there. I use a 1-inch cookie scoop to scoop and form my meatballs, but if you don't have one, just roll into 1-inch balls. Place on a cookie sheet covered in tinfoil and fitted with a wire cooling rack. This allows the meatballs to stand above the pan itself, so the fat can drip down off of them instead of letting them stew in their grease. If you elevate your meatballs, they become toothsome on the outside while remaining moist on the inside, which is exactly what you're going for. Place in a 375° F oven for 20 minutes, until the outsides of the meatballs are browning and quite a bit of fat has been rendered down into the foil.

Let those cook and then cool while you prepare the sauce.

In a thick-sided skillet, add the oil on medium-high heat. Sauté onions and bell peppers together until beginning to soften, about 4 minutes. In a mixing bowl combine brown sugar, rice vinegar, ketchup, mustard, Worcestershire sauce, and spices. Add to pan, pour in the water, and bring to a boil. Reduce heat to medium and add the cornstarch. Stir until thickened, about 5-7 minutes. Add reserved meatballs and cook through. Serve on white rice with sriracha sauce at the ready.

Orange Is the New Blah

"**Y**ou should come down here for Christmas," I told my mom over the phone in that flat, quiet tone people use when saying things that will never come to pass.

I don't even let her begin the list of reasons why that's not going to happen. They'd have to haul all the gifts down to Oregon. My siblings would have to get down here. No one wanted a Portland Christmas. I cut her short first:

"I know, I know. I'm kidding."

I'm wishful thinking. I'm crafting a fantasy of escape from the impending gauntlet of relatives who haven't seen me since this same time last year, a time packed with its own set of awkward questions: *When can we buy your book? Do you have an Amazon page? Did you know that J. K. Rowling was rejected 30 times before she published* Harry Potter? *I keep hearing about ebooks—you could give that a go, couldn't you?*

Last year was easier. I still had my lamppost in the hurricane to cling to: "Oh, you know. My agent is working on it." I could duck and come back for much easier questions on how happy we were to be back from Tucson after Matt's year-and-a-half job relocation, and how long it had taken us to unpack. I could tell horror stories about living apart when I'd found a job in Portland, and he was still waiting for his company to greenlight his return, and we could all laugh at the whole mess, now folded into our past.

Now I'd be heading in with way too much mess and artistic pathos to explain over stuffed mushrooms and cocktail meatballs. I could already feel the nods, the accidental eyebrow twitches.

"I don't know why you're so worried about it," Mom said. I

stared up from the couch at our Christmas tree, the most ambitious version I've ever attempted. I spent hours tying wire ribbons on the boughs, graduating from the messy all-ornaments hodgepodge approach of years past. It looked like a tree that wouldn't be kicked out of a hotel lobby. A tree worth driving to Portland for.

Hours I didn't spend writing. The evidence glowed with the intensity of 300 tiny twinkle lights.

"Besides, I thought you were feeling really good about your book," she said.

"I do feel good about it. It's going to happen," I reminded her with my latest absolution. For the first time in my adult life, I amassed enough vacation days to take the entire holiday chunk of work off. Ten whole days between Christmas Eve Eve and New Year's Day with nothing but me, my laptop, and leftover sugar cookies. It was like Breadloaf with fruitcake. And no bunk beds. And the only writer in residence was I.

It's an extremely exclusive program.

Here is what my day looks like: My alarm goes off at 5:15. I hit snooze every five minutes until 5:45. This drives Matt insane—*You can't even fall back asleep in five minutes!* he claims, but this is only because he is bad at sleeping. I try to explain that I cannot roll out of bed cold turkey, but there's no reasoning with some people. I drive to my office, a jaunt that takes anywhere from 30 to 60 minutes depending on the frequency of fender-benders, and I park underneath the parking lot's resident Douglas fir tree to finish putting on my makeup. Before I go up to my desk, a cubicle that feels like an adult playpen I've been plunked in for eight hours of daycare, I do a quick phone scroll of my feeds.

My east coast writer friends are already awake, scoping out the best spot by the window with lattes topped in foam ferns, proceeding to take over the world.

New day, new residency applications, their Twitter and Facebook blurbs shout.

Scones and The Sun Magazine. *#litsunshine*

If I don't finish my novel revision today, please come over and hold a gun to my head until results improve. Kthxbye.

When you follow a couple thousand people, it's easy for the greenest grass to stick out in radioactive neon. Maybe only a handful of my friends were full-time writers, but in the warped refraction of social media, it looked like I was the only dumbass heading into a day job.

I coveted their creative time with supernova intensity. *If only*, I lamented with every step up the office staircase. If only I'd committed to being a writer before we bought a house. If only I could clean up on *Jeopardy! Disney, Sailor Moon, and Titanic Trivia Night*. What I couldn't do with an unlimited spool of days with only two agenda items:

1. Survive.
2. Write.

I'd read so many craft books and author interviews set in this parallel universe where people sat home with their laptops and chapters, sometimes even getting *paid* to be there. Their schedule details were like porn. *Well, I try to get up around seven, and I simply can't start anything before I've had breakfast and coffee on my porch. Birdsong truly reactivates my heartbeat. I force myself to spend two hours in the desk chair, even if I'm not writing. Even thinking about writing, keeping that butt in the chair, is what matters. After that, I take the dogs for a walk. Make us all lunch. Indulge in a rich, decadent book. Switch mediums for a while—perhaps I'll move over to our studio out back and let my hands shape a lump of clay, or dabble some oil onto the canvas. After dinner I'll go back to my office for a while longer, another two or three hours, depending on the night. You know how it is. Some days are a thousand words. Some are five times that. What never, ever changes is an evening ended in yoga and meditation and blessings.*

This is why my novel wasn't finished. This is why I was falling behind in my paltry 180 words a day. I had no pottery wheel, no walks, no blessings.

I sat in my gray fabric cubicle that I'd plastered with reminders of everywhere I wasn't and the thousand places I'd rather be. My AWP conference badge hung next to my monitor. I covered the wall above my phone in buttons collected from literary journals: *Cheap Pop, Ploughshares, Split Lip*. The file cabinet cluttered with magnets from all the places I'd been, from my brief Sonoran Desert backyard to blessed Powell's Books. My desk had a disorienting level of flair. Don't-get-stuck-in-the-machine charms. Wherever I turned was a reminder that this company, this job, wasn't my end game. The art I couldn't support myself on was.

But there was only so much I could spin the reality. And as I churned out PowerPoint slide after PowerPoint slide, I couldn't help but think of how little my work at this company meant to anyone, let alone to myself. Forty hours a week penned into this same spot as the days and weeks and months and years tumbled faster than I could chase, quicker than I could even count, while I burned all of my time and concentration on tasks that only mattered so far as they paid the bills. I had one life, and I was spending mine here.

This is when my head would start to swim and my stomach seized, and I had to go outside and walk an obedient hamster circle around the parking lot until I could breathe again. This was my life, and until the lottery or the apocalypse intervened, I had to stay afloat within its boundaries. Boundaries my choices had drawn, a trade for the nice pans and kitchen cabinets. The envy and frustration is cyclical. I come back. *Get it together, girl.*

One morning when I got out the door and off the freeway early, I went over to the grocery store to get a chore out of the way. They opened at seven, but it was a loose seven, based on whenever they remembered to come by the door. I stood next to the sliding doors with my knuckles white on the shopping cart while an older man mused a pace away, hands in his pockets, leaning back on his heels. I checked my phone again. 7:05.

"It's not as if any of us have anywhere else to be," I said, readjusting how much time I'd have to browse berries before I'd need to be at the check stand.

"I don't!" the man said through a smile. "I'm retired."

I returned his smile, but he wasn't done.

"It never hurts to cut back the pace a little bit," he continued.

"I have to be at work," I said with the most polite smile I could fake.

"Y'know what my brother says? You'll never look back at your life and feel bad about the days you didn't make it into your office."

"Yeah, well, I'd like to look back at my life and die with a roof over my head," I said as the manager rushed over to her forgotten entrance.

The old man was still gazing up at the espresso stand menu when I bolted from the check stand, him the obvious winner of our impromptu fable.

"I'm not going to be able to write before Christmas," I said. To whom, I'm not certain. I might have spoken the words to Matt from the kitchen as he sat in the living room half-watching *Elf.* I was at the table, frosting sugar cookies with the same gags I'd been running every year—angels in bikinis, gingerbread men as mermaids. The dough was soft and cakey like the round pink cookies they sold in the coffee shops around Seattle when I was growing up. This is the only cookie worthy of holding the title Sugar: nothing thin, nothing crunchy. Their creation is an immovable and important tradition. I must carry it out, even if we shouldn't be eating them. Even if there aren't enough people I know still eating gluten to pawn them off. This is a magical time, only once a year. I still had days and days of writing time as soon as presents were opened.

"Don't worry so much about it," Matt said. Matt had nothing to worry about. Gifts were wrapped under the tree. Cookies cooled on the counter. His stocking would be stuffed, and his matching 10 days of vacation were void of any commitments. He lived in a calm, even, un-artist space. Once his work was done, he was free.

"Want to help decorate?" I asked. The dozen jars of sprinkles and icing pens were ridiculous for one person. I looked like I were throwing a decorating party for two dozen people. The woman at WinCo scanned them and smiled with a knowing wink, like, *Oh, those kids of ours! Always with the crafts.* At Halloween I'd played right along with the "How can we keep up with all these kids and their pumpkin parties?" small talk because it was easier to say, "Oh, I know. It's too damn much," than to explain, "No, actually I'm a 31-year-old woman who enjoys going to a lot of fuss to bake and decorate things I have to leave in the break room at work to get rid of."

"I'm no good at that," Matt said. It was the same reason he gave for not wanting to carve a pumpkin. Why leave the couch?

I didn't write on Christmas Eve. I made a cheese ball shaped like a tree with pomegranate seed ornaments and a cheddar star, and my cousin, Jessica, brought an identical appetizer. This is how Pinterest is destroying families. We took pictures with our twin trees and talked about what the temperature in Tucson must be right now.

"I'm so excited to have time off this year," I repeated in vignettes around the room. To my grandma by the punch bowl, my aunt filling a specially indented platter with deviled eggs, Matt so he'd hold me to it. "I've always had to use my vacation for my grad school residencies or whatever. I'm actually going to have time to just sit and write."

"You'll be able to get so much done!" everyone agreed. We reflected on what having time must be like—for my aunt to sew, my cousin to redecorate the finished basement, my brother to kayak every last inch of Puget Sound. We would all, it seemed, rather be Absolutely Anywhere Else.

It wasn't until we were back home on Boxing Day, unloading the anticlimactic sleigh of opened gifts in the back of Matt's truck, that I realized that no one had really asked me *anything*, not what I was writing or what it was about. Yes, these were questions I was trained in Writer School to abhor ("NEVER ask a writer what he's WORKING ON — You could BREAK HIM!"), but in their absence I felt a tendril of panic flitter in my heart.

By not hedging in for any details, there were no reactions to the details. Which meant, I could naturally assume, that my family had a telekinetic power to sense when something totally sucked and politely fail to bring it up.

"After all, you said my novel was a stupid idea," I reminded Matt, because he was the only human being around and as such default for scorn.

"I never said your book was a stupid idea!"

"Yes, you did! You said so at the bar that night when we went out," I culled up from half a year before. "You said nobody would want to read a book about friendship and loss."

"I really don't think I said that." This is usually where he would accuse me of putting the 'creative' in nonfiction, but as he set a pile of ModCloth shoeboxes next to our Christmas tree, he simply kept his side-eye on the exits.

"I remember. Distinctly."

"What do I even know about it, anyway? I'm not a writer. Don't your friends like it?"

I shook my head. "I don't know," I admitted. Not since I read the first chapter at the Sasquatch House had the emerging characters in my novel, Emily or Julia, existed in a world beyond my heart, my mind, the page, and Microsoft Word's Clippy. And that nosy paperclip was fresh out of suggestions. The two characters were still circling each other as I stared from the sidelines, trying to size them up, stalling for time, sending them out to do stupid shit like pick up tacos and visit peripheral characters. Why was Emily so ceaselessly cold? Why did she *need* to succeed at this new job? Why couldn't Julia move on from Emily and the company she didn't care about and the dead husband she couldn't fix? And why, most of all, should anyone care about these two figments of my imagination?

As I lost my focus on the women in front of me, I quit drafting their story. I started drafting their reviews instead.

Blankenbiller's characters are myopic insults to cardboard.

Time I should have spent caring about these characters consistently wandered to more interesting matters, like feeding my cat, and comparison-shopping car insurance.

Tabitha cannot write fiction.

"Maybe you need a break from it," Matt suggested. "You are on vacation, after all."

"I can't take a break! I've been on a break. We've been off for what, like, three days, and I haven't even opened the document."

"I'm just saying, you don't really seem to be in the mindset to accomplish much good right at this moment," he said, sinking into the couch. He turned on Netflix like an invitation. "You still have, what, like a whole week to work on your book. Don't do it when you're not enjoying it is all I mean."

I stood between the TV and its vault of marvelous stories and the Christmas tree. My laptop slept in the office. "What do you wanna watch?" I asked.

One episode of *Orange Is the New Black* turned into seven. We stayed up until two and slept until ten. Watched another while I sliced up Santa-shaped French bread for French toast. I dove headfirst into the tales of women whose identities were blotted out by the same terrible jumpsuit, making choices most of us viewers would opt for under far less favorable privilege. I didn't want to leave the living room because I didn't want to be without them.

"How do they do this?" I wondered aloud. "How do they make us fall so in love, so fast?"

Tuesday slipped into Wednesday as we left season one for two. *I still had time, I still had time,* I tried to convince myself. I could accomplish in one single day off five times what I could in a whole week of work-night writing sessions!

I could, but I didn't.

The days were shapeless. There was no set time for anything, no alarms, no schedules. Even our Netflix account ran on nothing but our whims, spooling episode after episode. I had no structure to encourage me back to my laptop. There was so much else to do instead.

I put away all the gifts. I broke down the cardboard boxes into the recycling. I hand-washed a December's-holiday-season worth of party dresses and sweaters. I threw away all the stale sugar cookies before I could gain back every ounce I'd fought to lose. We picked all the snowflakes from the chandelier, folded up our stockings, and hung the wreath next to my bicycle with its flat tires.

"Do you think we can put the tree back in the box without ruining all your ribbons?" Matt asked as we stared at the last boulder of our Christmas décor.

"I'll just have to redo them next year." We tore down every fake bough and dragged the refrigerator-sized box back into the garage.

"Everything's so … bare," he said. "It's kinda sad."

"It feels like this place is closing in on me," I said. "If I don't leave this house, I think I might start hallucinating." Bouncing between the couch and bed, I felt atrophy seizing my muscles. Could I end up with bedsores from lying in front of the TV too long? The longer I sat, the worse I felt—the greasier my hair, the scummier my teeth, the cloggier my pores. A vicious circle of feeling too disgusting to move, not moving and feeling even more disgusting. I missed the fresh swipe of foundation and powder in my structured mornings, a coat of lipstick after coffee. My routine didn't just get me out the door, it centered me.

"We've only been here for a few days."

"And I usually leave every single day!" I hadn't even put on makeup since Christmas Eve. When had I last washed my hair? How long did it take to go feral?

By the time my alarm went off to resume regularly scheduled office workdays, my laptop was still asleep. There was turkey jerky for my desk in my bag, new Christmas gift shoes on my feet, freshly vacuumed carpets and mopped floors in the house, talking points for my coworker who was anxiously awaiting the next season of *Orange Is the New Black*. I had done everything but kept my butt in the chair like those time-blessed writers evangelized. My butt had certainly been grounded, but my fingers idle.

"I didn't get anything done," I said in monotone as I toasted ham sandwiches to dunk in the butternut squash soup I spent the afternoon roasting gourds for. It was what I was supposed to say after squandering my PTO balance on nothing.

"Why do you always have to get things *done?*" Matt asked, flicking a game on his iPad.

"Because if I don't, who's going to do them?"

"Seemed like a pretty okay vacation to me," he said.

I didn't stoop to agree. I was, after all, supposed to be unhappy with this result. It was my penance for being a horrible artist.

I worked my eight hours. I ran to the grocery store on lunch as I almost always did, picking up the romaine and red onion and dubiously palatable avocados for January salads. I came home and tossed everything together, and watched *@Midnight* with Matt until eight o'clock rolled around.

"Goodnight," I said, kissing the sheen of his bald head.

"Where you going?" he wanted to know.

"I have to write."

He didn't argue.

I didn't have an endless horizon in mind. I had *l'heure bleue*, the last azure moments of dusk. This was time stolen from TV, chores, sleep. Nothing tastes as good when it's handed over. Without a full day of sitting around my house, wondering if what I was doing was good or important or special enough to be doing, the fear didn't have time to rise. It sputtered out. It left only the task: *keep moving it forward*.

The pages scrolled and scrolled. I went back to work.

Kaffee aus Äpfeln

Bikini Angel Sugar Cookies

T hese are not the best sugar cookies; they are the *only* sugar cookies. This is based on a King Arthur Flour recipe, with an important change—use vanilla paste instead of vanilla extract. The paste is thicker, richer, and much more like an actual vanilla bean than even the best liquid version. It also spikes the cookies with these beautiful, cinnamon-like specks of flavor.

They are perfect for the middle of an intense season of your current TV obsession, when making actual dinner would devastate your binge flow. The cream cheese will keep your bones strong, and lemon rind will keep the scurvy away during your binge.

- o   3 cups flour
- o   1 teaspoon baking powder
- o   ¼ teaspoon baking soda
- o   ¾ teaspoon salt
- o   1 cup butter
- o   1 ¼ cups sugar
- o   ¼ cup cream cheese
- o   1 teaspoon vanilla paste
- o   ¼ teaspoon almond extract
- o   1 large egg
- o   1 teaspoon grated lemon rind

Sift together the flour, baking powder, baking soda, and salt. You know, for the longest time I didn't sift. I was like, *Sifting is for losers*. Because I didn't have a sifter. Then, I got one at a local antique store for under $10, and not only does it look adorable on the counter, it makes lighter, better-textured cookies. So don't be a skeptical idiot like I was.

Use a stand mixer to beat together the butter, sugar, and cream cheese until fluffy. You could technically use a spoon, but ouch. Add the egg, vanilla paste, almond extract, and lemon rind. Mix until fully incorporated.

With the mixer on low, add the flour in several additions, allowing it to absorb fully before adding more. Form the dough into a ball, cover in plastic wrap, and refrigerate overnight.

Remove from the refrigerator 30 minutes before baking. Preheat oven to 375° F and prepare baking sheets with butter or parchment paper (or Silpat sheets. Whatever). Roll dough out to approximately ¼-inch thickness, then use whimsical cookie cutters to shape them into all manner of templates for your frosting and sprinkles. Don't have cutters, or don't care about themes? Use an upside-down glass or biscuit cutter for coffee shop-style round cookies.

Bake for about 10 minutes, until the cookies are just set and flushing golden along the edges. Remove and allow them to cool completely before decorating.

You can eat them as soon as your hand can handle them, though. And I highly recommend that you do. The spirit of Christmas doesn't arrive until you bravely sacrifice your well-being to test these fantastic cookies for your friends' and family's safety.

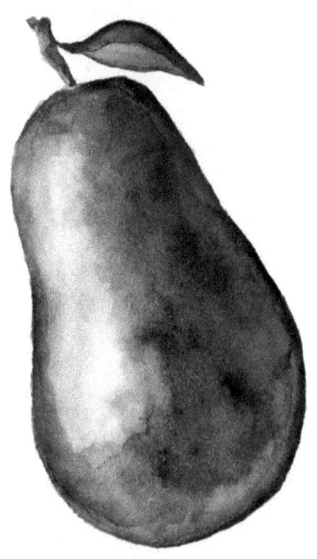

Soup at the *Ritz*

E very industry has its 'thing.' Whether you own a cluster of take-and-bake pizza franchises or approve loan applications for a credit union or arrange wholesale buys of quartzite, you're badgered into attending your trade's yearly Network-palooza at a far-off convention center. Excitement and acute social anxiety churn in your stomach with the bitter-stale airport coffee as you and thousands of your ilk converge into one city, one of the few chances you get each year to see people who normally exist only as email recipients and tweet mentions. You may be asked to get up in front of a sparsely populated meeting room and speak into a microphone about climate change's impact on the quartzite trade. Maybe you're tasked with sitting behind a table shrouded in your credit union's proud colors, smiling blankly as strangers snag pens and Hershey's Kisses while artfully avoiding eye contact. There are gems, like bar conversations that turn into lifelong friendships; there are minefields, like your one-night stand from Doughtopia 2006 who, no matter how many thousands of other people are streaming through this convention center, always ends up hunched over your hotel's lobby bar.

As a writer, this passion-rite-of-passage is no different. We are hassled to attend the Association of Writers & Writing Programs Conference, the Catalina Fucking Wine Mixer of literary gatherings every year. Around 12,000 writers book flights and cram hotel rooms past fire code safety for three days of panels, high-power superstar readings, and barhopping like Harper Collins is footing the bill. Promise to attend as many talks on pedagogy and transatlantic poetry structures as you will; the only reason no one wants to miss AWP is because no one wants to miss the year's biggest party.

The annual event is held in a different city each year, and though each individual conference has its own highlights and quirks, there are a few standby guarantees:

1. You will spend the equivalent of a month's rent on a hotel room for four nights.

2. You will attend a panel that makes you fall in love with all its participants and feel acute sympathy for anyone who didn't make it into the room.

3. You will attend a panel so lifeless and uninspiring you'll demand vengeance.

4. A writer you've long admired will endear herself even further into your heart, giving you a living template for how to evolve into a more generous version of your budding self.

5. A writer you've long admired will be a diva/lecherous asshole, and you'll spend the rest of your days rolling your eyes at his future accolades and award nominations.

And above all else, you end this weekend as a broken fraction of the writer who embarked—exhausted, hungover, inspired, and fulfilled just as deeply as you're wiped senseless and drained.

The 2016 conference was my third AWP, a fête I'd been planning for a solid year: AWP Los Angeles. I made the reservation at the chic JW Marriott conference hotel as soon as they opened up the room blocks. I then called the reservation line quarterly to ensure that they hadn't lost my room in a booking fire. I wrote up a panel proposal on one of my most favorite tortured subjects—body image—and rounded up people much smarter than I to buoy it up into an acceptance. I played it pretty cool when I was asked to read for five minutes alongside other, shinier writers, and narrowed my talk down to one of my favorite essay slivers.

I set the days of the conference out on a grid I'd sketched, and listed the obligations of each. The reading, the panel, the Night of So Many Offsite Events. I assigned each box two outfits, one for daytime that I could walk in, and my favorite fussy dresses with matching heels and necklaces for nights out.

"Is it that formal of a thing?" Matt wanted to know, tallying suitcase weights in his head. "You need a different dress every night?"

"It's just, I want people to see the best version of me, you know?" I tried to explain. Most of my writer friends lived in other time zones. Their best recollections of me surfaced through Instagram pictures and my Twitter avatar. If I didn't look like the girl in the living slideshow, I'd be a disappointment.

@TabithaBlanken Tabitha wears matching ModCloth ensembles every day and makes fancy crusts for her pies and keeps fresh-cut flowers on the table. I wanted to live up to my feed. I didn't want to be ordinary. I didn't want to be boring. I didn't want my game found out.

I looked up the Los Angeles Convention Center on Google Maps and zoomed out, orienting it around Hollywood and Malibu.

"I'm going to be really close to Disneyland," I mentioned to Matt.

"LA isn't close to Disneyland."

"Well if I'm flying into LA, I might as well go to Disneyland." I mean, there it was, just a smidge down I-5. It would be criminal to be that close to Splash Mountain and not ride it. I don't think it's physically possible for me to exist within the state boundaries of California and not make a pilgrimage to my favorite place on the planet.

"Sure, what's a few extra days off work and a few more hundred dollars on the AWP mountain?" he asked, mentally culling away at our tax return.

I was so glad he saw things my way.

Of all the people I gushed my AWP 2016 planning heart out to, only one was ~~brave~~ ~~stupid~~ daring enough to stand up beside me and proclaim, "Hey! I want in on that!" Enter Charlotte O'Brien, one of my MFA classmates. She was a first-time AWP'er, occasional Disneyphile. We skirted each other in our school years, sharing mutual friends and ending up in the same space for an open-mic reading or BYOB dorm party. I can't remember that we ever had a conversation together, a fact I verified when she picked me up from the airport curb and commented, "You have a lovely voice." I knew Charlotte had one, too, because, in a room full of Yankees, hers is impossible to mistake: an even, rosy accent I pegged for British but that had, she assured me, frayed with an Australian twang. I can't tell English accents apart. They are all a higher plane of tone existence than I'll ever reach.

During school I watched as she introduced writers to a rented microphone, this honey-haired girl with a cautious smile and cosmopolitan accent. She was a few years older than I, a 30 to my 25, packed with a few extra mistakes and revelations ratcheting her spine straighter than my slight tilt, an uneven girl who was headed in the right direction but didn't know it yet.

I decided that night during my second semester, hearing her

recite names amplified throughout the space, that she was far too cool to have anything to do with me. And so, as I am wont to do with everyone I honorably cast into that category, I didn't try to get too close. I stood back; I yielded. I crowned her queen without letting her voice a word to the contrary.

I wonder how many friendships I've let slip through the cracks this way, by falling back on my middle school-honed powers of self-rejection. Aloofness can be the overly earnest, awkward girl's only way of surviving adolescence, but it's a cold default that lingers decades past the last time you realized you were even doing it. My unconscious screening of everyone around me, filtering out potential exclusions before I can get close enough to introduce myself. It's how I made it through grad school, how I operated during every AWP. *Skate past before they see you. Don't let them smell your want.*

I'd missed Charlotte once already. How rare it is, a second chance. I jumped at it.

I admitted as much while we were waiting for our first ride, Pirates of the Caribbean. "Thirty minutes," I read from the line marker. Everything was a wait. It was the last week of March, which meant spring break, a concept I hadn't thought about in the nine years since my last college reprieve from classes. The rides were packed, lines at every one.

But it didn't matter, because I was actually here. On the shores of the Rivers of America staring up at New Orleans Square, my flip-flops treading cobblestones that appeared so frequently in my dreams—the reoccurring struggle to get to Splash Mountain but ending up trapped somewhere between Main Street, U.S.A., and Critter Country. This was the seventh trip of my life to Disneyland. It never lost its magic.

Did you know that Pirates of the Caribbean was the last ride whose construction Walt Disney oversaw before his death? Neither did Charlotte, but I went over it like a child introducing her favorite toy.

"New Orleans Square is probably my favorite land for theming, but it's also become the stronghold of one-percenting the park," I recited from my as-yet-unwritten dissertation, The Eisner Years and the Dismantling of Orange Grove Dreams. "Club 33 used to be a subtle, largely unknown enclave up in the rafters, but since corporate decided they needed more extraordinarily expensive event space, they tore up all these meticulously planned forced-perspective buildings to enhance a fraction of the park you'll only get to see for $12,000 a year."

Grousing about the Disneyland class system dovetailed right

into the most precious icebreaking topic there is: grousing about the people in your graduating class.

"I felt so isolated much of the time," Charlotte admitted.

"So did I!" I said. "I mean, there were people that just weren't nice, you know? And it's so frustrating because everyone acts as if they're the best, and if you disagree, then *you're* the asshole."

I could see her eyes squint behind her golden gradient sunglasses. "Are we talking about the same person?" she asked, and in a breath we harmonized the exact same name.

This, dear reader, is how best friendships are made.

My apprehension over being tethered to a person I only kind-of knew for this whole trip evaporated as we flew to the boat-loading dock on a conversation that never quite ended—the essays we were working on, where we'd been rejected, what popular Twitter people were doing, how we'd ever get invited to the swank parties at AWP, whom we'd gone to school with who was still actually writing, which ones had dropped away into that long goodnight (a career with a third the aggravation and actual pay and benefits). I hadn't talked so long in the whole past year. I could feel my throat clench like a calf muscle on its first run in an age.

"I'm so glad you're here," I reassured her while hustling to Tomorrowland for a Space Mountain FastPass, "but I'm afraid I'm going to kill you."

"You can't," she vowed.

But, oh, how I tried! We hiked circles and spirals between Disneyland and its adolescent sibling Disney California Adventure from morning rope drop until the overhead speakers sang us off to close and Main Street, U.S.A., became a basin of glassy-eyed wanderers hypnotized by the blinking marquee lights into picking up that last souvenir magnet, that sweatshirt they'd been eying all day. We clutched merchandise we wouldn't remember buying the next morning and bumped into each other, begging forgiveness as we clung to consciousness, squeezing the last sour drops from our $100-a-day passes. I marched until my feet literally bled from blisters bubbled by Grizzly River Run-soaked socks.

"How are you still walking?" Charlotte asked.

"Adrenaline?" The fact that I had no idea when my next chance to be there would come back? Months from now? Years? Trump could be elected president, and all future vacations would be canceled due to the apocalypse? The fear that underlies the audacious joy I feel of being in my favorite place on Earth—that I might never get there again. "I'm constantly afraid I'm not doing enough," I said, while we snaked through the gates at California Screamin'. "I come home; I make dinner; I write when I can."

"It's so hard to write after dinner and work," Charlotte concurred. As we were discovering, we really were the same person, traveling in concentric circles for all these post-grad years. Charlotte worked high-end retail and was a mother to two girls, an advanced version of my office and two cats, but neither of us the writers we anticipated we'd be. "I see everyone else, and they seem to be publishing something every 10 seconds. Like, I blink, and there's someone else landing in *The Atlantic* or whatever. And it freaks me out. What if I'm not doing enough, or I'm doing the wrong thing? What if I don't stay relevant, and all my work gets forgotten?" she said.

"Losing the momentum."

"Exactly!"

Never getting to this place again. One spin around the carousel, then yanked off the pony. I just had to enjoy the trip while I could. We fastened our restraints. The rollercoaster bulleted up the ramp, and my terror and dread emptied into the Anaheim air. The loudest scream my lungs could muster that only I could hear.

"I think I'll be okay," I said, while I bandaged up my feet in our budget hotel room. It smelled like old air conditioner and lowered expectations—*Well, I'm sorry, you guys, but the Grand Californian is, like, $400 a night.* I tried not to look at the unfamiliar, throbbing hooves as I wrapped them in little Band-Aids—skin puckered and pussing, most comfortable naked in a flip-flop, giving 40,000 people an unfettered (and unsolicited) view of the carnage. My out-of-shape legs were just as unhappy. I was walking with the grace of a jointless action figure. I'd be fine with a few Advil … if I were boarding a plane.

But no, because I'd bookended the most grueling event known to writerdom right on top of it.

The sad sack that drooped out of Charlotte's car into the lobby of the Los Angeles JW Marriott was not my best self. But I had to rouse her back. This was my once-a-year shot to be the writer I spent the rest of the year dreaming up alone in my room. Who knew who might be in the elevator or next in line at the bar, waiting to draw me into the most important conversation of my life? There were 12,000 people registered this week at AWP.

Twelve thousand first impressions. Twelve thousand chances.

The cruelty of a full heart and broken body was not one I was familiar with. Mind over matter, I decided, and as I limped my luggage to the elevator, I insisted that I was fine. *You're going to have a little Me Time*, I told myself, remembering the normally neglected swimsuit tucked between my dresses and pajamas. Pop some Ibuprofen, go for a nice rejuvenating soak in the jacuzzi. Splurge on a $20 poolside cocktail with too much sugar but tons of Instagram appeal. You've earned it, kid. You'll be good as new in an hour.

Wind was stirring the cool spring air, sequestering the paper-skinned Californians in their rooms. I had the pool deck to myself, which was perfect ... except for the shuttered bar. I settled for infused lemon water from an unmanned dispenser and sunk myself into the cauldron. Watching my hammered toes rise with the foam, the idea that for the next few days I was going to be fine was believable.

Something cold. Something cold. I'll feel so much better if I can just have something cold.

I was in downtown Los Angeles in a tapestry of neon and menus, on my third lap through the building. I'd left the conference for a break and found myself in the center of a city I did not know, feeling more disoriented by the second.

You're having a great time, I told myself. I didn't believe the inner dialogue, but it helped a little as I tried to navigate the barrage of shops and thoughts swirling in my mind, both competing for my attention.

An *Eater* article pointed me to LA's Grand Central Market— a century-old mishmash of restaurant vendors, ingredient experts, and artisan culinary specialists—which turned out to be a cousin of my lifelong love, Pike Place Market. There was a butcher shop claiming the city's best burger, served with a side of beef tallow fries. A completely vegan ramen shop. Straight-from-Berlin currywurst. This was an assembly of businesses with a soul and a heartbeat, and on any other day of my life I'd be happy to stumble in here.

Who knows when you'll be here again?

I'd made it through the first two days of the conference beautifully, despite my stiff legs and sore feet. I took cute selfies with friends from afar and said mostly intelligent things to the hundreds of tables of strangers representing journals, publishing houses, and organizations in the cavernous Book Fair. I maybe could have gushed less to the Coffee House Press editor who was debuting an essay collection about cats, but we all have our moments.

The panel I moderated was well-attended and resulted in no Angry Tweets or subsequent thinkpieces about how wrong and indicative of systemic problems within the AWP organization we all were. In the long nights of readings and parties and after-parties and bar-closedowns, I'd managed to drink and be charming without sip-slipping into a hangover. Maybe, actually, I could do this. Maybe I could create the Ultimate Traveling Writer Endurance Challenge and not just survive, but pirouette to the finish. Or maybe not.

I had tea with a friend on the promenade that afternoon. "This little scratch in my throat doesn't want to go away," I said. "I think it's all this talking. I've talked more this week than I have in the past whole year combined." We sat between the Staples Center and Wolfgang Puck's chain location and talked about our partners, how big and strange and surprising this city was, about all the work the day didn't leave time to tackle. I coughed. "See what I mean? I'm using up all my ability to socialize with everyone I love! I didn't get enough pre-AWP season training."

"What are you up to next?" she asked.

"I think I'm going to go off-campus for a little bit, maybe give my voice a rest before I read tonight." I'd been invited to a last-night-of-the-conference event in Hollywood on a bill packed with writers a million times more successful and badass than I was, writers I'd only worshipped from far off, publishing Goodreads reviews of their masterpieces and hoping they would see them—digital messages in a bottle. It was time to be my best self.

But my slight scratch had spiraled into a clawing, constant pain with every word and swallow. I felt kind of dizzy, a little off, like I'd been flicked out of my orbit. I read signs and menus with glassy, lagging eyes.

Something cold. McConnell's Ice Cream Parlor had a line around the stall, its own Splash Mountain queue. "Is it really that good?" I croaked out to the couple in front of me. I sounded like present-day Lindsay Lohan.

They scooted as far forward as they could without violently invading the bubble of another. "We've never been," the woman said.

I stood and I waited, convinced I was in line for my cure. At the counter they would scoop me two heaping helpings of get well. I'd freeze this pox away, and I'd be fine. I leaned against the side of the stall, shifting my weight from my blistered feet to my heels.

"Banana caramel and peanut-butter jelly," I ordered through a wall of phlegm. I carried the cone in one last slow lap around the market, confused and lost. Where would an Uber find me? Where was the front? Which street was up? The frozen dairy was like raking my nails across a colony of chicken pox. Orgasmic, but only for a nanosecond.

I held the cone to my lips in my left hand, my phone outstretched in my right. I opened my mouth as wide as I could, straining against the tender muscle, faking a monster bite. I brightened the focus. *NOM!* Upload. I listened to the Likes chime and leaned against the wall, willing the driver to my side of the market soon.

When I got back to the hotel, I still had two hours until the grand finale reading. My hotel roommates were absent, out fulfilling whatever fabulous plans they'd made for their last night. *I just need to lie down for a bit*. I chased the concept like a mirage down the hallway, as fast as my bloodied feet could hobble. Down comforter. More pillows than I owned in my whole house. A nest to cocoon myself, if only for half an hour or so. I'd emerge reborn.

I opened the hotel door and was about to collapse tits-first on my bed when I saw it: a silver-dollar-sized bloodstain peering up at me from the pure white linen.

"GUHHH!" The cry tore through my lacerated vocal cords, absorbed by the walls. I called down to the front desk and hissed into the phone as loud as I could, what I saw. Then I perched on the desk chair, mentally counting the minutes shaved away from how long I could rest and hide, pointedly ignoring the comforter.

Ten minutes later, a team arrived at my door, two managers in blazers and the housekeeping representative in starch black-and-white. The woman in the blazer held a plastic-sealed swath of white bedding, while the housekeeper clutched what looked like a biohazard bag.

"Thank you," I croaked as they rolled up the offending blanket as carefully as a funeral flag.

They fussed with the corners of the replacement—"We just got new bedding schematics, so we're still getting used to the technique," the woman in the blazer explained, and I ached to tell her to leave the blanket, to brush them all aside gently and dive into the linen mountain.

"How has your stay been?" the other, the man in the blazer, wanted to know.

"Wonderful," I said. "I wish I weren't so sick."

"Being sick while you travel, that's the worst. And then you come upstairs to this?"

"It's okay," I said. I smiled as broadly as I could at the room, feeling awful for the edge of indignation in my voice on the phone. It wasn't their fault; there were hundreds of rooms in this mammoth skyscraper hotel. Not every one of them can be perfect. "I just want to lie down and rest a little, that's all."

"My name's Dan," he said, forgoing a handshake for a wave from six feet away. "So if you need anything else, just call and ask for me. But in the meantime, I'm going to send something up to make you feel better, okay?"

"Okay, thank you," I said, waving as the emergency response team filed out of the room. The curtains were drawn to a tidy, seamless dark. I covered my eyes two pillows deep. I smothered myself from my last great responsibility. A few minutes. I'll be a little late. Surely my Uber will drive fast. Readings never start on time. You're not first on the program. Everything will be fine.

Three quick raps punctured the dark. "Hospitality!" a man called from beyond the door.

I tried to call back, but my voice had vanished. I dug myself out from beneath the covers and pillows and stumbled to the door. A young man in a dinner jacket waited with a full tray balanced on his right shoulder. His nametag was stamped with the lion profile crest of the hotel's upgrade associate neighbor, the Los Angeles Ritz-Carlton.

"We're all so sorry to hear that you're under the weather," he exclaimed, lowering the offering as he entered the room. "Hopefully this courtesy gift will help?"

A table magically appeared from beneath the desk, transforming our mutual phone-charging station into my own surprise café. I sat, my glassy, befuddled awe bouncing back from the mirror as he removed the cloche lid with a *Beauty and the Beast* "Be Our Guest" flourish. The hotel had sent up carafes of fresh-squeezed orange juice, a pot of tea with lemon, and miniature jars of honey, a bread basket, and homemade chunky chicken noodle soup.

"Is there anything else you need?" he asked.

What else could I have wished, save for my mother here in the flesh, bringing exactly what I needed to my bedside?

"No, thank you," I said, pushing all of the dollars I could find into his palm, anxious for his exit only to spare him from the sobs I could feel breaking loose. The moment the door eased shut, I tipped the soup bowl to my lips, tears salting the therapeutic broth. Never had I been away from home and encountered— or needed—such kindness. Rarely had I been gone so long, trying to stay On and Delightful for this many hours in a day. I cried into my English Breakfast tea with lemon, and then into my juice. I watched as my face flushed, and my eyeliner drooped into the crevices beneath my lids. In a few bites of salvation, I saw the entire artifice melt.

Fifteen minutes until the reading kicked off, and I was finally feeling the truth. I was exhausted. I was sore. I was feverish. I was not well. *Maybe I can stay here*, I thought, grasping the cool honey jar in my palm like a pebble. They won't be mad. There's always next time.

As quickly as she'd backed down, my inner perfectionist was back. What, fly all this way, spend all this money, just to weasel out on my last obligation of the whole hurrah? There's maybe two hours' worth of importance left. Then I'd have a whole year to sleep and take antibiotics and binge-watch *The Americans* or whatever other bullshit I needed to do in the name of 'self-care.'

A text message had arrived from Charlotte: *I've been sleeping for a whole day! I can't remember the last time I was this sick. What did you do to me?* What poisoned handrail had we grazed, who was the Patient Zero in the Haunted Mansion line, the sneeze that lingered in the Tiki Room? Forty thousand people to be the death of us.

I pressed the black-and-white Uber button on my phone screen. Alejandro would be here in five minutes. I glanced down at the wardrobe grid I'd left next to the TV. Saturday—Reading. Blue sailor dress with the white fishnets and red patent leather heels. The dress was hanging in the closet with my travel steamer waiting on the shelf.

"Fuck that," I choked out, and retrieved the flowing top I'd worn on Disneyland, Day Two with the stretchy navy leggings. My emergency flip-flops answered the call. I was comfortable; I was present. I would glide to Hollywood in a stranger's car. I would clear my throat and read my five minutes' worth of words between people with full lung capacity, and I wouldn't fail. In the microphone my voice would be a thick, powerful thing, its rasp less concerning and more mysterious, full of the clove cigarette wisps I puffed on in college. I'd be a picture for 300 seconds. I'd slip out the gallery into the cool darkness of a California night with all of its neon and possibility. I'd press another button and secure my getaway car. I'd return here to my nest. I would finish this.

I walked out of the room, down the hall to the elevator. As I waited, I felt another rock rise from my heart and lodge behind my tonsils. The overwhelming need to cry was a tsunami against my collected, poised plan. I was choked by a strange mix of appreciation for the unexpected kindness, a mourning that the trip I'd been so excited about was a few hours away from ending, the fact that I wanted to set the city ablaze with drinks and conversations and board the plane as I had every other year, hungover and running on a few scant hours of sleep, but was now struggling to remain standing. This conference's opportunity was so much more than I could be.

I was expecting the doors to open into a quiet space where I could collect myself before I reached the lobby and met my car outside, but through the gleaming streaks I saw that I was not alone, and the elevator opened like a curtain to reveal my melo-dramatic tableau waiting to board: girl at AWP a goddamn mess, losing her mascara, smelling of stale theme park and chicken broth. I was a one-woman performance to An Editor of Great Renown from the floors above. A career-launcher. An elbow you wanted to rub.

I slunk into the opposite corner. My red blob of a self was reflected in the mirrored edges, the ceiling. I felt the editor's eyes slide ever-so-slightly sideways, just to double-check what he'd seen. Yep, that was a girl in the middle of a meltdown. He jammed the Lobby button once again for good measure, then sank into the fascinating world of his cell phone.

The jig was up. And I had never felt so relieved.

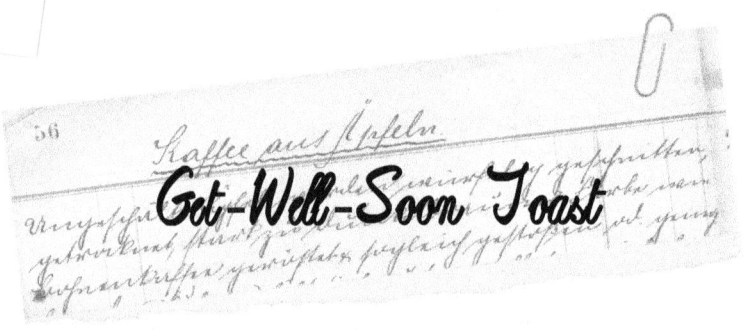

Get-Well-Soon Toast

*M*y mom wasn't anywhere near Los Angeles when I was sick and needed a hug, but thanks to Ritz trays, she was there in spirit. When I asked her what I would've gotten if I were lucky enough to be curled up on her leather living room couch instead of the hotel's double queen, this is the recipe she sent with the note that it's the same thing her mom always made her on those can't-keep-up-the-perfect days (along with the note: "She would have dipped it in warm milk after toasting for a sore throat"). I can just see this in my mom's immaculate cursive handwriting on one of her stationery recipe cards.

Mix ½ stick of butter with ¼ cup sugar and 1 ½ teaspoons cinnamon and a dash of vanilla and a shake of cloves. (Better yet, substitute cinnamon and cloves for equal amount of Penzeys Baking Spice.)

Smear white bread slices (preferably homemade) with mixture. Bake at 350° F for 10 min-ish, until golden and toasty.

The *Revolution Will Not Be Televised* on *Food Network*

My friend's face materialized on my phone screen at the chime of a bell. *You need to watch* The Great British Baking Show, her Facebook message demanded. *It's on Netflix. Add it now.*

Ok, I'll check it out! I typed back. Shorthand for, *I'm in the middle of* Orange Is the New Black *and cannot be bothered.* And even if I weren't, I had seen every baking show on and off the air in the last decade. *Ace of Cakes. Cake Masters. Cake Wars. Cupcake Wars. Food Network Challenge. Holiday Baking Championship. Halloween Baking Championship. Spring Baking Championship. Ultimate Baking Championship.* Years of sugar fantasies buckling and shattering under the unforgiving radiance of studio lights. I've watched these showcases mutate from artisan invitationals for the world's best bakers and pastry chefs to gather and broadcast their talents for the audience's awe and delight, into fondant-flinging, sabotage-heavy shit shows—now featuring 'celebrities'!

The dilution of the simple, beautiful premise of 'who can create the most outstanding cake' has traced the implosion of my favorite channel. It had been so long since I watched chefs create for the love of it, I could scarce remember what the non-spectacle looked like. *The Great British Baking Show*, I assumed without question, would be more shameless cross-promotion (Your challenge: to create a cake inspired by the new hit movie, *The Smurfs 2: Lost in Smurf York!*), dubious judges (Lou Diamond Phillips, the girl who played Pepper in *American Horror Story: Asylum*) and pointless hurdles (You've got to create your cake dough in this industrial cement mixer!) with British accents.

I knew that my friend was only trying to help. She saw how

much I loved to cook and how my vacations orbited around finding the best local markets, dishes, and ingredients to smuggle back in my checked baggage. She read my funky Food Network fan fiction stories. She understood that my heart and my tongue and my hands are tethered to the same nerve, the same vein, bleeding and gathering love.

She didn't know how much my heart could no longer take it.

My first apartment is more visceral in my memory than my childhood bedroom or freshman dorm. I can rebuild it down to the magnets on the fridge suspending postcards from friendships that have long unraveled. In the frozen amber of imagination, Matt is sitting on the couch cushion closest to the window. The couch is as old as my parents, a remnant from my grandma's basement and an era when sleeper sofas weighed roughly as much as cars. I'm in the kitchen, which no one, including me, has ever taken care of; the linoleum is fraying on every edge while the leaky window sprouts a fresh colony of mold spores along the sill. I haven't properly figured out how to clean a kitchen yet, so all of my cocktail shakers and bottles of flamingo-pink high-fructose corn syrup Cosmopolitan mixers are lacquered in a grimy peach fuzz of stove grease. At night after dinner, I run a Clorox wet wipe on the surfaces and hope for the best.

As I stand in the kitchen no bigger than my current house's master closet, grating too much lemon zest into pasta and piling 20 times too many toppings onto pizza, voices call out to me from beyond.

You always need to salt your pasta water. This is your only chance to flavor the dry noodles.

Rub a garlic clove along the toasted bread before topping it with the tomato bruschetta.

Always add a tiny bit of nutmeg to the pasta. Buy a whole clove of it and grate it fresh; the stuff ground into a jar isn't worth a square inch of your cabinet space.

When you're using just a few ingredients, it's important to make sure they're the best they can be. Never settle for anything less than pure, graded, good maple syrup.

Wisdom wafts in from our 32-inch square television, keeping me company even when I'm too busy to plant myself in front of the screen. Our basic cable was expanded just enough to include the Food Network, a luxury we couldn't afford as kids who ran credit cards for groceries, but we did it anyway, because nights where we couldn't tease and adore Alton Brown finding the most complicated, anal-retentive but admittedly logical, way to thread kabobs weren't nights worth living.

While I was growing up, my mom made dinner every night, the meals planned in advance. Every two weeks she sat down with her cookbook and recipe clippings to write The Menu. Her font-perfect cursive schedule of 14 dinners hung on the side of the fridge, and I read it before school to give myself something to look forward to. YAAASSS, BEEF SOFT TACO NIGHT. But since she was so meticulous and organized, I never needed to learn the survival skill of cooking for myself. Dinner was served family-style on the dining room table night after night. I was too young and hungry to see past the convenience and privilege into the future of how the hell I'm going to do this for myself.

Matt wasn't a huge help. "I don't think you can make bread without a bread machine," he said when Ina Garten's trip to a French bakery in Manhattan inspired a French bread day.

"How do you think they made bread before bread machines?"

"I think that's the only way at home," he doubled-down.

Giada De Laurentiis taught us how to smash garlic cloves with the back-end of a knife against the cutting board, which worked even with our cheap cardboard-like blades. Mario Batali introduced the wonder that is the leftover Parmigiano-Reggiano rind (even if the rest of my minestrone was soft, under-seasoned garbage). Watching *Iron Chef America* was like staring into the windows of Pottery Barn and dreaming of a future thousands of days and dollars ahead of us: *Someday, we'll be able to make scallops seared on a Himalayan salt block.*

As we upgraded apartments and jobs, my food improved. The dough in my pizza cooked all the way through. Breading clung to my chicken. My scrambled eggs fluffed instead of caked. I discovered that there are more seasonings than garlic salt. But at the same time, our default channel veered sharply away.

"Do you want to watch that new *Chopped* thing?" Matt asked one night.

I was in the kitchen, alternating sauce and Italian sausage and noodles in our favorite fail-safe lasagna recipe. It was 2009, and our steady stream of *Giada at Home*, *Barefoot Contessa*, and *Good Eats* was already being deeply undercut by *Diners, Drive-Ins and Dives* marathons. Which, yeah, was fun at first, but how many times can you watch someone shove a cheeseburger into his mouth and start describing it before he finishes chewing?

"I guess, if it's on before *The Daily Show*."

While we feasted on discount steak cuts, we watched chefs stumped by cruel baskets. Judges with Level 11 Resting Bitch Face gazed on, incredulous over the contestants' inability to cook down a brisket in 20 minutes. Ted Allen leered in the camera frame corners like a high-ranking resident of the Capitol watching a round of the Hunger Games.

"If you want that ten thousand dollars, you'd better get those desserts on the plate!" he demanded, dangling a teensy wedge of salvation to the contestants, whose troubles were reiterated in reality show confessional cuts. Shuttering restaurants, leaky roofs, mothers with terminal diseases who wanted one last glimpse of the ocean.

"Failure is not an option," they all recited.

We didn't learn anything, except never to serve Scott Conant red onions, nothing tastes good with durian, and that *pain perdu* is French toast in a dessert costume. We weren't inspired to make something new; it was just like everything else on every other channel—talent traded for drama, success measured in the way someone dodged a trap rather than executed a leap.

"I think we should start watching *Mad Men*," I said, rinsing the plates off in the sink. "I hear good things."

Nowadays when I come home from work and Food Network is on, I roll my eyes. "Isn't there anything else on?" I say, snatching up the remote from between the fat, furry flesh of our oldest cat and the back cushion of the couch.

"It's just background noise," Matt says. He's on his phone triaging the work emails that never end.

The voices against stock footage of spinning cupcakes are another track on the sound machine between Spring Rain and Tropical Rainforest. I make a point to switch over to a DVR'd episode of *South Park* or *Fixer Upper*. Every show was abominable, paused only for commercials previewing new concepts that were even more abominable:

Tia Mowry shows you how to make pot roast! Why? Why NOT!

You thought we found the Worst Cooks in America? *Think again! This guy can burn water!*

It's Chopped *... but with KIDS!*

Will you be able to tell if this dish were made by a Cook ... or a CON?

I couldn't tune out the idiocracy. In my ears, it amplified as an endless reminder of a friend I no longer knew. A presence that no longer existed.

When I arrived home at Portland International Airport from AWP, Matt had to scrape me up from the bottom of the baggage claim. I came back from the conference with strep throat so bad, I couldn't talk. I fell asleep on a plane for the first time in my life, just to escape the misery. That first day home, stocked with antibiotics and a doctor's note, I slept longer than my cats. I ate a popsicle for dinner. My mother called to check on me.

"Oh, my god!" she exclaimed, upon hearing my crypt-rasp of a voice. "I'm so sorry. ... I'll leave you alone. ... Just get better, sweetie!" and she hung up almost immediately.

The next day, I still couldn't speak, but I could keep my eyes open. I shuffled out of my bedroom to the couch and turned on Netflix. I scrolled past a mountain of garbage—*The Interview*, *Fuller House*, the complete and unnecessary *Friends*—until the cursor rested on a perfect chocolate-gilded cake. It was *The Great British Baking Show*, the recommendation I'd long cast away in the circular file. I hit Play knowing that at any moment I could X back out of it if I got monumentally bored—just as I had with the latest season of *Kimmy Schmidt* and every episode of *House of Cards*—and go check on my Neko Atsume cats. I could let *The Great British Baking Show* be background noise with much better accents.

When Matt arrived home from work an episode later, he found me on the edgiest of my seat as I could get (burrito-wrapped in blankets and slightly leaning forward). "How are you feeling?" he asked, unloading a bagful of Simply Orange juice and soft, delicately flavored soups into the refrigerator.

I pinwheeled my arm, ushering him into my domain.

"New Food Network show?"

I shook my head. "Netflix," I whispered.

I didn't need to explain the sheer optimism of the show, a concept so divorced from American food TV that I barely recognized it. There were no cuts to tenuous sob stories to force us into caring about the contestants. With *The Great British Baking Show*, we cared because we could see them pouring all of themselves into the proofing drawers, hoping to impress the two understated professional judges, not with a 10-foot Rice Krispie sculpture that could spit fireworks out its buttercreamed asshole, but with the ancient alchemy of turning flour and leavening agents into the best-looking, most delicious bread in existence.

No time was wasted undercutting one another. There was no side-eye thrown or passive-aggressive voiceovers. After the baking challenges, the contestants sat in a row, nudged together, clapping with feverish gusto as the day's winner was announced. If a fellow contestant was sinking, her neighbors came to the rescue. "What do you need? How can I help?" It was as if they were all human.

We kept watching the judges explain why a scone doesn't rise, and the merits of an egg wash versus butter brush, until my eyelids went on strike.

"We'll watch more tomorrow," Matt promised.

For the next week, we watched the show every night. Not while I cooked, not as background noise. We would not abide any distraction. My voice returned, and we bantered with each other in bad accents. "BAAAKE!" We cried out with the two hosts, women who managed to pirouette as comic relief without face-planting into being grating or smug. Instead of interrogating the contestants, the hosts politely asked if they could pocket an empanada for later.

"Do you like empanadas?" I asked Matt. Little meat-pocket pies were sorely missing from our meal rotation of chicken burgers, shrimp soft tacos, and beef stir-fry.

"I love empanadas," he said.

"I didn't know that! I swore you didn't."

"What's not to like? It's pastry and deliciousness."

"I should make some," I said, taking my eyes off the screen just long enough to Pin a *New York Times* recipe for Argentinean empanadas.

"Oooo, you should make some sweet ones, too, for dessert," he chimed in, as they switched over to a contestant spooning lemon meringue.

"That would require making pastry."

"Well, that's kind of a pain in the ass," he said.

"But I WANT to!" I shrieked. I wanted to watch the butter pulverize into pea-sized pearls, to feel the soft, velvety crumble of the dough between my fingertips. I had spent days sitting and watching the magic act. I craved a taste, not only of the treat, but of the trial.

"Well, then," he said, tossing his hands up in surrender. "BAAAAKE!"

"What do they win?" Matt asked when we finally sat down for

The Great British Baking Show's finale.

Two types of dough, sweet and savory, were resting in the refrigerator, waiting for the fillings I'd spent the afternoon slow-cooking and seasoning to slightly strong (Judge Paul was sure to note that flavors should be over-accented, since they mellow in the oven). Richard, Luis, and Nancy presented their showpiece cakes to the judges and went outside the tents to join their families in a picnic. The show's other previous contestants were scattered about the field, cheering on competitors who'd become friends. There were no pre-show reunions rehashing drama scripted between them, as we'd endured on *Food Network Star*. No one padded his inability to cook with the fact that he had a 'really great culinary point-of-view.' The best baker would win, plain and simple. I hadn't felt this nervous about filmed strangers since Ryan Seacrest and Brian Dunkleman held Justin's and Kelly's tender fates in their hands. I'd almost cried already when my favorite—17-year-old Martha—was booted off the baking show, victim to a bad batch of doughnuts.

"I don't know," I admitted. There was no $50,000 sugar ransom we'd been informed about. When the contestants spoke of winning, it was only in terms of principle. *I want to make everyone proud*, and, *It would be such an honor,* they gushed.

"They've got to win something," Matt insisted, because why in this country would people be on television if they weren't chasing a check?

But when The Great British Baker was crowned, there was no cash. There was a bouquet of flowers. There was an engraved cake stand. There were tears and hugs and a montage of contestant follow-ups that were worse for my eyes than scotch broom. *Luis is back at his office job, but still dreams of opening a bakery*. Oh, my god. SAME.

"Tabitha is rolling out her pastry for her sweet empanadas," I narrated like a loon as the credits rolled.

"May I have one for me pocket?" Matt asked, mimicking the host's tiptoe hover on my workstation counter.

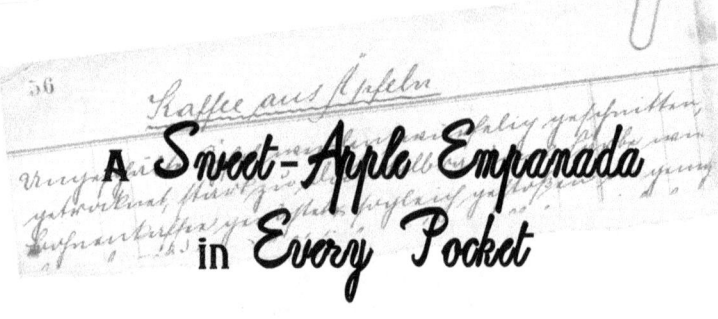

A Sweet-Apple Empanada in Every Pocket

he savory empanadas I made were pretty damn good (and I still have a ton of them in my freezer waiting for a lazy I-need-to-get-to-the-writings-ASAP kind of weeknight), but you know what was transcendent? Those sweet-apple empanadas Matt suggested as an afterthought. I found a fantastic pastry recipe online that does all the heavy lifting in a food processor, and I used apple pie filling that I home-canned last fall.

Wait. Did you not home-can your own apple pie filling last fall?

WHAT?

Really?

How very disappointing.

Well. I hope you've learned your lesson. Put that on your list for this fall, at least. Home-canned pie filling is one of the only things worth breaking out all the preserving equipment and creating a ginormous water bath for. Jam? Ehh. Pickles? Meh. Home-canned pie filling? Life-changing.

In the meantime, I'm including instructions for cooked apple filling. It will certainly do the job. You could also use any other favorite fruit or berry filling or whatever is in season. Whichever method you choose, these can't legally be eaten without a little vanilla ice cream.

For the Empanada Pastry
- 1 ½ cups flour
- ¼ cup sugar, plus 1 additional teaspoon
- ⅛ teaspoon salt
- 1 stick butter, cold and cut into cubes
- 2 eggs (1 for the dough, plus 1 for brushing)
- 1 tablespoon ice water
- 1 teaspoon cinnamon

For the Sweet-Apple Filling
- 3 tablespoons butter
- ½ cup brown sugar

o   4 large baking apples[*], cored and peeled and sliced into ½-inch cubes
o   ⅓ cup water, plus additional ⅓ cup water for cornstarch dissolution
o   1 teaspoon Penzeys Baking Spice[**]
o   1 teaspoon vanilla paste[***]
o   1 ¼ teaspoons cornstarch[****]

To Make the Dough

Add flour, sugar, and salt to the food processor and combine. Add the cold butter, one egg, and water, and process until a clumpy dough forms. Don't let it get too smooth. There should still be some pea-sized lumps. Remove the dough from the food processor (carefully! Don't cut yourself! Not that I've ever done that. Nope. I'm very coordinated.) and place on a lightly floured countertop. Knead approximately four times. Form into a disc, wrap in cling film (as the British say), and place in the refrigerator for 30 minutes, or as long as it takes you to make the filling and watch one more episode of *The Great British Baking Show*. If you're on the finale, do NOT allow Netflix to autoplay *Kids Baking Championship* featuring Duff the Cakedouche. This will ruin your day.

To Make the Filling

In a large, nonstick or cast iron skillet, melt the butter over medium heat. Add apples and cook for 3-4 minutes, until softened. Add the water, brown sugar, baking spice, and vanilla of your choosing and stir until combined. Reduce the heat to low and allow to cook for several minutes.

In the meantime, dissolve the cornstarch in the remaining ⅓ cup water. Stir into the apple mixture, then raise the heat to medium-high, until it comes to a boil. Allow to boil for about 1 minute, until the mixture is thickened and beginning to reduce. Remove from heat and allow to cool completely before adding to

---

[*] such as Granny Smith or Fuji.

[**] or Allspice, if your Penzeys supply is running low.

[***] Extract will work, too—but get yourself some of the paste. It will also change your life.

[****] I use the Clear-Jel style cornstarch, which is hyper-cornstarch and my addiction since the Great Teriyaki Meatball Debacle of 2007. It's also necessary to make your own home-canned pie fillings, so you're going to need some anyway. It sets up everything so much more reliably and buoyantly than the normal variety.

the dough.

To Bring Them Together

Remove dough from the refrigerator and roll out to about ¼-inch thickness. You're going to need something to cut 4-inch to 5-inch discs; you might need to get creative. If you have a round cookie or biscuit cutter in that size, you're a well-prepared individual. I went looking for a cookie cutter and realized my cookie cutter jar lid was the exact size I needed. You could also use a bowl, or cut around a dessert plate as a template. This is the part where you get to show off your resourcefulness. I've been waiting weeks to tell somebody about that cookie cutter lid trick.

Once you find your Weapon of Choice, cut the dough into discs, then place them on baking sheets lined with parchment or Silpat mats. Place about 3 tablespoons of apple filling in the center of each empanada, being careful not to overfill. You don't want these to leak and get messy. There should be an inch of dough space on all sides.

Whisk the remaining egg with ¼ cup water. Brush egg around the edges of each empanada, then fold in half and seal. I found that twist-twirling the edges, then crimping along them with a fork, led to a good seal. Do what feels right to you. With a sharp paring knife, cut 2-3 slits in the top of each empanada to prevent spontaneous combustion. Brush each empanada with egg wash. Mix the teaspoon of cinnamon with the remaining teaspoon of sugar then dust on top of each. Refrigerate for 30 more minutes before baking. You can also freeze them at this point and bake them whenever, but don't you want them immediately? Thought so. Now, this is very important: reserve the rest of the egg wash for a second brushing, so they're optimum golden and crispy. Where did I learn that? Martha, of course! Her pies were perfection. And so, too, can yours become!

Bake at 375° F for 21 minutes, or until golden brown with the insides bubbling away. Halfway through the baking time, remove from the oven and apply a second coat of egg wash, then bake for the rest of the time remaining. Allow to cool for 15 minutes before topping with ice cream and serving or popping in yer pocket.

I Am Not Going to France

This is not an appeal for help. I am not going to direct you to my GoKickMe page where I'll promise to bake you a baguette if you pledge $150 toward my discretionary travel fund. What I am attempting to do is the same thing I attempt to do with all other writing I hammer out: expose the manifestation of heartbreak. This morning it metamorphosed into an email I sent to an extremely kind, generous person I sort-of know. My message to her said, "No."

Today, I've tried to pinpoint the no's in my life that I most regretted. Not the simple no's, like not buying that breezy, made-for-my-long-torso cotton dress three seasons back at H&M before it vanished, or the chocolate cake I passed up at Disney World as a child because I was too busy trying to catch Minnie Mouse's attention. I'm talking about the Gwyneth-Paltrow-in-*Sliding-Doors* no's, where one decision—in or out—pivots the course of destiny.

There are a few declines I made in the past that I mourned initially, but when I pedal back from this distant vantage point, I can soothe them away in hindsight as an eventual path to good. Like the job offer I received from Nordstrom during my last year of college. They wanted me to be their Urban Decay girl, the sole ambassador for the edgy makeup brand that infused glittery metallics into grungy greens, purples, and grays. What if I'd gone for fashion and beauty full-time, instead of keeping them sidelined as a hobby? Would I, a decade later, be invited to Hollywood's Nokia Theater for my Best Makeup Oscar nom? At least be invited backstage to touch up the eyes of small, luminous superstars?

But you couldn't have taken a full-time job while you were still in school, I tsk myself. *And what, did you want to work retail for the rest of your life? Unpredictable hours, no weekends? See, you did the right thing.*

Leaving my first office job at a specialty food distribution company seemed, on the surface, like a monumental mistake. I was young and stupid and greedy and leapfrogged into a bad position at a new company that I wasn't qualified for. I ended up being let go only six months in, right at the crest of 2008's Great Recession. It took me almost a year to find another job—any job—and I landed in the most dysfunctional, toxic place I've ever been. Shady-dealings toxic. Chauvinistic toxic. Had-to-go-in-for-weekly-therapy-sessions-   just-to-keep-my-head-above-the-rapids toxic.

Still, I shake my head at that sad, panicked girl aching for the gentle world of cheese brochures she left behind. *Now, if you weren't pushed onto the edge of a precipice, if you didn't feel the earth giving way beneath your feet, why would you ever have gone to grad school? How would you ever be a writer? You should be writing those assholes a thank-you note.*

And I'm certain that a wiser, more balanced version of myself—who's become better at contouring and has finally followed through with that concept of taking yoga—will be waiting years down the road to tell me just how fantastic it was that I did not go to Paris in 2016. She will be right, of course. That bitch always is.

But I am only as wise as today. My contouring is still janky, and I remain unwilling to give up an hour of my week to teetering on a foam mat. And that No is killing me.

It started as a Facebook post. One of those links that gets shared by half your friends, then a dozen of them post the same story to your timeline because the headline hollers your name. On this day, it was the headline: "Now You Can Stay in Julia Child's French Cottage," teased with a provincial porn shot of the most rustic-perfect kitchen you'll ever see. Julia's potato mashers, meat tenderizers, and measuring cups hung from a corkboard on the wall, each utensil lovingly traced into its place by her husband, Paul. A bowl of lemons waited on the island. A continental sunrise coaxed the herb garden awake.

I clicked Like.

Julia Child's preserved house felt as real as Igloo Village in

Finland or the Giraffe Manor in Kenya. I realize that it's there, but I can't imagine any scenario in which I'd be able to participate: too distant, too expensive, too fantastical. Maybe they'd build a copy at the Paris Las Vegas that I could visit and take a selfie in. The Strip was my only semblance of international travel.

Later in the afternoon, the Julia Child cottage appeared in a different spot. A writer friend posted a picture of the house in a group, along with a call for enrollment:

Friends, I'm putting together a small writing workshop at this divine location in the fall. We'll be staying in Julia Child's house to produce new work in the French countryside. I even have a chef friend coming in to teach our own private cooking classes—in Julia Child's kitchen! I've only got four spots available, so let me know quickly if you're interested.

I read the description three times over, processing the au gratin potato layers of decadent, carb-loaded divinity.

Writing in the French countryside.

Cooking classes.

Julia Child's kitchen.

For the first time all day, I clicked through into the actual article and viewed the slideshow. I saw single beds lined like petit fours with lemon buttercream bedding. I saw the terrace with Tiffany-blue-painted shutters. I saw the hilltop medieval village and its market, where I imagined myself standing, winded, with my shopping bag and camera and very little French, memorizing every scent and sight and sound. From that moment to the last day I drew breath, I would remember that time I walked and cooked and wrote in the footsteps of The Goddess.

I could have saved a sea of heartbreak if I'd just closed the window and allowed the future French apparition of myself to vanish with the afternoon. I could have been kind instead of opening up a new email message.

There's no way I can afford it, but just out of curiosity, how much is the workshop?

Already an undercurrent was swelling underneath my sane-sounding message. My greedy, gluttonous heart was worming in for a way.

"What is it?" Matt wanted to know as soon as I walked into the living room.

I hadn't even set down my purse and bag yet. I was planning

on counting the beer cans in the recycling to gauge my possible success and ease my way into a most uncomfortable conversation. He sensed my hurricane of want from the I-5 freeway exit.

"What do you mean?" I asked, through Cheshire-grinning teeth. That dream image was a light I couldn't snuff out. My lust was an unmistakable tell.

"Out with it," he insisted, tipping his Coors can to the sky. "Ask me now so we can get on with it." Damn this man who'd been with me for 11 years. Damn my honest face, screaming every joy and crestfall and secret.

"Let's say, theoretically, that there was going to be a writing and cooking workshop in France. In Julia Child's house." I tried to describe her kitchen, the lemon beds, the sunshine and the herb garden, and the croissants and cheeses waiting in the medieval hillside village.

"When?"

"This fall."

"How much?"

Matt did not see the cottage or the beds. He didn't try to imagine the village. His mind went straight to the ledger. Black in, red out. My withdrawals tallied sins. I could hear the beads of the abacus clicking my transgressions: MFA. AWP. Disneyland. Platinum blond touch-ups and purple shampoo. When it came to my income-to-input household ratio, I was getting worse than the cats. Every inch of progress I eked forward—a tiny raise, a bonus—I spent 10 times again before it actually went through.

"Nineteen hundred dollars."

"No."

It landed heavy between us, Matt behind the kitchen counter choking his empty beer, me on the loveseat curling into as little space as possible. I felt ridiculous for even asking. He'd never once asked for a $1,900 lark. How small and stupid this dream felt when oxidized. Matt's shoulders caved underneath his light cotton button-up.

"But I have enough to cover it in my 401(k)," I said, laying out the careful plan I'd been drafting. I had decades to fill the account back up again, and besides, I was a millennial. There was no way I'd be retiring before I was 80 anyway.

"That shows up on our credit report. That's another ding against our credit in a lifetime of dings." Wedding, ding. Car, ding. New double stove, ding.

"I didn't know that," I said. I had no other aces.

"Now I'm the asshole," he said.

"I'm the asshole," I corrected, although both assertions felt true.

"We need to start doing the *right things*," he said, and I knew that everything I was chasing was in the Wrong category. "No more of this two-thousand dollar vacation, spending like there's no tomorrow bullshit. How are we ever going to get out of this house if we don't pay off our credit card? How are we ever going to pay off our credit card if we keep burning money like it's kindling?"

I didn't say anything, because I've said this before, to him, to myself. We're on opposite sides of reasonable desire and preference: he wants an upgraded structure, while I crave a shot of adventure. This wasn't a conflict I could win. "I'm sorry I asked," I finally conceded.

"I'm sorry I have to say no."

We were both bad liars.

There was no fight that night, though I ran through the argument in my head. I played out the childish, impotent rage of slamming my foot into our linoleum and insisting that I follow through on my scheme. "This is for my career," I could claim.

Oh, yeah? he could say. *Just like going to grad school was for your career? Or the* Tin House *workshop was for your career? Or every year AWP is for your career? Why don't you go ahead and tell me how much your 'career' is contributing to our lives?*

I might rage about the once-in-a-lifetimeiness of this opportunity, but I'm overexcitable and he'd call my wolf's cry. The biggest chance was always brushing up against my fingertips. Everything was a 'must.'

I couldn't win this fight on flow-chart logic. There was no winning at all, because it was an argument rooted in the deepest chasm between Matt and me. He wants to build a fortress, strong and true, around himself. Every day he spends at the office is another millimeter toward a yard that will separate him further from obnoxious neighbors. A finished basement he can burrow into. A garage large enough to house every hobby he's yet to desire.

I want to travel. I want to fly far from this nest and spend time as my actual, contented self. It's a personality that peeks out from hibernation a few days after my Out of Office replies start going out, when I'm miles down the road or up in the sky. The traveling version of myself is open. She asks questions and strikes up conversations with strangers. Her smile does not dim. Every place has something to teach her; she's constantly surprised. She comes back and wants to take everyone she's ever known to see what she has seen, to eat the same foods and meet the same waiter who told ghost stories about the hotel bar.

We are two people who love each other immensely, but this doesn't change the fact that in the 11 years that we've known each other, we've grown into people who desire different things out of life.

Our Saturdays are usually spent tethered within a half hour of our house, running errands. We have breakfast at the same restaurant because there are only a few places serving brunch south of Portland. While we're waiting for pancakes and scrambles to arrive, we argue over what we're going to have for dinner. We buy meat at Costco and produce at New Seasons. We're early risers and usually get back home around lunchtime. I camp out in the kitchen to prep ingredients, while he nestles into the couch. In a few hours, the whole house is singing with notes of onion and garlic and olive oil and bacon, and the cats come out and build a fort of blubber and fur around Matt, and he'll turn to me and say, "I sure do love the cozy life." This is the best version of being alive to him: warm, fed, and loved in his own space, surrounded by the reliable and the familiar.

My friend, Melanie, came to visit last summer from Tucson. She was the one strong connection I made in the city—one of the only coworkers my age at the mining company. We chatted in the company bathroom and outside hallway, where the truth about who we were seeped out. Me and my writing deal; she was a belly dancer and soccer star. We bonded over these secrets and our not-so-hidden desire to get out of the dusty, dying city. We picked out the most promising bars and drank ourselves into darkness.

"I trust you!" she said when I prodded for Pacific Northwest visit wishlists. "You'll be the best tour guide."

And I was. The Japanese Gardens, Multnomah Falls, Willamette Valley wineries, downtown rooftop breweries. On the last weekend we drove up to Seattle for her first Major League Soccer match, watching my beloved Sounders play the San Jose Earthquakes. We got a cheap hotel by the airport and took the train into downtown, wearing our bright green jersey and knit scarves.

A family in Dallas sweatshirts sat across from us with their checked luggage bags and asked, "Excuse me, what are the Sounders?"

"Soccer," I said.

"Like a high school team?"

Any other day this would be the point at which I'd check out, when I'd pull out my Beats headphones or pretend my phone was ringing or start live-tweeting how I was next to ignorant Sounder-less imbeciles. But today, I was on my third day of PTO, and I was on a train coasting into the heart of my favorite city, where there would be the freshest sushi and beers of Sounders victory, and such joy was nothing but contagious.

I explained the Sounders. I explained where CenturyLink Field was and how it was different from Safeco, and where to find the best fish and chips, and how to pick up the Monorail. "It's Seattle!" I cried when the car crested over the hill, and the horizon transformed into the skyline, and we all erupted into cheers.

"Can you do this for a living?" Melanie asked.

"I don't think there's a big market for tour guides."

"You're just so good at it."

I am a hopeless lark. I adore airports. My heart lilts when a plane takes off. I want to regard the world as a place I still have a thousand chances to discover. Home is a pause between the real lives I want to live.

I'm afraid I just can't make it work, no matter how I run the numbers, I typed into the Facebook message box. When I read it over, the reasoning seemed sound. How many people had several thousand dollars chilling in the bank waiting for just the right writercation? Who would fill the yellow beds of Child's house? I wondered. Who were these women who can devote themselves to writing, one of the least lucrative things you can be good at, and still afford international travel and lodging in famous people's old addresses?

Maybe they're the ones who are serious, another quadrant of my brain chimes in. The voice is the version of myself I'd be if I were alone, maxing out whatever card, credit line, and resource I had to stretch one millimeter closer to a dream.

Hate Lasagna

This is what I made for dinner that night, after I'd snuffed out the root of our fight with a single message. It's my mom's recipe (Hi again, Mom!) that I've been making since Matt's and my first apartment days—one of the few meals that always turned out. In the decade since, I've played around with the meats and made it my own. But that night, when I cut out a giant wedge and set it in front of Matt, he greeted it with a leery side-eye.

"This is Hate Lasagna," he said.

"You hate lasagna?"

"No, this isn't a lasagna you made with love. You hate me. It's poisoned with hate."

"For the love of cheesus, there's a whole bunch of the good sausage in here," I snapped. The delicate pasta furls. The three kinds of meat. The 'preferably good' Italian red wine I picked with surprising blindness, realizing that my vino knowledge didn't spread far past the west coast. I twirled a fistful of saucy pasta onto my fork and airplaned it across the table toward his lips.

"Okay, OKAY, I can do it myself," he surrendered.

He took a bite. Then I took one. He forgot I was a spend-thrift succubus, and Paris managed to slip out of my periphery in the face of a meticulous-ridiculous dish. The chasm between us bridged for another day.

For the Not-Hate Marinara
- o   3 cloves garlic, minced
- o   ½ cup 'preferably good Italian-style wine'
- o   2 tablespoons tomato paste
- o   1 generous teaspoon sugar
- o   ½ teaspoon red pepper flakes
- o   Salt and pepper to taste
- o   32-oz jar home-canned or San Marzano tomatoes

o 1 cup diced onion[*]
o ½ jar your favorite quality tomato sauce[**]

For the Lasagna Assembly
o 1 box dried lasagna noodles
o ¾ pound Italian bulk sausage[***]
o ¾ pound lean ground beef
o ⅓ cup chopped pancetta[****]
o 1 tablespoon Penzeys Tuscan Sunset seasoning[*****]
o 32-oz container cottage cheese[******]
o Vegetable oil for cooking
o Salt and pepper to taste
o 2 cups sliced mozzarella cheese[*******]

To Make the Marinara
In a small Dutch oven or large saucepan, warm 1 tablespoon vegetable oil over medium-high heat and add the onions, stirring until softened and golden, about 5-6 minutes. Add the garlic and cook for one additional minute. Deglaze the pan with the wine, scraping the pan to snatch up any brown bits. Add the remaining ingredients, stirring to combine. Bring to a boil, then lower to a slow simmer and allow to cook for an hour. This can also be done in the Crock-Pot on low for half a day.

---

[*] about one small onion or half a huge onion. Onion size in Oregon is a total inconsistency ranging from baseball to basketball size, so 'one onion' in recipes always drives me nuts.

[**] I've tried a ton of marinaras over the years, and using a little jarred sauce as a starter always turns out the best.

[***] I'd recommend avoiding sweet varieties and going normal or spicy, although the chicken varietal would be fine.

[****] Our local New Seasons Market sells the end bits and pieces of pancetta for recipes; if you can't find such a thing, a sliced salami chub would work just fine.

[*****] or Italian Seasoning, if you're not going to go with Penzeys like I've been telling you this entire time!

[******] Yes, I like cottage cheese over ricotta, although if you're going to be a real snob about it, you could use ricotta instead. Just be warned that your noodles aren't going to cook up as well if you do.

[*******] either the dry type or fresh style, pressed lightly with paper towels to absorb excess moisture.

To Make the Lasagna

In a skillet, warm a tablespoon of vegetable oil over medium-high heat, then add the ground beef and sausage. Sauté until browned, then remove the meat onto a plate. In the pan drippings, lightly brown the pancetta for another 3-4 minutes, just until it's beginning to crisp and to become fragrant. Remove and add to the meat mixture. Sprinkle the meat with the Italian seasoning, carefully tossing to coat.

To assemble the lasagna, start with a generous ladleful of sauce on the bottom of a lasagna dish (or 15-inch Pyrex pan) and coat the entire bottom with marinara, adding more if necessary. Cover the sauce in a layer of dry noodles. Evenly distribute half the meat mixture over the noodles, followed by half the cottage cheese, then a third of the mozzarella. Add another layer of noodles, and cover with an even layer of sauce. Repeat with the second half of the meat, cottage cheese, and mozzarella, topping with a third and final layer of noodles, and finishing with a third layer of sauce. Cover the dish tight with aluminum foil, then bake for 45-60 minutes, until ferociously bubbling with golden noodles curling up the sides. Remove the lasagna, top with the last third of mozzarella, then turn off the oven and allow the lasagna to sit in the cooling hot box for 15 minutes. Take out, and allow to sit for 15 more minutes before slicing into this monstrosity.

Any sauce left over? Use it for spaghetti or dipping breadsticks, or freeze it for next time.

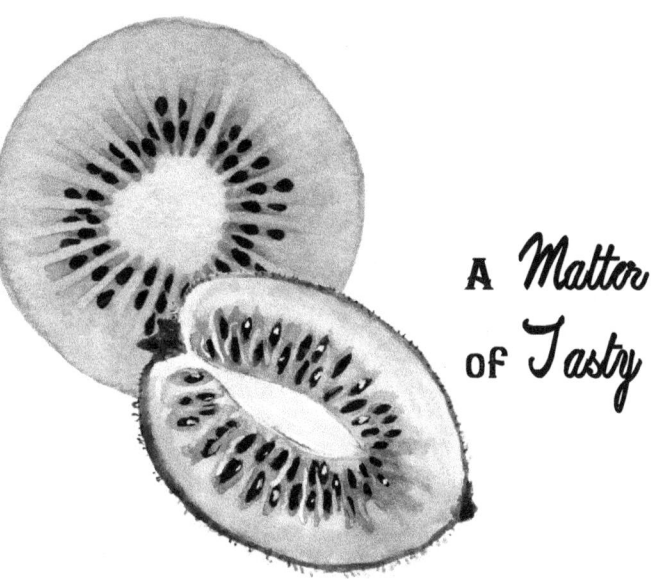

A Matter of Tasty

*J*anuary—Matt and I discovered in 2016—is when Portland hibernates. The not-outlandish hotel rate should have been the giveaway: "Remember that sketchy La Quinta in Stockton on the way back from Tucson?" I reminded Matt while we waited for the emerald Art Deco elevator. "We paid more for that night than this one."

Our room was tall and narrow, like a shoebox you could fit two La Quinta guest rooms inside. This was our first hotel room together that wasn't picked because it was the cheapest rack rate on Hotels.com, or because it had enough room in the parking lot for a 20-foot U-Haul. The minibar was stocked with locally distilled rums and cheeky pleasure kits. There was a button on the phone I could press and receive a hand-delivered pint of Salt & Straw ice cream.

The hallways were quiet. The parking options were boundless. The Multnomah Whiskey Library, with its club-member-only reservation policy, walked us straight upstairs to a front seat at the bar. "How is nobody here?" I wanted to know. It was a Saturday night, and the most crowded corner was a couples date of tanned (and thus assumed) tourists taking selfies with the drink cart.

"Everywhere is pretty much dead this time of year," the bartender explained. "There's no more holiday travel, and everyone's made resolutions to quit drinking, which they should be breaking any day now."

So I didn't think, when we woke up the next day on our get-drunk-on-fancy-things-in-the-city-and-use-this-nice-restaurant-gift-card-my-boss-got-me-for-Christmas weekend, that we would have any trouble getting into downtown's Tasty n Alder for brunch. But the line just before opening curled around the corner, where people flicked through their phone apps while their partners tracked down coffee at surrounding cafés.

I turned to Matt, expecting him to shake his head and pivot away with a hard "NOPE!" But he was filed in place, counting the tables inside the restaurant versus the hungry guests in wait. "If it's this good, I want to at least try it," he said.

I puzzled behind him, too groggy and under-caffeinated to realize—he didn't remember. We'd been here before.

Tasty n Sons, the Northeast Portland version of the Tasty family, occupied an industrial space that was modern and chic, with generous natural light beaming through the floor-to-ceiling garage window front. The utilitarian look was softened by gleaming dark woods and communal tables, blending contemporary aesthetics and practical comfort. Like a play on savory and sweet, the look toed the line just right.

We first visited in December 2011, after I'd spent months craving a taste of the tapas-style small breakfast plates, which were extolled in every foodie publication I picked up. My opportunity came when we were heading out of town, which brought us through the city center and near off-ramps that led to destination neighborhoods. When I was a dorm-dwelling college student in Portland, I was only a few miles from the burgeoning Boise neighborhood where Tasty n Sons currently hangs its shingle. I later came into the city every so often for literary readings and happy hours with friends, but snagging Matt in tow was a rarity. He seldom agreed to venture into the closest neighborhood for dinner, let alone 45 minutes each way into the city.

A 10-foot chalkboard mounted next to the entrance detailed the local purveyors curated for the menu. I read off the names of those I'd tasted as if recounting celebrity acquaintances— "Olympia Provisions! Oh, I just love their kielbasa. Provvista— they import the most a*maz*ing cheeses."

Matt tapped through his phone, messaging his coworkers who also spent Sunday mornings loitering in their company email. We were seated at a communal table's corner, overlooking the streetscape, which, at the moment, featured a solid line of Portland Waste recycling bins. How urban! How vogue! The perfect table details: the miniature pepper mill and salt pinch bowl, the French-style decanters of water, the handsome hipster couple in the table's opposite corner nibbling on tiny plates of artfully-stacked French toast and egg sandwiches (between Portland's staple-du-jour, the haute biscuit).

At the other end of the eight-foot table, a couple about our age huddled together over a collection of miniature breakfasts. Their experience was completely intertwined—the woman buried her fork into a leaning tower of French toast, and her guy followed suit. They shared a gaze of carb lust and made low comments to each other I couldn't hear over the garbage trucks and nearby kitchen. No gushing, just contentment as she fluttered open the *Portland Tribune*, and he drove the coffee press into the ground abyss.

I effused over the menu as if reading a grand poem. Roasted apple with bacon lardons and cheddar. Burmese Red Pork Stew with Brown Rice and Eggs Two Ways. Cast Iron Frittata with Roasted Squash, Buttered Leeks, Feta, and Fried Sage. The bravado of ingredients that paraded across the distressed parchment menu card kicked up my pulse. This was where food culture was being born, where cooks transcended into chefs and mere sustenance was elevated into fleeting works of art.

After I set down my menu, confident in my selection of Moroccan Chicken Hash with Harissa Cream, I noticed Matt was still scanning up and down the card. And not in a *Wow, this all looks fantastic—how can I possibly decide?* way. His pursed lips, slumped shoulders, and tired gaze suggested a person far less enthralled by the possibilities at hand.

"What are you thinking?" I asked.

"I don't know," he mumbled, always a bad sign.

If he wasn't salivating over at least three choices by now, he wasn't happy. Dining out is its own holiday, and at a restaurant Matt likes, he'll order an appetizer and entrée. If we're out for Thai, make that two entrées to guarantee a haul of leftovers. His idea of a great restaurant discovery is one that is located within 20 minutes of home with a giant parking lot and portions so outlandish, the attraction lies in the spectacle. What is 'good' compared with getting a forklift of food, like at McRae's in Oregon City, the diner Matt found on Yelp that didn't involve crossing into Multnomah County.

The morning we set out for McRae's, we followed the GPS directions up the hill, past Fred Meyer and Dollar Tree, to a building that had been a Skippers seafood restaurant in a former life. The porthole windows still remained. *Home of the 12 Egg Omelet!* the sign proclaimed to those passing on their way for Les Schwab tire rotations.

The table was covered with a plastic gingham tablecloth that clung to my elbows and made them smell like disinfectant and Minute Maid. The menu was diner classic: stacks of French toast with macerated strawberries and whipped cream, sausage hash, Denver scrambles. I ordered my safety (one pancake) while Matt went for a full-sized ham-and-cheese omelet.

"I'm not taking home a scrap," he vowed.

And he didn't. Every last bite of egg, American cheese, and cubed ham, plus the frozen hashbrowns, were devoured from a plate the size of a Thanksgiving turkey platter. I ate half the flapjack, which was large enough to take two bites of and use the rest as a ski mask. From that day on, whenever I breached the subject of where to eat breakfast, his answer was always McRae's.

"But what about Pine State Biscuits?" I tried to steer him, pointing to Guy Fieri on TV, stuffing his face with fried chicken between mounds of soft buttermilk pastry.

"Northeast Portland? Are you kidding?"

Unless I wanted to kick off an argument that would culminate in an angry grudge-drive into the city, Matt glowering while I pouted, then, yes, I was kidding.

When we signed our name 50 times for the house in Hubbard, I thought these sojourns into the city would be part of our rhythm, like picking up cheese at the store and going to Macy's for new towels. Our real estate agent strummed my need as I quizzed him on the community: Are there any good places to eat? A grocery store? A farmers' market? (Nope. No. Never.)

"You're just moments from the freeway out here," he said in the middle of the Great Room living area/dining nook/kitchen combo, which he promised would be a super-desirable feature when we eventually decided to sell the place to old baby boomers who couldn't move around much. "Thirty minutes, and you're in Portland with a cocktail in your hand, just in time for happy hour!"

After two years of living in a town with no diversions, Matt had burrowed in. Work, home. Work, home. A steady job, a couch, cold beers, and snuggling cats waiting back at the house. I wanted to rip the surrounding hazelnut groves open with my bare hands.

When we visited the original Tasty n Sons in 2011, I suggested that Matt order the Southern Pride Omelet with Hot Link Sausage, Red Onions, and Housemade Pimento Cheese.

"I don't think I'd like the hot links," he said.

I felt a souring of impatience. *Really? Don't like hot links? You eat the shit out of hot links at home, you liar.*

"Why don't you just order for me?" he resigned, tossing the card on the table with the chill of a big-shot director rejecting a crappy screenplay.

I felt personally affronted. This isn't just food! It's fashion; it's culture! How dare you toss genius aside! "We could leave," I suggested in my calmest voice, which doubles as my most condescending. "Why don't we hit the road and swing through McDonald's?"

"Now you're just being an ass."

"What?" I batted my eyelashes in shock, but I was getting too old, and we'd been together too long for this game to work.

I didn't remember us always being this way. When I look back on our first apartment years of digging for meat from the Fred Meyer bargain bin, I don't recall having to fight and barter to live a life. We began our time together in Tanasbourne, a dense jungle of restaurants, stores, and long traffic lights. A short walk from my apartment, and I was sitting down to sushi, or shopping for jeans, or picking up short ribs at Trader Joe's. A family ran a wine store across the street from our first apartment and hosted free tastings every Friday night. We would visit and talk grandly with the owners about notes and overtones.

"I'm sensing bacon," Matt would claim.

Nowadays, I would roll my eyes and hiss at Matt to *Shut up, or you'll embarrass me in front of the sommelier*, but for years I would laugh and move the conversation to something I had caught from the bottle label, like strawberries and pepper. If we had just been paid that week, we might pick out our favorite from the five tastes and pop it open at the apartment, drawing out our bliss.

Sometimes I would be driving home from work or school, and he'd catch me on my cell phone.

"I feel like pool and drinks," he would tell me. "Let's meet up!" Back then, he would stand behind me at the pool table to line up a shot, sneaking a grab of my ass before ordering another round. Or we'd sacrifice a precious 10-dollar bill and play the lowest bet the slot machines would allow. I'd sit on his lap, pushing the button on the machine in the secret 'Lottery' back room you had to enter through the saloon doors.

A miniscule jackpot, maybe five credits, would send us into a tailspin of high-fives and kisses. I couldn't believe the dead-eyed regulars around us, hunched over machines like they had grown around them, the same expression when they won it all as when they lost the house.

"We'll never be like that," I vowed out loud. "Let's always be excited."

The waitress at Tasty took our order of the two dishes that seemed the most Matt-pleasing of the bunch: Patatas Bravas with Overeasy Eggs and the Open-Faced Monte Cristo Sandwich in Spiced Maple. The food will come out as it is finished, the waitress explained, so sharing plates is encouraged.

"Great!" I said with a stupefied grin. Did you hear that, honey? No warmers!

The first dish to arrive was the potatoes, coated in a mild tomato and paprika sauce, topped with a dollop of housemade aioli and eggs with yolks as smooth and sensuous as butterscotch.

I stabbed a potato with my fork and popped the bite into my mouth. A slow, uncontrolled *Mmmmm* rose from within, coaxed by the richness and crisp-creamy texture combination that felt divine to every sense involved. "These are exquisite," I proclaimed, but Matt stared them down with the same look he gave the argyle sweater I bought him to wear last Christmas.

In that moment, I realized that I married a man who hates Tasty n Sons, and patatas bravas, and morning drives into the city, and so much else that brought me joy. And I imagine that was the same moment when Matt saw me as a woman who laps up foodie-hype hipster bullshit. There we were, our two opposing cores laid out on the communal table. Me, the person who sees every weekend as a new potential adventure, who wants to be part of what has just emerged and is best loved. He, the quiet homebody, who wants nothing more than the comfort of his own familiar walls, away from crowds and hustle and the unknown.

As much as food can bring people together, how far can it tear them apart? Some of our deepest grudges have arisen from what's been on our plates. I seethe when I recall the day I'd spent hours prepping and slowly simmering scratch spaghetti sauce, only to watch him scrape 80% of his plate into the trash. Too much basil, he claimed. And I can't count how many times he brings up the fact that I hate his recipe for macaroni and cheese. For god's sake, it's noodles, evaporated milk, and big slices of cheddar all congealed together. I need fresh and eclectic; he craves a canvas of comfort he can paint with hot sauce and roll in a tortilla. These are not differences to compare or apologize for, but they are differences. Some days our digressions are charming, but on days like these, they're chasms that teem with bitterness.

I paid the check as soon as possible. We walked to the car, passing all of the trendy businesses on my must-try list: Chop Charcuterie, Pix Patisserie, Eat Oyster Bar. Dark, polished wood grains, sleek track lighting, natural daylight, small plates, bold flavor. I didn't ask how he liked breakfast because I knew the answer would only piss me off. And I knew if I were to return to the neighborhood for another taste, it would need to be on my own or with a like-minded girlfriend. My revelation was hardly startling: we are very different people. The fear that this was a spark onto a much more explosive fuse—this was new. How separate could lives be lived before they were apart?

It's just a restaurant, I thought, shoving my inconvenient fears away. I didn't want a fight. I didn't want to hurl 'always' and 'never' across the car for three hours. If I spoke my fear, then the chasm wouldn't be mere paranoia; it would be a rift we'd have to traverse. Something we may fall into. A place we could sink. No. It was nothing. Only a matter of taste.

"These potatoes are fantastic," Matt said, spearing the warm, starchy paprika bundles between bites of Tasty fried chicken.

"I know," I said. Six small plates in, two rounds of Water Avenue coffee, and Matt hadn't betrayed the tiniest sense of déjà vu. "You've had these before. Don't you know?"

"When?"

"Here."

"We've never been here."

"No, but we've been to their sister restaurant, Tasty n Sons, over in the Boise district."

"Oh, yeah?" He scooped more of the chicken-fried pork cutlets onto his plate, a second round for one of my picks. We'd each made three menu selections, ending up in an accidental harmony of petite mains and generous sides. "When?"

"About five years ago. We were on the way to that Eagles/Seahawks game?"

He blinked back at me, nothing recalled.

"We got in a big fight because you hated it, and I wrote a whole essay about how it was a metaphor for the differences between us, and it was in my MFA thesis, and then it was published last year?"

"Oh, great," he groaned. "Well, it couldn't have been that big of a blow-up if I can't even remember it."

"I guess we worked it out," I said.

Five grown-up years later, we were still together: Matt, a little more open to untread flavors, and me, willing to admit that I don't want dinner out of a micropipette. Here we sat in an unproclaimed truce: a sometimes-trip with the wind at our backs and the crowds at home, pretending *this is the year!* they're going to kick the expensive bar habit. We'll be tourists in our nearest metro, just as we are on every other vacation, our common ground paved in the fact that tasty is always better than trendy.

Patatas Bravas Worth Breaking up Ouer

*H*opefully, these Spanish-style breakfast potatoes bring you more harmony and less existential dread over whether your soulmate truly gets you. Give him a minute to come around. After all, what kind of monster doesn't like perfectly spiced potatoes?

- o 2 pounds Yukon Gold or heirloom red potatoes, halved[*]
- o 2 tablespoons olive oil
- o Salt and pepper to taste
- o 1 tablespoon smoked paprika[**]
- o ½ teaspoon cayenne pepper
- o 1 ½ cups chicken stock
- o ½ onion, finely chopped
- o 1 tablespoon flour
- o 3 garlic cloves, minced
- o 1 bay leaf
- o ½ teaspoon tomato paste
- o 2 tablespoons butter
- o Fried eggs, in the quantity you desire[***]

Toss cut potatoes with olive oil, salt, and pepper. Spread in a single layer on a baking sheet, and roast for 1 hour in a 400° F oven. Turn and stir the potatoes halfway through the cooking time.

Melt the butter on medium-high heat in a skillet (preferably cast iron—are you sensing a trend in my kitchen yet?). Add onions and sauté for 2 minutes. Add garlic and tomato paste, and continue to cook and stir for 5 minutes.

Add bay leaf, paprika, cayenne, and flour. Mix well until incorporated. Whisk in chicken stock and allow to come to a boil.

---

[*] Don't mess this up! Artisan potatoes only need apply.

[**] I use the Hungarian variety.

[***] cooked to your favorite consistency to serve on top. I recommend a soft yolk that will drip and mingle with the lovely saucy potatoes, and this is what Tasty n Sons believes in, as well.

Simmer for about 10 minutes until slightly thickened, then remove from heat and (safely! Don't burn your fingers!) extract the bay leaf. Allow to cool for several minutes.

Now, this is where an immersion blender would be immensely helpful. If you've got one of those, blend in the pan until smooth. No immersion blender? Carefully add the liquid to a blender, and purée until smooth.

Add potatoes and sauce back into the skillet on medium heat until all is warmed through. Season with salt and pepper, and top with one (or two, if you're super hungry) eggs. You can also make it extra pretty with fresh parsley and green onion garnish. I'd also add a dollop of Greek yogurt whisked with a bit of roasted garlic, but that's because I'm a fussy food snob.

They Killed Portland, You Know

In February of 2013, I met Chloe Caldwell for lunch. I was two weeks away from moving out of Oregon for Matt's job transfer to Tucson. I was reluctantly going along because that is what spouses do and what marriage is about and all that.

Chloe was one of my favorite writers. Her essay collection, *Legs Get Led Astray*, was a pivot point in my work, a true revelation in that marvelous MFA-student tenure filled with false prophets. Caldwell's sashimi-fresh prose reconfigured how I arrived at the page. She excavated what was possible in essays and memoir. Like many other artists I'd recently fallen in love with, she was also local. This was the beauty of living in Portland; writers lurked as thick as invasive blackberries. We were an insatiable force.

With only a few weeks until our U-Haul departed, I had nothing to lose. I'd already cried on my therapist's couch about 'losing the community' I'd come to treasure more than anything. I didn't know when, and if, we would be back ("We might really love Tucson!"), so I emailed Chloe. *Want to eat sandwiches with a fan?*

I was used to writers taking me up on these random invitations because we were a small world and loved food. We were all loosely connected: friends or representatives of a person or organization that the other knows (or wants to). I'd become accustomed to people like Chloe saying, "Sure!" It was a Pacific Northwest quirk I took for granted for a lifetime. A month later, when I moved to Tucson and cold-emailed one of the only writers I loosely knew, I was caught off-guard with a rebuke. *Sorry, I'm, uhhh, really busy finishing up a novel. Good luck with your move.* I felt my ears ignite as I read the reply email, my audacity smacking me back with blunt force.

"But, we're all writers!" I kept myself from typing back to the Arizona rejector. "Aren't we supposed to be friends?"

Chloe and I met for lunch at Cheryl's Café, built a few blocks up from Powell's Books on Burnside Street, at the base of old-city stately apartments. Not so long before this, a belligerent drunk guy chased me down this very block until I dove into a cab, but the cheery cupcakes and latte art of Cheryl's was a tentative step toward changing the area. A year and a half from this lunch date, when I moved back to Portland, my BOLT Bus driver would pull into the Portland station where a titanic, mirrored condo building rose over the restaurant's new northern neighbor. The LEED-certified glass was a glimmering Silicon Valley warning, a beacon of transparency churning out the grit that used to quicken my steps in the dark.

That afternoon with Chloe, we talked for over an hour about finicky lit journals, small presses, Portland passive-aggression, and our futures. "I'm actually moving away, too," Chloe admitted. Back to New York. Of her own free will.

"Will you come back?"

She shrugged through a bite of veggie and hummus sandwich. "I don't know. It kind of doesn't seem like the same city it was, you know? I feel like I may as well be in Brooklyn."

I periscoped my vision down to my tuna-cado baguette, ignoring the creeping cranes and construction chainlink fences that surrounded this corner that used to be known for riding crops and dildos, where the closest thing to brunch used to be a Roxy's 24-hour hangover diner. The city was my heaven and refuge and muse. Portland was a heartbeat. Portland was us. If we loved this place, if we stayed, if we kept making art, how could it change without our permission?

June, 2014. The Doug Fir Lounge, a Don-Draper-as-Lumberjack bar in a converted roadside diner. The entire Jupiter Hotel is a 1960s Travelodge, gutted and lacquer-antlered into a hipster cove slinging Shiner tall boys and hosting bands in the basement.

I had a room on the second floor that looked like an Ikea 'look what we did in 250 square feet' showroom. A futon bed, Austin Powers plastic chairs, free condoms flicked on the bed. I got green and red ones, like Christmas. My carry-on suitcase was propped open on the desk table next to a stack of *Portland*

Monthly magazines. I packed nothing but my toothbrush, my MAC makeup collection, and an interview outfit I revised a dozen times before tucking it into my cheap, cat-shredded suitcase. My navy belted dress and cardigan said business casual. My houndstooth stockings stamped my passport to Southeast Portland. Perfectly fashionable, edgy, and pretentious. My vintage leather saddle purse hinted at the trove of creativity and whimsy Rogue Brewery would reap once they added me to the team.

In the 15 months I'd lived in Tucson, I'd morphed from wistful adventurer to petulant southwest detractor. I hated the weather. The traffic. The snowbirds. The one not-Barnes & Noble bookstore. The lack of teriyaki shops.

The roots of my misery were slightly less superficial: I hated my job. I was doing tedious, unfulfilling work that contradicted all my lofty quit-ravaging-the-earth principles as a technical editor for a mining company. The commute was a nightmare. I didn't know how to make friends as a grown-up in a new place. We didn't have kids or religion, the easy access points into young adult belonging. The manuscript I'd written wasn't selling, and it was easy to blame that on being away from my Portland writing community. *If only I were hanging out at Wordstock,* I thought, *HarperCollins would HAVE to jump at this.*

I can't remember what the catalyst was, what passing comment or dark-hearted afternoon drove me out into the office parking lot where I hid behind a cluster of cholla and tapped out an email to an old friend, Nick, my boss from a few years back, a guy who'd always been in my corner. *How are things at Rogue? Any way you'd want to work with the best copywriter on this side of the Mississippi again? I really need to get back to PDX.*

I hit Send, not expecting to hear anything back. Sometimes the smallest effort, a bit of betrayal against your current situation, is enough to ferry you through another day. As I started-and-stopped through the 33 stoplights that stood between our rented house on the opposite side of the city and me, a response pinged on my phone. Nick:

Let me talk to HR!

Before I pulled into the driveway, I was on the phone with the brewery's corporate recruiter, with a formal Skype date set up a few days later. A week after that, I was on a plane bound for the Rose City, a guilty claim of 'family emergency' on my supervisor's voicemail. My ticket home was one nailed interview away.

The night I flew in, Aaron Burch was touching down in the

city on a book tour. He had published a series of essays of mine on *Hobart*, and was one of those far-off people who'd changed my writing life. The reading was held at Ristretto Roasters, a sleek coffee shop owned by writer Nancy Rommelmann, who'd shared a coffee and one of those unexpected, random, beautiful AWP conversations with me in Seattle. The glass-and-hardwood space was Twitter come to life, inhabited with people I'd yet to meet or hadn't seen since grad school. I got my Aaron bear-hug. Nancy cupped my chin in her hand and kissed my cheek.

"Welcome home!" she said.

The after-party migrated to the Doug Fir, where we took over the fire pit. Whichever cluster of people you leaned into, you heard the frenetic conversation of word nerds cut loose from their desks. *McSweeney's* and *submission fees* and *Ta-Nehisi Coates* drifted into the smoky and cool, cloudless sky. One of my best writer friends, Cucumber Risotto Susan, appeared beneath a garland of patio lights, and we didn't stop talking until a guy in plaid-and-Warby-Parker-glasses = a uniform broke in.

"I'm sorry to interrupt," he said, "but I just wanted to tell you—I loved your *Hobart* essays."

I drifted back upstairs to my room, high on midnight espresso, Mason-jar cocktails, and the warm elixir of belonging. The kind of night that makes you think that every other can be just like it.

The next day I kicked the shit out of the interview. Because my life depended on it.

While I was living in Tucson, I made promises. Portland resolutions. When I get back to Portland, I will:

Go to every event Powell's has.

Sign up for all the workshops.

Attend each reading series like an auditory stalker.

Eat at all the new restaurants instead of reading about them.

Never take this city for granted.

You know my secret, though: I didn't live in Portland. Never did, at least not since my college dorm days in the early aughts, living off Alberta Street before it had an artisan ice creamery, or *Top Chef* contestant restaurants, or a Bikram yoga studio or French bakery or collage supply shop. Matt and I worked in the suburbs south of the Multnomah County line. Hubbard debatably fell within the boundaries of Portlandian civilization, though we only grew the hops fueling the craft beer revolution, and the free-range chicken eggs were shuttled in for brunch.

Five years ago, when I was still in grad school and uncovering the riches of the city's lit scene, my masquerade as urban-dweller felt seamless. I had the boots and the scarves. I could layer sweaters and book bags as well as anyone. I'd leave my office at five in the afternoon, and in 30 minutes I'd pull into my favorite parking garage, the one between Anthropologie and Whole Foods, catty-corner to Powell's. I'd meet Susan at Fish Grotto for cocktails shaken by fellow MFA grad, Drew. As a technical outsider, I could still participate. I had everything—a burgeoning life in the city, a quiet home in the country.

When I was in Arizona, feeling marooned and lonely and hopeless, I obsessed over those nights. I'd reconstruct them in my head, filling in the details to make sure I hadn't forgotten them. If I couldn't forget them, they couldn't forget me. I traced the steps back to that place I'd been off Burnside Street, overconfident about my stuffed Submittable In-Progress queue. One plane ticket. One MAX ride. One text, one drink. Home. That strange, suspended time before gravity caught notice of the graduation afterglow and Portland's polish to gold before the rush.

While I was away, Fish Grotto was gutted and sold, part of an entire block parcel steps from Cheryl's Café. They turned it into a shopping boutique with designer backpacks on pedestals and handmade, flavor-forward lollipops. Drew had stuffed his Subaru from floor to ceiling and made a hell-run to Louisiana. After majoring in literature and devoting my life to stories, I missed the most obvious inevitability on the page: you can never go back to the Shire.

Last summer, I went to a reading in Southeast Portland. My office was 14 miles away. It took me an hour and 15 minutes to arrive. There was no accident or construction project. The bridges were not lifted. No brush fires or spewing volcanoes. Just a chokehold of cars serpentining around the city center, red brake lights chaining a scorpion tail tracing the river. My gateway from the suburbs to culture had become a wall.

When I'm pinned into my car, I go feral. I scream. I throw my hands up. I curse anyone with out-of-state plates, no matter how rationally he's attempting to merge. Friends, cocktails, food, words are only a couple exits down, if only *please* could we quit cutting each other off and switching lanes and just drive?

I arrived late. The first writer was already on stage. Everyone was two drinks in, unwound.

"You made it!" A friend from grad school caught me in a hug. "It's been so long! I never see you at stuff anymore!"

There's more than one way to choke out a region's original proletariat. The residents get notes on their doors and hikes to the ceiling. The commuters get barred from the inside out. The price we pay—the time, the gas, the patience—grows steep. That was the last time for months that I went to a reading after work. I'd planned on going to half a dozen in the time since. I checked 'Going' on the Facebook event. I wore my favorite sweater dress and boots to work. I brought my copy of the book for signing. I instructed Matt to eat the leftover casserole in the fridge.

Then I clocked out of my office and walked to my car, contemplating the left turn that every other car was making. I opened Google Maps and saw a line so deep red, they had to deepen it to maroon to designate it from just normal, everyday badness. I think, *There will be another time. I'll catch that author later. No one's going to miss me. I can get tons of writing done if I go home, eat dinner, stop fighting.*

I tell myself that community is overrated.

It is difficult for me to parcel the fault of this disillusionment. It lies in the gray area between an adolescent city's shrewd, lumbering awkwardness and my own slip into something inevitable: a woman who is no longer as young as she was in her twenties.

You've read it before. Portland is dead. Seattle is dead. San Francisco is a zombie eating our West Coast brains. Blame the tech money, the foreign money. The newly rich, the ever-powerful. It's not that the story isn't true, because gentrification and housing instability and displacement are real, tangled, terrible problems.

But this isn't a story about eviction or homelessness, just like most of the stories you hear about livability's decay aren't—stories written by those like me with the luxury of time to write them and the privilege of a platform to share them. We are the ones who lament the closure of our favorite bar that we can't—through the Vaseline-smeared lens of nostalgia—admit was kind of disgusting.

The change, and sometimes exploitation, of a region hands us an easy narrative—a boogeyman. No one is keeping me out of Portland, but it feels good to say they are. If I really wanted to participate in the scene, it's there. Better than ever, growing more diverse with writers from all over the country moving in and out and through, incorporating new art forms and ideas. We have a monthly writer collage night, and a mix-tape reading, and open mics in Tiki dives. It might not be as easy or fast to get into the city from the outside, but it's not impossible. The bar has only been raised a few inches.

I toss around the idea that my world has changed because the more I lob it around, the more it distracts me from the fact that I've changed. A 25-year-old writer is inevitably different from a 32-year-old one. The glitter on my mind's marquee has flaked as the novelty of being a 'writer in a literary city' wears. I've done the things—the readings, the signings, the festivals, the workshops. They were marvelous in those glimmering days of discovering this world. They still are, on the occasions when I've got the energy and desire to draw back in. But unlike that girl at the start, who felt like she was contributing by witnessing, I'm no longer satisfied by simply being present at a place. I'm in the thick of the work: working on my 180 words amidst keeping up with columns, squeezing in reviews, and lending whatever hand I can give my enduring and scattered tribe. Keeping pace with this load doesn't grow easier with time and a full-time job to support a home-owning, Whole Foods-shopping, new model Prius-driving suburban lifestyle I chose and committed to years ago. No one forced these obligations on me, and the universe will not mourn if I ditch to the writing part. The realities are the param-eters I've drawn and the space I must now work within. Pretend-ing otherwise is as fruitful as shaking my fist at every California-plated car that zips into the stopping distance I try to maintain on the freeway. They're not going back to Los Angeles, and I'm not getting any younger.

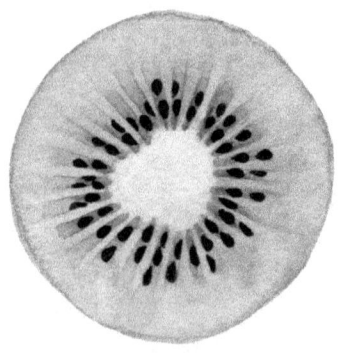

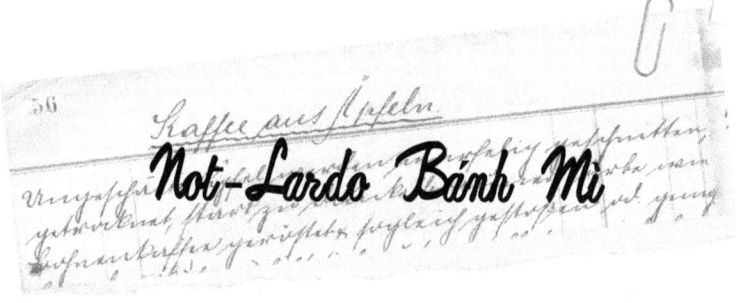

Not-Lardo Bánh Mì

Across the street from Cheryl's Café is Lardo, a gourmet sandwich shop with some of the most unique, delicious creations I've ever had between bread. My first order at Lardo, right after I moved back from Tucson, was a bánh mì sandwich. The classic meatball sub from Vietnam is served on a baguette, combining the toothsome French loaf with the vinegar crunch of slaw and spicy mayo tang. It is one of the most pleasing combinations of flavor and texture I can name.

Not long after my Lardo experience, *Bon Appétit* (as they are wont to do) ran an exposé on this sandwich and included this recipe, which I've adjusted a bit to meet my own pantry's contents and to accommodate my personal belief that meatballs should be roasted instead of fried. As I've worked with the recipe over the years, I've been back to Lardo on sporadic occasion. And each time I skip over the Phở'Rench Dip roast beef or Korean Pork Shoulder in favor of the bánh mì, I leave a teensy bit disappointed because, well … it's fabulous, but it's not mine. And mine is kinda transcendent.

The city can be inspiring, but it's nothing like what you're capable of at home.

- o   1 pound ground pork
- o   1 long, crusty baguette from your favorite bakery
- o   ¼ cup fresh basil, chopped
- o   1 tablespoon fresh minced garlic
- o   6 green onions, chopped and divided
- o   1 tablespoon fish sauce
- o   2 tablespoons sriracha, divided
- o   1 tablespoon sugar, plus ¼ cup, divided
- o   2 teaspoons cornstarch
- o   1 teaspoon salt
- o   1 teaspoon pepper
- o   ⅔ cup plain Greek yogurt
- o   2 tablespoons mayonnaise
- o   1 cup cilantro, roughly chopped
- o   1 cabbage, grated
- o   ¼ cup rice vinegar
- o   1 teaspoon salt

- o   1 tablespoon sesame oil
- o   2 carrots, grated*

As soon as you get home, grate the cabbage and carrots (or open the bag of slaw mix) into a mixing bowl and toss with rice vinegar, 1 teaspoon salt, cilantro, and sesame oil. Set aside while you go change into yoga pants and take out your contacts.

When you're starving and ready for a sandwich, preheat oven to 400° F. In a mixing bowl, combine the ground pork, basil, garlic, a third of the green onions, fish sauce, 1 tablespoon of sriracha, cornstarch, 1 tablespoon of sugar, 1 teaspoon pepper, and 1 teaspoon salt. Squish together to combine with your hands until the ingredients have just combined (Don't overwork it), then roll into 1-inch balls in your palms. Place the balls about an inch apart on a prepared cooking sheet lined with foil, with a cookie cooling rack fitted inside the sheet. We have a cookie cooling rack that we use exclusively for meats to cook in the oven this way, like meatballs and bacon strips. The fat drips down, but the meat remains crispy. Bake for 20-25 minutes, until the meatballs are brown and sizzling. Remove and keep warm.

Meanwhile, while the meatballs are cooking, pay attention. You've got shit to do. Combine the yogurt, mayo, green onion, and 1 tablespoon sriracha in a small bowl. While you're at it, slice the baguette lengthwise and hollow out most of the beautiful chewy middle. I know, it seems like a violation, doesn't it? It will, however, make the sandwiches much easier to eat. You can feed these extra bits to hungry squirrels or birds that may loiter on your back porch, or dip them in some oil and vinegar as an impromptu aperitif.

Spread the mayo mixture on each half of the baguette. It is now *fin* and ready for assemblage.

On the bottom of the baguette, spread a generous layer of slaw. Dot the top with a dense line of meatballs. I angle them at a bit of a diagonal to ensure maximum meatball in each bite. Top the meatballs with the other layer of baguette, then slice into desired wedges of sandwich. Serve with leftover slaw, scallion pancakes (Oh, god, I'm so doing this tomorrow), or kettle chips. Commence laughing at all the people fighting for downtown parking to get a comparable bite of your masterpiece.

---

* The cabbage and carrot form the slaw that tops the sandwiches, and to be perfectly honest, I sometimes skip the separate ingredients and pick up a package of cole slaw veggie mix from the grocery store to make things go easier, if it's a worknight. I'll shave off 15 minutes of grating time that way.

Writing Is Magic

*W*riting is magic. If someone tries to tell you different, he is peddling something. Probably a write-your-novel-in-three-weeks workshop.

No, it's not magic alone. And all the magic in the universe isn't going anywhere without putting in the hours (and hours) in the chair, fielding the rejection, tempering the weight gain and liver swells. That's the process. But that indescribable, fleeting, unexpected, manic inspiration that opens something up in you that you never dreamed existed? That is magic.

I was lamenting an essay slog with a friend of mine, the way that a topic that had seemed so fresh and full of potential sagged on the page. Each word felt lifeless, stringing together into heavy, stinking cadaver sentences. Whole paragraph massacres.

"I know this doesn't sound right," she admitted, "but when I'm writing something good—really good—it's so easy. It just happens. It all comes out, and I don't have to do anything. I barely even have to revise it."

"Me, too!" I said.

Yes, I have to commit the time to writing it and to editing out my random garbled garbage, maybe tweaking the structure a smidge. But the story, it lilts. It feels effervescent on the page, and as I type, I don't groan. I feel like I am strumming an instrument rather than plodding on a machine. I don't ever know when that feeling is going to strike or why. It's rarely on deadline. Not normally on whatever thing I think I should be writing. I have to enjoy the moment when it arrives, make the most of it, then not despair when it departs.

I can attempt to recreate the magic, to force or beg or will it into being—make sure all of my favorite knickknacks are in their desk spots, switch from laptop to vintage Smith-Corona typewriter, play the *Inception* soundtrack softly in the background. My failure to manufacture a spark is more disappointing than its mere absence.

Which is a theme I find in my other beloved art form: cooking. Most nights when I come home from work, I'm not using a recipe. I have a carousel of techniques and standbys that I know by heart, and these rotate in and out of the kitchen. The whatever's-in-the-fridge curry. The whatever's-in-the-fridge pizza. They are normally fine, sometimes pretty good. Every so often, there is a rejection funneled straight into the garbage can, but this has become increasingly rare with unrelenting daily practice.

But then there's a night—maybe once every few months, maybe several times in one mystical week—when the mishmash in my refrigerator inspires me. I run away with an idea, an odd combination of unlikely harmonizing flavors striking me into action. It's like being on *Chopped*, when a basket of random crap and Ted Allen's Brooklyn smirk give way to divinity.

The last time this happened was last week, when I was at my corporate-job desk trying to decide what would be for dinner. I was sick to death of chicken, sandwiches, things stuffed into pitas, and potato wedges baked in the oven. My imagination rifled through our freezer and came across the package of curry-flavored sausages I bought on a trip to Leavenworth, Washington. My German heart beats for a good sausage, and I'll put up with all your low-hanging jokes to say so. The sunny turmeric-laced links reminded me of mangoes, the ones I'd gotten much better at peeling while living in the Southwest, their sweetness, their ability to cool a muggy summer evening. I also remembered the chicken sausage salad a friend of mine brought for lunch last week, how blessedly different from most tidy salads it was, how original.

Curry sausage salad.

It came together while I drove a Whole Foods cart through the produce section maze on my lunch—banana chips for crunch, the in-store avocado tangy vinaigrette to temper the curry and mango sweetness. The guy at the cheese counter sold me a few tablespoons of artisanal corn nuts.

"They're for a salad," I explained, and he was intrigued.

The excitement over eating one of the best salads in my memory is the sadness with which I write down the recipe. I know I won't have the curry sausage again for months, maybe ever. Mangoes are some of the most fickle fruits to find in prime condition. In-house dressings love to disappear. That dinner was a flawless plate, and now it's gone, just like my writing inspiration from day to day. It's the believing that the magic will return on another plate or with another pen—that this one celestial feast will not be my last—that keeps me trudging forward in the kitchen, on the page, and in all tiny things in between.

Fleeting-Inspiration
Curry Sausage Salad

- 1 package of curry sausage from Cured in Leavenworth[*]
- 1 head romaine, torn and washed
- 1 perfectly ripe mango, peeled and cut into chunks
- ¼ cup dried banana chips
- 3 tablespoons artisanal corn nuts[**]
- ⅓ cup feta cheese
- ½ cup Whole Foods Avocado Dressing[***]
- 4 green onions, thinly sliced

Grill sausage and allow to cool slightly before slicing into ½-inch pieces. Toss all ingredients together, season with pepper, and serve.

For the Scratch Dressing
- 2 avocadoes, pitted and peeled
- ¼ cup Japanese mayonnaise[****]
- 1 tablespoon fresh lime juice
- ½ cup cilantro, chopped
- ½ teaspoon salt
- ½ teaspoon pepper

Combine all ingredients in food processor and purée until smooth. Adjust salt, pepper, and lime juice as necessary to your taste.

---

[*] or something similar, if you're not living near Eastern Washington right now.

[**] If you can't find these, Marcona almonds would probably be the best bet.

[***] or the scratch dressing recipe I've given.

[****] You can get this from Asian grocery stores or order it online, and it has a magnificent texture and slightly sweeter flavor that knocks dressing out of the park. Go ahead and use regular mayo if you must, but you have to track down and try this life-changing ingredient at some point.

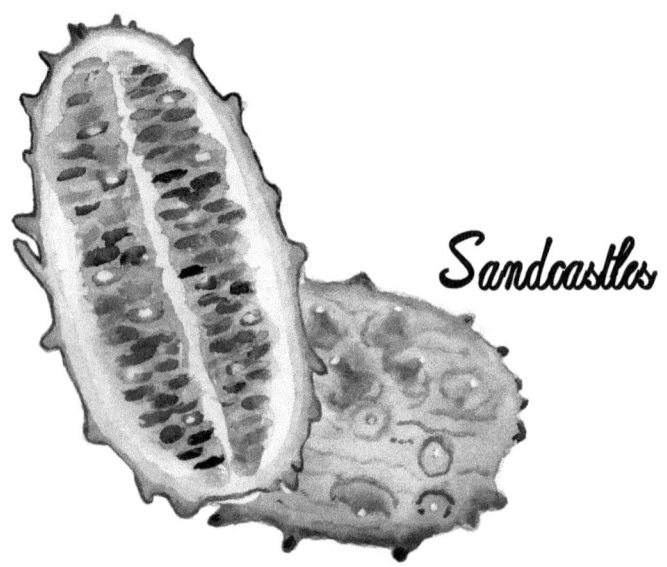

Sandcastles

"**Y**ou know I love lemon meringue pie, right?" Matt said, skulking in the corner of the kitchen. It was a Tuesday night, not a time that the flour bags and egg separator normally got a workout. But this wasn't any normal Tuesday. This was Beyonc-Eve.

"I'm going to have a bunch of ingredients left over," I promised. A bowl of lemons, a full canister of graham crackers to toss with butter and press into crust. "I'll make you one this weekend, okay?"

"I don't want a pity pie," he mumbled.

"Oh, for god's sake, it's not my fault you're not going up to see Bey."

Matt doesn't 'do' concerts anymore, he'd informed me. The act sat on the list of things he used to do that predate knowing me, like barhopping downtown or eating Papa Murphy's Chicago-style stuffed pizza. And even if he did, Beyoncé's Formation Tour was not the concert where you brought a husband as a date. It was a destination for girlfriends or, in my case, Christian and the Twirls—one of my oldest friends and his Seattle crew, who had, over the course of a few Seattle visits and way too many drinks, elevated from far-off acquaintances to almost-friends.

They were an alternate life up in my birth city, quoting *Girls* and shutting down Capitol Hill. They fed my favorite lie, that if we moved back to my home, I'd have a social life. Happiness was one U-Haul away.

I was the satellite girl who watched the *Lemonade* premiere alone, texting Christian about "Sandcastles." I wasn't a Beyhive fanatic until that Sunday after Matt went to bed. The buzz for Beyoncé's mysterious 'film' in a prime HBO time slot was deafening, and I didn't want to be the only one on Twitter not grasping the next day's memes. I liked and respected her for her contributions to my TRL adolescence—"Say My Name" is a time machine back to the South Hill Mall food court of my youth. I screamed at the TV when her badassery was interrupted by Coldplay's dad rock set at the Super Bowl. When I needed a GIF expressing pure joy, fearlessness, and confidence, it was her image I went hunting.

Not until that night, though. Not until Warsan Shire's poetry poured from Beyoncé's lips.

So what are you gonna say at my funeral, now that you've killed me?

Here lies the body of the love of my life,
whose heart I broke without a gun to my head.
Here lies the mother of my children,
both living and dead.
Rest in peace, my true love,
who I took for granted.
Most bomb pussy who, because of me, sleep evaded.
Her god listening.
Her heaven will be a love without betrayal.
Ashes to ashes, dust to side chicks.

Under the frothy pop distraction of her husband's alleged infidelity, Beyoncé hid a subversive ode to intersectional feminism and racial injustice in America. While every idiot news outlet was busy trying to track down Becky with the Good Hair forensically, the Queen was empowering women of color never to be sorry, to remember that winners don't quit on themselves. The lush visuals embossed themselves on my heart by a bass line. As soon as it ended, I watched the film a second time through. The next day, I downloaded the Tidal app (cleverly owned by her husband, Jay-Z) and listened to the music five times over.

Christian, though. Christian and the Twirls were hardcore tenant Bey-lievers long before I got serious. They'd bought their tickets to her Seattle tour stop when they went on sale months ago. There was, of course, no Portland stop. For the upperest echelons of superstardom, Portland was the flyover beltway between Los Angeles' Staples Center and Seattle's CenturyLink Field.

"Even if I wanted to go, it's sold out, isn't it? It's not as if I could even get a ticket."

I never had tickets. I'd been to two concerts in my life: a

garbage show by Modest Mouse at the Paramount before I was old enough to drink, and an emotionally eviscerating night of raw, bleeding art with Fiona Apple in 2012. Everyone else I adored—Lady Gaga, Norah Jones, Britney Spears, Arctic Monkeys—were added to my Ticketmaster cart, but lost when I chickened out on the hefty purchase price.

"I think they're still on StubHub, and they're not that bad, actually," Christian said.

Which is how I ended up in my kitchen on a Tuesday night baking a tribute pie for the Beyoncé pre-party, a suitcase with leather pants and kitten heels bound for Seattle waiting next to the door.

I had to take a day and a half off work in the middle of the week. I had to drive seven round-trip hours. I had to hike up to the 300 level of the stadium, the land of seagulls. I arranged three ice packs in a cooler bag to keep a toasted meringue pie from collapsing in on itself. It's only now, writing it down, that the trip seems excessive in any way. At the time, her pull was insurmountable and unquestioned.

Even Matt got it. "It's Queen Bey," he said, checking our freezer for pizza stock for the long, tough night he'd have fending for himself. "You've gotta go."

A Seattle bartop table on a Thursday midnight. The owner of the industrial-ceilinged, copper-accented, modern downtown speakeasy was bartending alone; apparently he didn't check event listings at the stadium less than a mile from his bar's door. We ordered a round of Moscow Mules, and I tried to convince myself that there was not, in fact, a blister being birthed on top of my big toe. My Steve Madden heels were ravaged by the city's porous Gold Rush sidewalks. "Uber surge pricing is crazy right now," the urbanites said, opting to hoof it from the top of the stadium toward Capitol Hill.

"I'll pay it," I offered, waving my phone as a baton.

"It's not worth getting into a car," someone shot down from the front of the caravan. "I can practically see it."

I'm ... going ... to ... die, I death-chanted under my breath—what little escaped from my lace-up corset. I'd dressed like a woman who would dance until a comfy escape through the parking garage.

The Twirls were hardcore, training all year with their city apartments and weeknight last-calls. At this point in the night, I was struggling to cobble together a sentence. They were planning the after-after-after party.

"I hate to say this, but I was a little disappointed," Christian announced. "I was hoping there was going to be a through-line to the show. A story. I wanted her to take us on a journey, and it was just basically her greatest hits."

I sat silently with so many questions. Do most concerts have a through-line plot structure? How could anyone possibly recreate the intimacy of the film, *Lemonade*, in a stadium built for 68,000 people? She'd performed for two hours straight, through water and pyrotechnics. She spat fire, danced in and out and around a giant spinning cube of light projecting her image 50 feet into the night air. She had a red carpet's worth of costume changes and a 20-strong backup-dancer squad. I wanted to ask smart questions, to stoke the table discussion, to be the fierce shade-throwing debater who would defend the Formation World Tour's honor.

I wanted to express how powerful it was to see this pop culture mammoth grow up before our eyes, from her winking mention of "Some of you may remember me from Destiny's Child" to her caped walk down the aisle to a lagoon, singing "Freedom." How inspiring it was to watch a woman appear so poised and undeniably happy, adored by thousands. Creating art. Becoming powerful enough to control fully the tone of her voice and its purpose, independent of what record labels were pushing most other female artists to say and to be.

Such notions stayed half-formed in my head, flitting butterflies, and me without a net. All I wanted was bed. I fantasized about sneaking outside, requesting a ride, texting my sincere regrets.

I watched the bubbles dissipate in my $14 glass of ginger beer with its traces of booze. I felt too tired to drink, too wiped to be buzzed. My midnights were usually fast asleep or, if shit was really getting wild, hunched over my laptop describing the pizza that Emily was ordering in the latest chapter and making myself ravenous by proxy. What's happened to me? I used to be interesting. I could live on cheap vodka and Gardenburger patties, walk trails and stairs in my heels, and rock lingerie-as-outerwear. These long, spontaneous nights used to be a treat, not a punishment.

I was the most mediocre version of all my selves: wiped, sore, done, blank. Thank god I didn't live in Seattle after all. Christian would figure it out; they would all figure it out. I was absolutely no fun. I was a bore. I was too old for this life, and too old to pretend I'd ever wanted it.

Christian and I met in the most early-aughts stereotypical way possible: through a mutual friend on *LiveJournal*. I was tibby-hime, a Japanese modification of my nickname. I was super into anime and thought I could watch enough *Sailor Moon* to qualify for Japanese citizenship. Christian was upthebuttgirl, a *Sex and the City* reference I couldn't resist connecting with.

"I have to tell you, that's my favorite Charlotte scene ever," I commented when I'd worked up the nerve to transcend my lurking status. We both wrote about dating as almost-grown-ups, which meant mostly dreaming about the possibility of dating. I would twist my one-sided attractions and rejections-by-way-of-no-acknowledgment into relationships reflected in characters far more chic, successful, and desired than I was. "I think we're a Steve-and-Miranda kind of dynamic," I'd say about a guy in my drama class with whom I'd exchanged three sentences.

After months of long comment threads on each other's posts, Christian and I made a date to become official IRL friends. We met at the Denny's in Federal Way and shared chili cheese fries, marveling over this glimpse behind the avatars. He was not Charlotte York, and I was not Sailor Moon. But we still made sense to each other—tall, narrow Christian with his sharp, impeccable jawbone and frenetic, full-circumference hand gestures that were only rivaled by my own. Me, the virgin Victoria's Secret salesgirl. I paid my half of the meal with allowance and met my mom outside at precisely 2:00 for my ride back to Buckley. We were children.

"Oh, wait, we have to get a picture!" one of us said with our point-and-shoot film camera. I remember our heads tucking into each other and the shutter-snap. The film, the print, I haven't seen in a decade. Dissolved evidence.

We graduated high school and kept in touch, giving each other behind-the-scenes DVD extras of our blog misadventures over the phone. Christian was there for all my horror stories, like the time I got stood up at Lloyd Center Mall by a guy I met in a *Yahoo!* chat room and was walking back to my car when my super-sexy pair of underwear with side laces came untied and fell down around my ankles on Broadway Street.

"No one saw!" Christian promised me. "A bus didn't stop, right? If anyone caught a glimpse, they probably figure they were hallucinating."

He was the first person I called when a guy insisted we go out to The Old Spaghetti Factory because he had a coupon, and then argued with the waiter over its validity, because he had ordered water instead of the required soda. When I met a Match.com connection at Peet's Coffee, and he showed up so high he could barely walk down the street—and I literally turned and bolted while he was distracted by some way-beautiful flowers in a window box—I dialed Christian on the way back to my minivan and asked, "Why do we date men?"

"Because we are cursed, Tabitha," he reminded me. "Eternally cursed."

Two years into college and atrocious dates, I met Matt. I moved into my first apartment and first cubicle. I set our wedding date without a proposal—just came home one day before graduation to serve Matt his fate. He was sitting on the couch watching *Good Eats* when I got home from work. I stood in the entryway, purse tucked in the crook of my arm, hands on hips. I was 22. I was running out of time. Charlotte York would be with me on this.

"So, I found a wedding dress, and I'd really like to get married next September," I said. "Is that okay?"

"Uhhh, sure," he said. He decided that was the best answer.

"I can help, right?" Christian asked later. "I can be your wedding planner?"

"I couldn't have a wedding without you."

He managed a linen-rental debacle, covered the getaway Tundra in streamers, and caught my garter. My favorite shot in our album is our hug on the dance floor, me nearly lifting him off his feet, my second vow of the day—*I'll love you forever.*

Matt and I moved further out from urban outskirts to suburbs to rural farmland. We signed off on small percentages of our incomes diverted into 401(k)s. I started learning how to cook. Matt figured out how to keep green grass growing on a fenced plot of earth. We raised our children together (and by children, naturally, I mean our two beloved cats).

Christian didn't leave the city. He graduated from the small-time South Sound world of Tacoma to apartments overlooking the Space Needle and EMP Museum in Seattle. He got a job on the 33rd floor of the Columbia Tower, where he could take an elevator to a Starbucks. He amassed enough bad date stories to fill another six seasons of HBO.

In any logical narrative, this is where the characters normally would part ways. But that's the magnetism between us. We didn't talk every day. We didn't know the intricate details of each other's everyday churn of stress and drama. Catching up was an occasion, a curiously old-fashioned heart-to-heart where we skipped over our Facebook feeds and went deep into what was really going on in that rare meeting moment. We squinted across the wide space that divided us, each one seeing an opposite side teeming with luscious green grass.

"You're such an adult. You have all your shit together," he'd say.

"That's shorthand for boring. You're out there meeting people, visiting places," I shot back.

A decade rolled by. The vintage knickknacks in my living room came together. Christian moved to a narrow, light-filled townhouse on Queen Anne and learned to read Tarot. I couldn't keep up with stories about the city and dates and late nights—*Staying out until closing time on Capitol Hill sounds like a blast, but wait until you watch this video of my cat snoring that I filmed last night in bed at 10!* Christian was too kind to voice the truth; I wasn't even a Charlotte anymore. I was that woman whom Carrie knew from college, the one who was put out to pasture in Connecticut to die.

At 7:30 on post-Beyoncé Thursday, a garbage truck grumbled up to Christian's four-story townhouse. I heard it grunt right outside his bedroom window and heave the recycling bin brimming with Rainier cans into its guts. We'd gotten back just before four, but spring sunshine was ecstatic over Lake Union, as tough to ignore as our cat, Max, when he's ready for breakfast.

I muffled the light with my arm against my eyelids. Groggy. Zero headache. I drank slowly and weakly the night before, buffing out the sparse doses of vodka with a Jucy Lucy burger and a fat slice of Lemonade Lemon Meringue Pie. The only alcohol they were serving at CenturyLink was more of that hipster pisswater Rainier and a high-fructose shot-to-the-heart of Mike's Hard Lemonade. Apropos, but disgusting.

"I'll just skip it for now," I opted as the Twirls loaded up with double-fists. I'd lose my mind after the show and enjoy the Queen fully capacitated.

But I didn't lose my mind. I soured as my feet swelled. I trailed along to the club on Capitol Hill that was playing Beyoncé videos all night. I ordered a Surfbort (Sprite, blue curaçao, vodka, and maraschino cherries) and followed the gang up to the third-floor dance pit, where a hundred sweaty men and their tagalong girls pulsed in one entangled mass.

Good god, this has to be a fire hazard, I thought, turning around and walking down to the second floor, a refuge with sofas and darkness. One of Christian's friends, Arlen, found me in the corner and poured half a screwdriver into my glass.

"Did you escape?" he said. "That dance floor is such a nasty meat mess."

"It can't be up to fire code," I said.

"No way! This place gives no fucks." We sipped and talked blogging until the staff herded us downstairs for last call.

"Get out, or we'll kick you out! Down those drinks," a voice prodded the crowd. Were clubs usually this cranky? I couldn't remember the last time I closed a tab after 10.

Arlen took my arm as the cluster turned up Republican Street. The after-after-after apartment party. Christian was blocks behind us in the arms of a man he'd been texting for a while. Or something. I couldn't hear the story through the blasting "Flawless" remix and crush of men clamoring for their last drinks and last chances.

The apartment was an old Seattle studio that had a one-small-person-maximum kitchen and a showcase window with all-original crown molding and a sill wide enough to cover in pillows and live in the skyline. It was the kind of Carrie Bradshaw rental *LiveJournal*-Tabitha imagined herself graduating dorms into and filling with Hello Kitty appliances.

The studio crowded with Twirls and strangers—other building tenants? New friends from the walk up the street? I couldn't tell if anyone knew them or not. I yanked the laces on my corset loose and let my heels clatter onto the original wood floors. It was time to go to bed, wash the Avril Lavigne eyeliner job off my face, and return the fake eyelashes to their plastic MAC coffin.

Watching the city kids break off to gossip in tiny cliques, slip into the bathroom and make out, and fill whatever coffee mugs were clean with New Amsterdam gin, I had been too tired and comfortable to chide myself for being old. That came now, the morning after, at last delivered to the quiet and relative familiarity of Christian's home.

Seven-thirty a.m. I was beating everyone else to consciousness by five hours.

Way to make friends. Way to prove you're interesting. Way to get invited back.

How did they do it? I wondered while I quietly folded my leather pants back into my suitcase. Brushed my retainer. Swept a line of moisturizer underneath my eyes. Why was I so dreadful at keeping apace?

I pulled the comforter back to cover the mattress and fluffed the coordinating yellow-and-gray pillows. Christian's bedroom looked like a Joanna Gaines project, with its oblong yellow nightstand and purple loveseat. Framed Mariah and Streisand albums were cheeky winks from the walls. He could wear Modern Whimsy like a pullover sweatshirt. Effortless.

For so many years, Seattle was my secret backup plan, that place I kept friends and options banked away, a relationship security deposit box. If I moved back, I could slip into that other girl I thought I was, the one who wore things like the old Frederick's corset in my suitcase. Pull the strings and transform. *I'm a city girl at heart*, I would tell myself any time I felt unsatisfied or out of place. If I were back in my element, I'd be everything I was supposed to be.

It wasn't until escaping that morning from the Fremont House onto a pristine early sidewalk, shared with no one but old women walking their miniature dogs, that the truth cut through years and years of padding around my heart.

You don't belong here, either.

I was stuck between early and late: too early to go back home to Portland and waste a day off work, but not wanting to stick around so late that Christian would be up and ready for brunch. This side of Seattle was not my native side; we were a South and West family, my dad and grandpa building condos you can still buy on Alki Beach for a mere million dollars. I spent my late high school summers working at a heating and air-cooling company on the hill between Rainier Valley and White Junction, carpooling with Claire's dad, who'd gotten us the intern gig. Our first house that exists in a smattering of memory flashes—the Mickey and Minnie Mouse decals on my bedroom closet, the satin blue thread of my mattress, the dark-forest paneling of furniture bought in the late 70s—is around the bend from the city's south Junction, with its old-school German deli and new French pâtisserie. These were the circles in the city that were mine. My family's steps.

I searched on my phone for Metropolitan Market, my favorite grocery store in the southwest Admiral district. It was the street where I watched *Beauty and the Beast* in a grand old palace theater when I was five, the movie's chandeliers and golden frescoes merging and becoming one with the scrolling velvet seats. The phone's GPS voice guided me onto an almost-empty freeway recovering from the morning commute. I'd never actually driven myself here, I realized. I only visited when I was up here to see my family and luxuriating in the wonders of someone else driving me around.

I passed the lookout viewpoint over the city, where I always made everyone pull over for a picture. I turned at the Baskin-Robbins my mom worked at during high school, alongside a sleazeball who tried to get her out on a date, gave ice cream away to all of his friends, and went on to hold an illustrious career in Washington state politics. I made my way through the store with all the precision of a woman without obligation past bringing her favorite treats back home to Oregon.

The aisles were empty, and the shelves freshly stocked with tidy rows of boxes and jars promising they were 'Made Local.' Apples and avocados stacked in pyramids. Cheese wedges huddled together to recreate their former wheels. I read all the mustard flavors. I lingered over the trays of fat chocolate-everything cookies (Met Market's specialty) and the to-die-for poke that was so ephemeral it couldn't survive the 3-ish hour drive back to Oregon before turning. Employees with checklists and carts of boxes paid blessed little attention, sticking to their morning routines of stocking and gossiping before the waves of lunch shoppers and dinner-grabbers.

Reaching for a crottin of Vermont hand-churned sea salt butter, I caught myself in an empty, silent aisle with the same molar-flashing smile I'd worn to the concert last night. The one I hadn't had since Beyoncé finished singing "Halo" and the stage swallowed her whole. The solitude, the newness of the world yet to weary from the day, the beautiful ingredients that could be coaxed and transformed into any possibility you craved. This was the happiness I was so embarrassed to possess. I was the old lady early bird with her tidy little packages, loading up her Prius Wagon to shuttle back into the 'burbs.

But everyone knew this. Christian knew this. The Twirls knew this—I was introduced as "Martha Stewart, but in the very best way; I promise."

Even though he knew how boring and prissy I'd become, how he promised to love me anyway, I didn't trust Christian to accept this version of me, not with his cooler friends and higher tolerance. He was my oldest friendship now. He held the record. I loved him and was petrified that he'd change his mind about me. The well-traveled, Metro-riding friends churned an insecurity in me that I'd thought I'd kicked. I was terrified of losing my now-oldest friend to a circle I couldn't keep up with. I would inevitably drop away because I was, inevitably, not cool.

My self was a proven liability.

I paused in the gift aisle and held a golden sticker in my hand for a good three minutes. It was an outline of the state of Washington surrounding the word HOME. The sentiment felt right, and yet, I couldn't think of a place I could stick it that would work. Sticking things on my car was a sure sign I'd stopped caring about it and would soon total it, and my office cubicle sagged with souvenirs of all stripes. I left it and proceeded with my jalapeño cheddar hamburgers and brioche buns.

When I got back in my car, I felt a gravitational pull down the hill. It was still early enough in the day; I could walk on the beach. The clouds moved on that had unloaded their wrath on the city the night before, and the entire world was blue. I set my GPS for Spud Fish & Chips, a deep-fried family favorite since long before my parents went on their first date, but I scarce needed the voice and its turn commands.

Usually when we visited the beach on those same Met Market family runs, after Sounders games or while killing time, the oceanfront was like Greek Row during pledge week: topless Jeeps and convertible imports wielded by techbros willing to murder each other's firstborn for a spot along the boulevard, bonfires and blankets pitched on every square inch of sand.

There was a giant parallel spot the size of an Escalade on the main drag. I joined maybe three other souls, a round of brawling seagulls, and a Jack Russell Terrier as the Alki morning population.

What is it about you that I can't erase, baby?
When every promise don't work out that way.

While I watched the ferries from the shoreline, a thought I'd been trying to trample since I parked had sneaked up from the deep. It was here, on this street, at the Thai restaurant, where my parents saw my ex-best friend and real-life Emily: Claire. Was she here now, one set of steps removed from mine, ordering coffee at Tully's or walking an animal? How long would I have to wait on this beach to see her?

"Fuck," I spat into the rock-shard sand.

Why, of all the neighborhoods and outskirts in this metropolis, did she commandeer this one corner I could trace my roots to? I was supposed to think of my mother here and my dad, and how they met at West Seattle High School over Bunsen burners. This was once the home of my step-grandmother and her ocean-facing diner, now Pegasus Pizza. I wanted to remember this neighborhood for the summer mornings spent picnicking at Lincoln Park when I was still in preschool—and that girl who tried to steal my McDonald's Happy Meal blow-up boat toy, kicking off an era of labeling everything I owned in Sharpie—not where and when I might catch a glimpse of a ghost.

Two ferries passed each other on opposing journeys—one downtown, another to sleepy Bainbridge Island. *We built sandcastles that washed away.* My favorite song from the album on loop in my head, the one Beyoncé didn't perform. The angst felt real, but it wasn't total. This place was still *mine*. I still wanted to come here, not because I wanted to find lost Emily.

Because, I suddenly realized, she's not here.

Claire doesn't live here.

Claire wasn't at the Thai restaurant.

There is a woman who lives on with Claire's first name and a new last one and a partially shared past, but the woman I fell in love with no longer exists, just as the girl who fell in love with her no longer exists. Maybe she wasn't being unkind 13 years before, when she predicted our demise on a swingset. *We're not going to be friends forever.* Perhaps she was more objective than I was, more pragmatic. She may have known what was now only cresting my understanding—that for every long-haul, easy-to-pick-up-the-pieces friendship were dozens of conditional relationships. Friends that did not weather distance, or job changes, or diverging choices, or clashing opinions, or the transition from high school zygote to kind-of adult to freestanding woman. Maybe Claire was never the love of my life that I lost. We were crutches to each other in a place in life we couldn't stand alone. Once she could walk, she did the only natural thing. Walked away.

This novel I saved on my hard drive and carried as I moved through the world was not about that stranger. Emily and Julia were both completely me—one side eviscerated, the other reflected. All of my worst tendencies on one side, and the imagined opposite who didn't want to deal with me anymore. The question and the multitudes. Artifice, but more honest than my essays often reached.

I understood the truth. I understood the fiction.

I felt a hinge loosen between my shoulders. Finishing my novel? Such a thing would never bring me closer to Claire. If revenge or reclamation was my goal, I might as well pitch my hard drive into the Sound. Words I wrote, no matter what echelons of literary success they might reach, could not raise the dead. I could only hope to become closer to myself—the parts I can't hide, the parts I flaunt and amplify, the parts I break down to make, and the parts everyone can see but me.

There was a worry folded into the embarrassment over admitting what I was working on—the question of motive, why I wanted to write a book based on a broken heart. I didn't think I was after an absolution. I knew a book worth reading could not be conceived from such an indulgent place. It wasn't until that morning that I knew I wanted to know Me, not her. The woman Christian could continue to love; the same one that whomever Claire had become could not.

We are contradictions. We are multitudes.

Like a superstar with 20 costume changes, I was everything that I treasured and denied. This beach was a home. I turned to head back to another.

Sorry I bailed, I texted Christian. *Just needed to get home. Xoxo!*

I am so sorry I slept in so late! he sent back hours later.

Don't be. I had an important day on Alki. I'll tell you about it later, I promised.

We'd catch ourselves up. There would always be a next time.

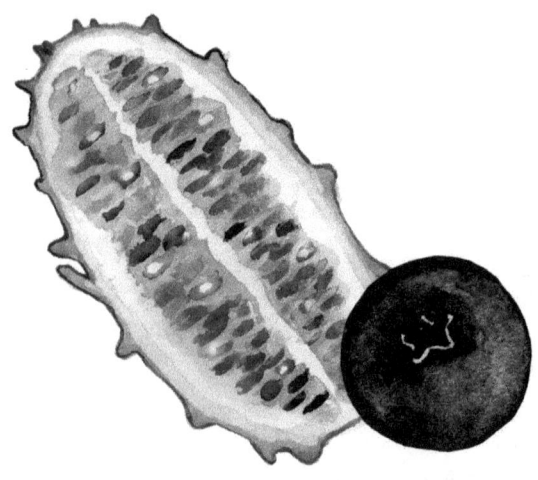

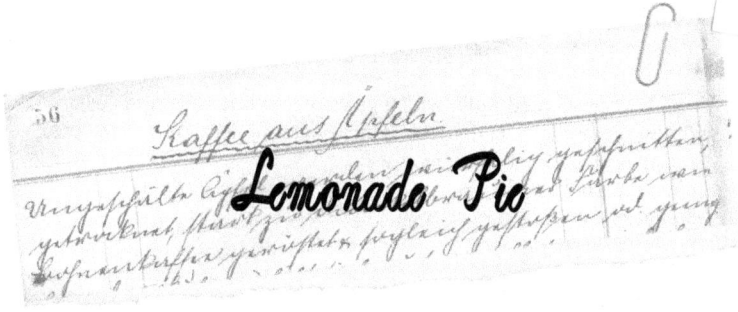

Lemonade Pie

hough I wanted to make a Beyoncé-themed pie for my Seattle trip (because as much as I don't want to be that lame PTA rank climber, I also want to be remembered for impeccable desserts in the presence of guests), lemon meringue pie and I have bad blood. I was afraid to make the pie for years, only ordering it on occasions when professionals were willing to craft it for me. It seemed awful difficult, what with that rich, springy sunshine curd and mountain pass of marshmallows up top. And I know you'll see people on cooking shows and in their food blogs pooh-pooh your fears, assuring you that their lemon meringue pie recipe is 'so easy!' and 'not fussy at all!' and 'never fails!'

They lie. Oh, how they lie.

Lemon meringue pie is fussy, and it fails. How bad does it fail? Let's talk about the lemon meringue pie I finally decided to make while we were living in Arizona, a pie that was supposed to ring in Matt's 35th birthday. I pulverized a batch of homemade gingersnaps in the food processor and baked them into a lovely crust that made the tile and terra cotta kitchen smell like Christmas. I tempered the lemon curd according to the recipe's directions, being sure to keep the temperature low and to coax the correct texture out gently.

When I poured it into the crust, it looked like lemon soup.

"Is it going to set when it bakes?" Matt asked over my shoulder, as he is prone to do only when I'm in the midst of a disaster. Perfect kitchen days are his times away.

"I'm sure it will," I reassured us both, glopping meringue on top like icebergs in a sea. After 20 or so minutes in the oven, I pulled the pan from the rack, sloshing a tsunami of lemon glop over the side to sizzle on the element below.

"How'd it turn out?" I heard from the living room.

"FINE," I called, and, holding the hot pan as steady as I could, I walked to our garage chest freezer and placed the pan on top of a box of Costco chicken bakes. Icebox pie. That was a thing, right?

Hours later, the meringue had slid off. The middle wasn't freezing. The edges that did crystallize weren't edible so much as had become lemon ice shards.

Matt ended up with birthday deep-dish pizza for his pie. Not a bad consolation prize, but the wound cut me deep.

When I went looking for my next lemon meringue pie, I went

for an ace: condensed milk, which gives the texture of lemon custard without the asshole tendencies of making a perfect curd. You can sneer at my Midwest housewife ways all you want, but screw you. I'm eating a delectable pie that all of the Twirls were thankful didn't slide out of a box. So. Bow down, bitches.

For the Crust
1 ½ cups graham cracker crumbs[*]
⅓ cup sugar
6 tablespoons butter, melted

For the Filling
1 can condensed milk
⅔ cup lemon juice
1 ½ tablespoons grated lemon peel

For the Meringue
4 eggs[**]
½ cup extra-fine sugar[***]

In a small mixing bowl combine the graham cracker crumbs, sugar, and melted butter. Press with your hands into a pie pan, covering the bottom and sides evenly with the crumb mixture. Bake at 350° F for 10 minutes. Remove from oven and allow to come to room temperature.

Whisk the condensed milk, lemon juice, lemon peel, and egg yolks together in a bowl. When the crust is cool, pour the mixture inside.

Beat the egg whites with a hand mixer until stiff peaks begin to form. Gradually add the sugar while you continue mixing. Continue to beat until the sugar is fully incorporated and stiff peaks form once more. Use a spatula gently, with a swirly frozen-yogurt-cone motion, to top the lemon with the meringue. If you're really going for that fair blue ribbon, you could use a piping bag to pipe the meringue onto the pie, but if you're planning to schlep the dessert any long distance (say, PDX to SEA), I wouldn't recommend it. You're setting yourself up for some Saran Wrap disaster heartbreak right there.

Bake at 350° F for 15 minutes or until the meringue is getting golden like a marshmallow you're patient enough to elevate above the campfire flames (vs. me, the girl who sticks it in the white-hot center to set it on fire). Remove from oven. Serve. Flawless.

---

[*] You can also use the same amount of gingersnaps.
[**] Separate and reserve 4 whites; you only need 2 yolks.
[***] Don't bother buying it special—just let regular sugar spin in the food processor for 30-60 seconds.

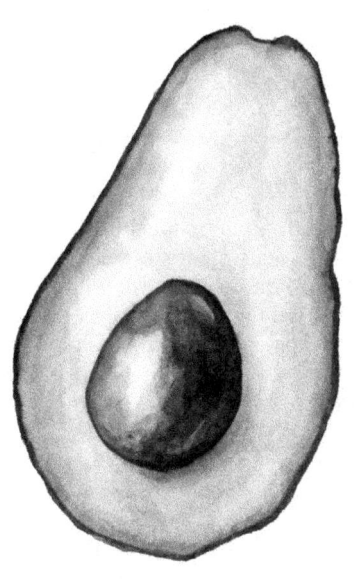

Pioneers and Perfection

*M*y first post-college office job was at a specialty cheese distribution company. Our frigid warehouse housed hundreds of cheeses flown in from Italy, England, California, France, and the Basque region of Spain. Mammoth wheels of Swedish Emmentaler and Parmigiano-Reggiano were air-freighted over to Portland, cut into hundreds of vacuum-packed wedges, then trucked to grocery store cheese counters up and down the I-5 corridor from Bellingham to Medford. We were fromage middlemen.

I was an intern-turned-Marketing-Assistant, meaning I'd come on part-time as a lackey knowing enough Photoshop to be helpful to their overtaxed promotions and events team, and sweet-talked my way into staying on as a full-fledged employee once I'd graduated college. I was essentially a professional bull-shitter, writing copy on wine and cheese pairings for triple creams I'd never tasted with grape varietals that Google thought would be a good match. I tossed in some of our company's favorite words like 'pastoral' and 'unctuous' and added clip art of a sheep lazing in the Alps.

In retrospect (and even, I think, I partially grasped at the time), it was a sweet gig. Where else do monthly meetings involve a new cheese vendor, anxious to impress, coming in with a counter of free samples? Where you're sent home from trade shows with wedges of Ossau-Iraty and Grana Padano the size of the family Bible, so that soon your humble apartment's refrigerator deli drawer holds more value than your checking account? A time when you're paid to wax on and on about your favorite subject, something that genuinely speaks to your heart, instead of the Internet and phone services, disaster restoration, and light switches that would follow?

Surrounded by cheese and cheese people and cheese knowledge, the world of couture curds shaped my impressionable 22-year-old self. I adopted the food world's lenses into my own corneas. I was generous and shared this golden perspective with others in my life who may not have yet heard the gospel.

Oh, you NEVER should buy pre-grated cheese. The moisture evaporates and makes it sawdust.

You know you don't even need to refrigerate Laughing Cow wedges? They're processed out of a dairy designation.

Why bother with a cheddar that isn't aged over a year?

Why bother with fresh mozzarella if you're just going to melt that perfection on a pizza?

WHY BOTHER TO LIVE, YOU UNCULTURED, TILLAMOOK-WORSHIPPING IDIOTS!!!

I may have come off the teensiest bit sanctimonious. On rare occasion.

Like when I went to visit my mom's house up in Washington and curled my lip at her chunk of Somerset apricot-studded cheese. "Ugh, British cheese is every joke about English food personified," I said, fishing in the drawer for anything edible—a slice of Jarlsberg, perhaps. "They'll toss whatever crap's just laying around into the curds. Blueberries, mustard seeds, an ass-ton of caraway. You know that no one who actually made *edible* cheese would ever cover it up like that."

"Is that so?" Mom said, in a voice honed from years of parenting self-proclaimed subject matter experts.

"You should get some thinner crackers, too. The thicker and more adorned the cracker, the more it robs from the true essence of the cheese."

"I see."

I packed my plate with the pantry's thinnest crackers and shaves of Beecher's Flagship cheese and sat down at the family laptop to check my Facebook. When I woke the sleeping computer, I landed on a Firefox page stacked with tabs from someone who called herself The Pioneer Woman.

"She's actually got some really good recipes," my mom mentioned as I scrolled through a Typepad-hosted, photo-heavy page on cinnamon rolls.

"But who is she?"

"She's a woman who lives on a ranch in Oklahoma," she said.

Ew. Landlocked. "What's a chef doing out on a ranch in

Oklahoma?"

"She's not a 'chef.' She just writes about her food. And her dogs. She's got this old lazy hound named Charlie who's the sweetest thing."

I caught the comment count just beneath the recipe. Three thousand shares, 427 people discussing this. I couldn't be sure that 427 people even knew my name. "So she just decided one day that she was so wonderful and good at things, without having ANY training or actual culinary education, that she was a kitchen authority?"

"She's been cooking every day for a big family and their ranch hands."

"Yeah, and she puts Kraft Singles on her burgers," I pointed out on the next post.

Of course this is because Kraft Singles are the only cheeses you should ever melt on a true authentic American hamburger; not to mention the fact that she pointed out that all the work of prepping toppings and gently pressing and grilling the patties will all be for naught if you don't toast the buns on a butter-slicked griddle before slipping a morsel between them. And that her family and friends raised a hefty share of the cattle that fed us. All I saw at the time was a much better kitchen, hundreds of thousands more followers, and way nicer pictures than I had.

"How's the cheese?" Mom asked gracefully, skirting away from a no-win with her post-adolescent idealistic-phase daughter.

"Good, but it's always good," I said, pressing a slice between two cracker shards in a sandwich. "Beecher's is what stores stock when they want to look like they're being artisanal but don't actually want to take the time to learn anything about real cheese. It's practically Boursin at this point."

"Interesting," Mom claimed.

Before I was finished chewing my last bite, she whisked the plate away and into the dishwasher.

Almost 10 years later, I was sitting at the same kitchen counter on the same iron-scrolled bar stool, visiting for the weekend as I did every month or two. The kitchen hadn't changed much; Mom upgraded to a much fancier MacKenzie-Childs checkered teakettle from the old whistling cow of my youth. Dad bought her the Ruffoni copper pot of my dreams. She moved all the cookie sheets and baking stones into the pantry, fitted with new spice racks with every Penzeys Spices catalog option.

"Would you like a snack?" Mom asked. It's comforting to know that you never age out of being a daughter.

"No, thanks, I'm good," I said, sticking with my Diet Coke pilfered from the garage soda fridge. A new version—the last soda fridge melted down on their camping trip to Yellowstone, spoiling a freezer full of bacon and Trader Joe's treats.

I, too, had undergone modifications. Upgrades, downgrades, severe setbacks, recalls. My cheese head had inflated so large it exploded in a fondue of ego and hubris. "I'm 22," I'd ranted to anyone who would listen (mostly myself). "I should be *managing* shit by now. I should be making *so* much more money." I quit my modest cheese marketing assistant job and hopped over to a rural telecom company, which had a business model based around landlines and the notion that a small town with an elderly population would rather undergo 12 root canals than hassle with switching cable providers. I arrived green as pasture and bursting with New! Exciting! Ideas! to really spice up the place's snoozy promotions mix!

I lasted six months.

They handed me my last paycheck and COBRA paperwork in July, 2008, a month before banks folded and the market cratered. I spent the next nine months in our apartment refreshing Craigslist's scant job postings and my email, attending rare interviews for bottom-rung positions that ended up being cattle calls of women (always women) brought in for auditions as if we were up for the role of Busy Mom #2 in a Skippy peanut butter commercial. In the Great Recession economy, no one had a reason to hire me. So they didn't.

These became months I learned to fear mailboxes with their bills and apocalyptic notices ("We're writing to inform you that your unemployment benefits are scheduled to expire"). Months where I'd wake up at two or three in the morning terrified that some check or autopay transaction had gone through a day early, triggering an avalanche of overdraft fees. You have never felt so unwanted as when no one will permit you to do the most menial of tasks his business holds. The crush of an endless swath of time, waking up morning after morning with no one expecting to see you. Nowhere to be.

By the time I was at my mom's counter, shaking off the three-hour drive from Portland to Seattle's far-far outskirts, I'd been back to work for seven years. The first place that would have me was a disaster-restoration company, meaning that when your house caught on fire or someone left a faucet on and flooded your basement or a contractor pocketed a few thousand dollars on your house instead of insulating it properly from mold spores, you called us, and we sent a crew out with drying fans and hazmat suits to wade through the filth and take 10 times as long as we said we would to rebuild your life. It was owned by an ex-University of Oregon Ducks football player and his buddies, a man who decorated his office with mounted elk heads, their glass eyes keeping watch over his framed jersey that hadn't seen on-field action in over 20 years. He ran the company like a frat house, something I should have realized my first morning at the job, when the president and my new boss (the latter a Jared-from-Subway doppelgänger) came into my brand-new little office and shut the door.

The president, Jason, was red-faced and blubbering: "Mmmmy w-w-w-wife is l-l-l-leaving meeee!"

Turns out he'd been having a yearlong affair with the recently departed receptionist, who had been promoted to Vice President within a few months because she showed a lot of 'initiative.'

"Jason needs you to find him a semi-permanent hotel," my new boss instructed.

"With a pool," Jason sniffled.

And so it went for several soul-crushing years. I made Jason's hotel reservations, booked his fishing trips, wrapped his Christmas presents, and picked up and thawed hamburgers from his brother's ranch out in Prineville. I edited together his hunting videos and added his favorite country songs to footage of wild turkeys brawling in the eastern Oregon desert. I Photoshopped Paris Hilton onto an Oregon Ducks helmet to accommodate some in-joke he had with the other VPs. I assembled his King Cake kit for Mardi Gras. I wasn't a Marketing Coordinator; I was the walking embodiment of Other Duties as Assigned.

You can only tell yourself, "At least I have a job," so many times, even when the worldwide economy is in freefall. For me, it was over a year into this catastrophe when I left the house with the same thought I had every morning before work: *Maybe I'll get in a car accident and not have to go in today*. This particular morning I was creeping up a crowded I-5 a few feet from my exit when the minivan in front of me slammed on its brakes. My Toyota Corolla accordioned on the back bumper.

I had to fill out a police report, ride in the tow truck to the auto body shop, call the insurance adjuster five times, and finesse my way into a rental car. My premium was leaping; my back was sore. But my mantra of peace and relief was: *It could be worse; I could be at work*.

This, I realized, was a problem.

I knew that if I had to do a job like this for the rest of my life, if this stalled and crash-landed engine fire of a career was all I had to measure my worth and mold my passion into, I didn't wish for my existence to be a long one. I remember calling my eventual graduate school from the office parking lot on break to figure out the soonest I could theoretically enroll in the MFA. I chatted with the bubbly administrator under the pretense of changing my life, sheltering the hard fact that she was saving it.

My first year of graduate school was a year of recovery. I was detoxing from my lost almost-year in our apartment in all of its consuming uncertainty. The setback had absorbed me— stripped the overconfident girl who flipped her hair and condemned substandard cheeses into one who made little eye contact and felt her throat close up when she tried to talk. Once I began working on projects that I actually cared about, everything else about me had the purpose that I'd misplaced. I shed the 40 pounds I gained by chewing and swallowing my sorrow. My hair was trimmed and cropped and cut at a smart, sharp angle to match my newly squared shoulders. I stopped believing Jason and his fellow Executive Council members when they dismissed me for being too young, inexperienced, non-omnipotent, or emotional.

It's not me, I realized. *It's you.*

I waded through everyone else's disasters for another year until I submitted my cordial two weeks' notice to leave for the mellow day job comfort of the lighting controls company. A broken girl in baggy sweaters entered; a stranger with spine departed.

"Do you have time to go through those cookbooks?" Mom asked while I leaned on her granite kitchen countertop.

"Sure," I said.

Still a few hours until Dad would be off work, and we could head out to the Seattle Sounders game. My sojourns home were usually like this—drives into the city for games and Metropolitan Market shopping and brunch with whichever old friend I could book, coupled with downtime in our old living room, switched out with new couches and a bigger entertainment center and much nicer lights. Staring out at a backyard shaded in trees I'd seen planted as saplings. A homestead as grown and unrecognizable as my heart.

"How many are there?" I asked, gesturing toward the

recipes.

"Just a box."

Mom had purged before, but the cookbook collection was mountainous. Not only were there the dozens upon dozens of tomes she'd bought over the years as our family's head chef, but the inheritances of aunts and great-aunts stretching back to the midcentury to my favorite cookbook I've ever held, my Great Aunt Eva's copy of *Cut-Up Cakes*. It was a promotional leaflet from Baker's Coconut, flawlessly preserved over the years, just as Aunt Eva kept hundreds of *Ideals* magazine editions creaseless for decades. Each recipe was the same: bake sheets of cake, slice into a pattern, then frost and decorate with coconut dyed with food coloring and candies. Like a 1950s handheld version of Pinterest, I adored the pictures of perfectly frosted butterflies, giraffes, and knockoff Minnie and Mickey (circumventing copyright law as Myrtle and Milton Mouse). I especially loved the Hobby Horse with its white coconut coat, black licorice rope reins, and Life Savers candy spots. I dug the book out from my mom's ever-growing bookcase of cookbooks countless times as a kid to look at the garish, warm Technicolor photographs and imagine the parties I could throw someday, when I'd knock the socks off everyone in the room through the power of sponge and coconut.

"It's just upstairs in the office," she said.

I unpacked the new millennium's burnt-out trends and fading stars, like the cringeworthy *Deen Brothers' Grilling Guide* and oddly gendered *Mad Hungry: Feeding Men and Boys*. Between a copy of a Tom Douglas seafood love letter and recipes from a long-shuttered Tacoma New American restaurant, I found a copy of Ree Drummond's *The Pioneer Woman Cooks: Dinnertime*. It was Mom's extra after ordering a signed copy from Elliott Bay Book Company.

On the Pioneer Woman's first cookbook tour during my first year of graduate school, Mom and Dad had gone down and stood in line for two hours waiting for a personalized signature. "She stayed there until every single person in line was signed," Mom praised.

"I just really wish they wouldn't waste all that valuable bookstore space when they could be hosting, like, Joan Didion," I said, high on the fumes of my new writing life venture.

"There's plenty of space for both, don't you think?" Mom asked with a patience my child-free existence will never evolve to know.

No. I did not think.

On the cover, Ree held a roast, likely a former member of the ranch's herd of cattle. She wore a bright floral tunic—flowy but with enough shape to suggest a silhouette, and bright enough to remind us that she's here, the queen. She was looking just over her shoulder with a startled flash of joy, as if she'd heard her favorite voice in the world. Her smile wasn't steely or frightening like Giada's, nor was it the muted East Coast elegance of Ina or Martha. Unlike Paula Deen's Photoshop-dentistry veneers or Guy Fieri's aggressive, insistent charisma, Ree was simply warm. I was weary of food as personality and theme and brand. I was tired. I wanted dinner.

"God DAMMIT, Ree!" I cried from the kitchen.

"Is it bad?" Matt asked, rushing up from the couch as if summoned into the ER.

He was waiting on a plate of Sloppy Joes, one of our rotating easy weeknight favorites. Crack open can of Manwich, brown hamburger, spoon on whatever bun is around. Feel happy and taken care of. Except I'd come home from work that evening certain that I had a can of our sauce staple in the pantry when, in fact, the can shelf was nothing but garbanzo beans and Ro*Tel tomatoes.

"No, of course it's not." I barely had to type "Sloppy Joe Pioneer Woman" into Google before her scratch recipe appeared, made up of essentials that lived in our fridge and spice cabinet since the dawn of apartment time. Ketchup. Brown sugar. Chili powder. "It's the best, most perfect Sloppy Joe meat I've ever tasted, so now I'll never be able to go back to cans again."

"You can still buy it in the can for when you're lazy," Matt promised. He understood the prerogative of not giving a fuck after work. Or before work. Or during the workday.

"No, that doesn't make sense," I said, spooning the spicy-sweet beef onto toasty pub buns lightly coated in butter and pressed into my cast iron skillet. Regular butter that comes in a 4-pack from Costco, not the pure Irish stuff with its rich fat content and Willy Wonka golden ticket wrapping I used to insist would be the only fat to grace my fridge door. "Honestly, it only takes me a few extra minutes to stir the ingredients into the pan instead of pour the can into it."

Matt plucked a clump of seasoned beef from the skillet and popped it in his mouth. "Oh, god, yeah. Sorry. You're going to have to take the extra few minutes."

She did it to country biscuits and gravy. Pea salad. Creamed corn. Frittata (oh, god, the frittata). Even raita, the minty, cucumbery Indian condiment I wanted to drizzle over homemade tandoori chicken. Yep, she just wanted to use up some of those pesky herbs that grow so vivaciously in her ranch garden! Her recipes were simple and quick but never sacrificed depth of flavor. They tasted like the food was cared for. They tasted like you, the cook, cared. The meals were the same little cheese plates, turkey sandwiches, and grilled hamburgers set down when I came up to my mom's house. A thank you for coming; an endless welcome.

My phone rang immediately after the cell phone picture went through. "I can't believe you actually went into a Walmart," Mom marveled from the other end of the line.

"I had to," I said as I drove back toward my office. I'd hopped across the street to Target for an aura cleanse, but I still felt like I needed a shower. I entered a Walmart with the frequency of the summer Olympic games. There are a few principles you never waver on, no matter how old and tired you become. "It was the only place to get her pie plate." The pie plate from Ree Drummond's signature kitchen and housewares collection, exclusive to my least-favorite retailer on Earth. On the last episode we watched, recorded on the DVR while we were at work (Food Network only airs its anemic lineup of actual cooking instruction programs during soap opera and talk show hours), she used a pair of them to make dueling quiches for her best friend, Hyacinth, and a few other friends to try.

"You know a freakish amount about her friends and family," Matt pointed out the night before, when I explained who the elderly guest Edna Mae was (Ladd's grandmother) and why daughter Alex wasn't present (away at college and according to her Instagram, having a kickass time).

They are my Kardashians, a royal family of food and property I watch through the filter their matriarch designed, wishing that my food pictures got a fraction of the likes, that I could spend my workdays picking fixtures and finishes for a restored 19th-century country store, that Land O'Lakes thought I was a sponsorship opportunity worth chasing, that I could buy and store that many varieties of cast iron skillets.

The scrolling blue flower pattern on my new pie plate,

speckled with coral pollen, was pure Anthropologie whimsy. It was the closest I could get to her Pawhuska restored mercantile store without booking a flight to Tulsa.

"And to think, a few years ago you didn't even *like* her!" my mom pointed out when my new pie plate picture appeared in her Instagram feed.

"I ... didn't ... hate her."

"You didn't think she was worthy of being in a bookstore."

"I just," had no leg to stand on. "Well, her backstory seems kind of cheesy, you know. Until you actually watch her. And there's so many shitty personalities on Food Network that the crappiness taints all of them."

Moms are nice because they let your bullshit slide. They let you hide in the forts of backpedals and justifications you build to defend against the truth's invasion. I was a snobby, full-of-it, self-appointed cheese genius with no room for those who hailed from Oklahoma, or raised kids and cattle, or sometimes used cream of mushroom soup instead of making a scratch roux. My identity was too small and fragile to accept that I had a hard, expensive way of doing things that wasn't right or wrong, but was simply preference. When you've whittled your scope down that narrow, you're left with no room. You become flimsy and unkind.

You can stay closed, or you can open wide enough to discover that a happy, functioning world exists outside your dogma. I realized that Velveeta really does melt better than anything aged in a cave. That Laughing Cow wedges may be shelf-stable, but they're also a divine snack when you're trapped in your cube for hours and need something that hints at the concept of real food. I did stock my pantry with Manwich because I ended up in a life with two full-time jobs, one feeding the bank account and another my compulsion to express all of the joy and anger and concern and revelation that brews while I'm driving my commute and scraping soft taco mung from a nonstick pan.

Ree cooked as though she loved the process, from the long trek into Pawhuska for groceries to the ravenous friends and family descent on the table. But she made concessions and found loopholes and allowed for all of the obligations and surprises that cut in and ahead of crafting meals. She gave herself permission to be more than a chef. She cooked as though she was living.

I came home last Saturday with five bags full of homemade ramen ingredients. You don't need five bags from the Uwajimaya

Asian Grocery Store to make ramen, but I didn't want just *ramen*. I wanted the experience of those deep-welled ladle-spoons, the radiant clay cup warmth of gunpowder green tea, the plump bao dumplings smuggling a belly-full of spiced pork. I wanted that last trip to a Portland ramen shop tonight, without the commute. Learning to recreate a culinary niche at my house was becoming less of a hassle than going out to visit it.

While I unpacked the noodles, leeks, pork shoulder, and cauldron-sized soup bowls, I turned on the TV for background noise. I'm like a puppy in the kitchen; I want to feel like I'm not cooking alone. I selected the stack of *The Pioneer Woman* episodes recorded on my DVR, which has become the signature voice I want to hear behind my ruckus. The list began with a new episode—a rarity, as I've seen every existing episode of Ree Drummond's Food Network show five times over.

Her blog, long predating her TV show and cookbooks, brought the Drummonds' remote homestead to the rest of the country—and funneled the world into Pawhuska (population 3,477). Although we're able to watch and read and Pin her from anywhere, Ree Drummond is very much in a Place. A secluded microcosm of a 450,000-acre place far from all other Places. Her closest neighbor (Cowboy Josh) is two miles away; the bright lights of downtown Tulsa are almost two hours' drive each way. There are no beat-up Hondas dropping off Jimmy John's or congealed stuffed-crust pizza, no white paper boxes of rice and noodles to save a night where you'd rather peel your toenails off with pliers than put a pan on the stove. Takeout only comes from a freezer.

It is in these secluded spaces that necessity yanks growth at a pace most city and suburban kitchens never need to muster. It is why Ree Drummond gets tin bento boxes shipped in from hundreds of miles away for her "Cowboy Bento" episode, why I spend my Saturday morning finding the Chinese red bowls that are ubiquitous at the trendy noodle shops along Portland's Alberta Street and Mississippi Avenue. When we exist as satellites of the culture we love, our pots must contain the universe.

"Today I'm making phở," said Ree.

I cringed at the way she pronounced it—"foe." A Vietnamese coworker was kind enough to correct me eons ago. Drummond Ranch was likely short on those. I finished unwrapping the new Japanese teapot and sunk down into the loveseat, giving the Season 16 premiere my absolute attention. "Go on," I pressed the animated image.

"We're going to start with some ramen noodles." Which

isn't how you start phở. Phở begins with rice noodles soaked briefly in hot water. And Ree did not turn to retrieve a package of fresh, lightly bitter Japanese ramen noodles from the refrigerator. She reached into what could have been a five-year-old junk drawer and revealed a packet of Top Ramen, which she smashed into clumps (as one learns to do in college), and sprinkled the freeze-dried starch log with the packet of 'Asian chicken flavor.'

IN THE NAME OF PHỞ.

"Oh, my god, no!" I cried aloud as she smiled, slicing a par-frozen chunk of steak into razorblade strips thin enough to cook in the hot pot. She covered the mass in sriracha and stirred the Entire Asian Continent Soup.

I could just imagine Ree, who'd wrapped 15 entire seasons of food in her lane—marinated pork chops, cherry dump cake, fried chicken, beef tostadas—assigned to New York to meet with the bigwigs they parade for *Food Network Star*. Susie Fogelson and Bob Tuschman, who looked like Kermit and Miss Piggy cosplayers, and demanded that contestants consider what their 'branding message' will be and what 'narrative' their cooking show will follow. They liked to see big, GIF-able personalities, people who would really shine on the YouTubes.

They did not care if you turned off the TV knowing how to debone a chicken. That was not a lucrative demo.

"We'd like to see you branch out into more Aspirational recipes," I imagined Susie telling Ree, as Bob nodded along with each syllable. "I want to see less of bringing the ranch to the world and more of bringing the world to the ranch."

"Me and the kids love a good Top Ramen lunch," she might offer, trying to suss out what the hell the execs were getting at.

"We could work with that," Bob would massage. "Phở is so hot right now."

Ree would leave with notes. She'd know that no one (except the Cheesecake Factory menu) can be an expert at every cuisine on Earth. Some shortcuts veered off a cliff, and some dishes were worth waiting for the next trip into town. After all, you needed some reason to fire up the truck. Then again, she was on a pre-production deadline. She'd open the junk drawer. She'd shout downstairs to Ladd—"Bring bourbon!"

Ladd, as always, would oblige.

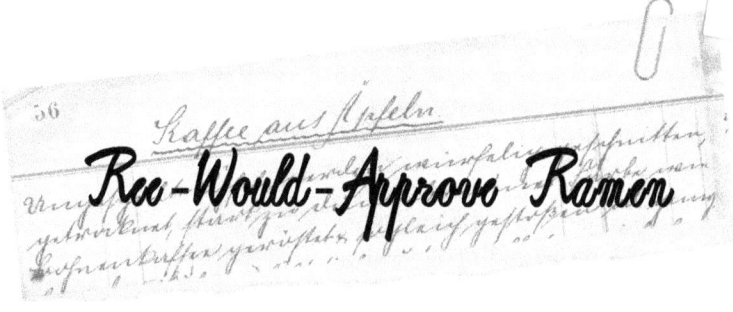

Ree-Would-Approve Ramen

I don't make phở. If I can't get to the Vietnamese restaurants that are remarkably common around northwest Oregon, then it's not happening. The broth is labor- and time-intensive, built with bones and lemongrass. I have instead gone chasing the art of Japanese ramen, which comes (unpackaged) in thousands of iterations. I prefer the soulful miso versions, while Matt is a big fan of the pork-belly-based tan tan ramen. This recipe pleases both of us, and I imagine would win the Pioneer Woman's seal of approval with its blissfully easy Crock-Pot prep. I originally found the recipe online and tweaked it with my own favorite toppings—one of the most fun parts about ramen: they're like tacos.

I've always wanted to have a ramen party with a tableful of toppings (soft-boiled eggs, seaweed salad, braised bok choy, scallions, julienned carrots, teriyaki tofu), but if you can't get anyone to commit to that nonsense, slurping bowls in front of a TV playing your favorite HBO show of the moment is a good alternative. It's also super fun to eat out of all that authentic servewear, but hey. As long as you're not dumping seasoning packets over dehydrated noodles and calling it phở, I'm happy.

- 3 pounds boneless pork shoulder, cut into 3 equal pieces
- Kosher salt
- 2 tablespoons vegetable oil
- 1 onion, coarsely chopped
- 6 garlic cloves, chopped
- 1 (2-inch) piece fresh ginger, peeled and chopped
- 8 cups chicken broth
- Soy sauce
- Sesame oil
- Chile oil
- Sriracha
- Toasted sesame seeds
- 4 eggs
- 4 green onions, thinly sliced
- 2 carrots, grated or julienned fine

- o 2 cups bok choy, seared and chopped
- o 1 leek, halved lengthwise and coarsely chopped[*]
- o ¼ pound mushrooms[**]
- o Shichimi Tōgarashi powder[***]
- o 1 ½ pounds fresh ramen noodles[****]
- o ½ cup wakame salad[*****]

Rub the pork with about 2 tablespoons vegetable oil, and season with salt and pepper. Place a cast iron skillet (or Dutch oven) with an additional splash of oil on medium-high, and sear each side of the pork until it is well-browned, about 3-4 minutes per side. Remove the pork and place it in the patiently waiting slow cooker. In the fat of the departed pork, add the onion and sauté until browned, about 5 minutes. Add the garlic, ginger, and 1 cup of chicken broth, scraping up the browned bits as the mixture sizzles for another minute.

Dump the sautéed onion mixture, along with any remaining delicious fats and oils, into the Crock-Pot, where the pork waits for its friends. Include the sliced leeks, ¼ cup soy sauce, and the remaining broth. I like to assemble this the night before so that all the flavors receive extra marinating time, but it's not mandatory. What is mandatory is allowing the mixture to cook for 8 hours on low (or however long it takes for you to leave for work and come back). Switch the Crock-Pot to the Keep Warm setting, and proceed with the fussy prep steps.

----

[*] white and green parts.

[**] There's this outstanding mushroom stand at Portland Farmers' Market that's been on the corner spot for as long as I've been going, and when I make this recipe, I pick up chanterelles from them. They are otherworldly. But if you don't have access to chanterelles, or they're just ridiculously expensive, creminis would be nice, too.

[***] I picked up my shaker in San Jose's Japantown, after seeing them on every ramen stand around the block. You can also order them online from your favorite conglomerate retailer.

[****] Fresh ramen noodles are, as I've come to learn, tough to find. I thought I could waltz into Whole Foods and pick up as many as my heart desired, but it turns out, they're only interested in stocking fresh udon. All other grocers I visited were the same story, save for Uwajimaya, the incredible Asian grocery store we're lucky to have here in the Pacific Northwest. For the real deal, try the national chain H Mart, or if you're in real dire straits, switch them out for fresh linguine or spaghetti noodles. Just please, say no to the packet.

[*****] a seaweed salad that is completely optional.

Remove the pork chunks from the broth and place on a cutting board. When it's cooled ever-so-slightly, use two forks or a set of pork-shredder Wolverine gauntlets (a highly recommended minimal investment) to claw the pork down into bite-sized shreddy morsels. Discard any chunks of fat you may encounter on your journey. Return the shredded pork to the broth, along with any residual juices you may have extracted. Add soy sauce, sesame oil (Careful! A little goes a very long way, and I got turned off on this miracle ingredient for almost a decade after misusing it around Teriyaki Meatball time), and chili oil to taste. Let that all sit and think about what it has done.

To cook the noodles, add fresh ramen to lightly salted boiling water for approximately 3 minutes. Remove and distribute evenly between waiting serving bowls (This will generously feed 4, and you'll likely have leftovers). Simultaneously, if you can swing this level of multitasking, place the eggs in a saucepan covered by an inch of water and bring to a boil for 5 minutes.

Ladle a couple scoops of broth and pork into each bowl and top with a carefully peeled soft-boiled egg. Top to preference with bok choy, carrots, green onions, sesame seeds, sriracha, Shichimi Tōgarashi, wakame salad, or whatever else you recently had at your favorite ramen restaurant and want to try at home.

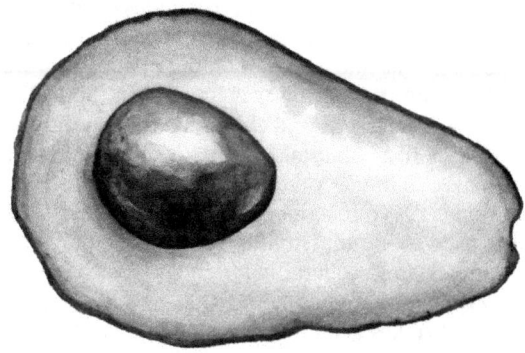

Clock People

"Is there anything I can help you with?" A woman in a blue dirndl approached us as Matt and I entered her store. Light was blotted through the windows by dense shelves of German imported knickknacks, from standing-room-only crowds of Hummels to genealogy mugs bearing the crests of hundreds of European surnames (minus Blankenbiller; no one stocks a Blankenbiller). Almost three decades after my first visit into the shop on one of our many family day trips to Leavenworth, holding my mom's hand as she warned, "Don't touch," I was still tucking into myself. Elbows and shoulders squeezed to center, my purse held at my hip. I was as clumsy as the stock was delicate.

To the uninitiated, all the shops that line the main street of Leavenworth, Washington, might appear the same. Leavenworth is a mountain tourist town with all the structures sporting the same city-mandated Alpine flourishes: chalet window shutters, Tole painting accents, loft balconies overflowing with snappy red geraniums. Originally a logging boomtown that hit a sharp mid-century decline, the rebranding plan to turn Leavenworth into a Bavarian destination was hatched in the 1960s. With a citywide facelift, a strange and charming destination was born. Now every commercial building, down to the McDonald's and Starbucks, makes full use of old-world wooden signage and calligraphy fonts. I love imagining the corporate marketing departments assigned to an unassuming Eastern Washington franchise location and having a branding standards meltdown. *Too … many … unauthorized Pantones …*

It takes a lifetime of popping into each shingled door—Die

Musik Box, Mainz Haus of Rock, Kris Kringl—to learn each one's quirks and specialties. There was a personality to each shop; the trick was finding the nook in Leavenworth that matched you. Like the themed stores and carts dotting Disneyland, you'd find repeats all around town, like the pretzel magnets and headless dirndl torso pens. A truly special souvenir was a hunt, and in this charming mountain enclave just east of my childhood home, I was a seasoned tour guide.

I opened my mouth to say, "Stein"—the reason we were taking a second trip down the street before we had to go. A bag from my favorite sausage shop was hiked on my shoulder, with more of my beloved currywurst, and a new rub for Matt's ribs. We were picking up our last souvenirs before heading the five hours back home. I was after a lederhosen-shaped blown-glass Christmas ornament. Matt, we agreed, would return with a fresh beer stein to grace the liquor cabinet.

But Matt was quicker on the draw. "We'll take that," he said, pointing directly to a Black Forest cuckoo clock carved with maple leaf details, pinpricked by delicate red flowers, crowned by a sparrow stretching on the brink of flight. A true chiming, ticking, dancing cuckoo clock—the kind it was my dream to own since we'd first rented walls together.

The blue dirndled associate scampered into the back room, and I stared at Matt, who was a shade under blushing. "I thought you said they were too expensive."

"I want it," he shrugged, and I filled in the empty spaces with the palette you amass from living with the same person for 11 years. He loved the nod to our shared, unseen homeland as much as I did. He was a man on the downhill side of 30. He worked far past the 40-hour workweek threshold. God dammit, if he wanted a cuckoo clock, he was going to buy a cuckoo clock.

This rationale for the occasional indulgence didn't work as well for me. I had more interests, more possibilities vying for shopping cart space. My heart's desire would bankrupt us. When we were back at the hotel the night before, eating complimentary cookies from the front desk, I nodded when Matt nixed the idea of adopting our very own Black Forest clock baby.

"Two hundred and sixty dollars is way more than we should be spending right now," he said, like a grown-up. Two hundred and sixty dollars on top of the cost to come here: gas, a sauerbraten and fondue feast, beers at the sausage *garten*, this rented bed and bathroom at the Courtyard by Marriott.

This long summer weekend trip to Leavenworth was an accidental vacation for two people growing weary of the same daily scenery. The weather forecast was bad, and hotels were remarkably open. We still had the reservation in the fall for Oktoberfest, but the possibility of making it was dimming: our friends might not be able to make it after all, I had an obligation in Seattle the night before, and my novel was not yet done.

"We have to paint the house, too," I reminded us both. Last summer, the entire neighborhood retouched their houses. In the course of an August, we went from status quo to shabby.

"We can always get a cuckoo clock," Matt said. "It's not like Black Forest is going to stop making them after 300 years of nailing it."

We finished our free dessert and burrowed into bed, matters settled. We would leave the next day with sausage and a stein. Matt's first trip to my childhood wonderland was already a high-light reel of my favorites: coffees at the Gingerbread Factory, a bakery designed like a candy house; dinner at Café Mozart, eating *spaetzle* and sauerbraten; a walk down the promenade to the Enzian Inn to watch a man in lederhosen bellow an alphorn ode to Washington's Cascade mountains. We had to keep a few dreams to chase for next time.

"It was meant to be," Matt declared as he stood back from the liquor cabinet, a distressed teal-tinted piece we bought while living in Tucson.

We collected a few of these small furniture pieces while we were there, to match our stucco and tiled house: a coffee table, a runner for the hallway. Their bright presence now hinted at our broken Oregon streak. The spot above the cabinet, formerly home to a vintage Olympia beer sign, was the only place in the house where the cats couldn't access the clock chains. The cuckoo clock, fresh from its box, settled immediately into the easy ticking rhythm that would soon become our home's heartbeat.

"Looks good," I said. And it did. With the mini whiskey cask and elkhorn knife atop the cabinet, it gave the corner bridging the kitchen and living room a Gaston's Tavern feel.

"Do we have enough clocks yet?" he asked, as our mantel clock chimed, a few minutes behind.

A carved antique gift from my parents, a close match to a version I grew up with, it was old and quirky, only keeping time when the left front leg was balanced perfectly on a washer. A few feet away was our original housewarming gift, a polished chrome clock with spatulas, forks, and spoons in place of numbers. It looked like a midcentury Mary Blair starburst. Then there was the non-functioning Tramp Art clock on the mantel, and down the hallway a hanging timepiece my grandma gifted us during one of her clutter purges.

"I guess I didn't even think about it," I admitted, taking stock. "I never sat here and counted them before, but yeah. I think we might have a problem."

"It's okay," he said, standing back. His shoulders tipped behind him, his chest inflated with pride. "We're clock people."

The shutter opened, and the yellow wooden bird poked its head through the archway. Five cuckoos, a retreat. Consciously or not, we had one more reminder that our time was flying away.

I am quietly obsessed with time. I count it like rosary beads: how much has gone, how much I have left, what I've amassed in the space between. I tally how many hours I've spent at my laptop with Microsoft Word open versus how many hours' sleep I would get if I went to bed right this second. I divide the time by how many projects I've promised I'll complete. I subtract the Facebook checks, the Twitter updates, the trip to make tea or to rummage for the last square of chocolate squirreled away at the back of the drawer.

This spring, my sums weren't working out. My 180 words a day was somehow not adding up to a full novel draft. By the time I booked an early hotel in Leavenworth, the *Emily and Julia* document contained 35,000 words. The halfway mark was in sight, but I was only a few months away from the end of my year deadline. My mountain wasn't being built steadily, shovelful by shovelful, night after night. It grew in tectonic shifts between long, neglectful slumbers. I wouldn't open the file for a week at a time, caught up in writing an essay that manifested on my commute ("I need to write about class discrepancies evident at Disneyland RIGHT NOW.") or not writing at all (coming home and making dinner and watching *Full Frontal with Samantha Bee* until suddenly I am asleep on the couch with another night gone).

The next week I'd carve out an hour at a coffee shop, avoid learning the Wi-Fi password, and hammer out a thousand words, diving back into Julia's neurosis and Emily's distance as if I never left them. I made a mess of their worlds, trying to accept that it would eventually amass to a clouded, befuddled first draft but that I would be able to work through that. Don't look back, I demanded, instigating a strict No Scrolling Up rule to curtail my cannibalistic self-editing. Push ahead. Just get the first draft done. You have so little time.

A lot can happen in a year, we said. When I glanced back at what this last year had been, I focused on what hadn't yet happened. I saw the missing pieces and the chasms of all I had set out to do but had failed at achieving. I didn't give myself enough credit for what I had done.

I didn't see the new publications I chased, tackled, and could finally proclaim on my résumé. No acknowledgment of the readings in which I participated, or the panels on which I served. None of the small, strange, heartening moments of kind 'I loved your essay' emails from strangers, or much-needed kudos from my heroes. All the minuscule steps forward dotted the calendar not in bold strokes, but tiny tile mosaic. The relentless ant's mountain grew beneath me despite the doubt and the impatience and the knockbacks. All of the life I thought I could put on hold in exchange for work I'd made myself believe *had* to happen.

"We should go somewhere before the summer is up, maybe Leavenworth?" I asked Matt over dinner as my self-imposed deadline closed in. Summer had yet to begin officially, but Portland had already hosted its first 100-degree stretch. The air conditioners and flip-flop hunts ushered in the end of my writing year.

"That's probably a good plan," he said, a reaction I wasn't expecting, since the suggestion hadn't been much more than an inner monologue slipping out to fill a lull. "I mean, we don't know if we can actually go to Oktoberfest, do we?" he continued. "Has everyone confirmed that they're really going to make it?"

"I haven't heard."

"That's not usually a great sign, is it?" Matt shared my trust issues on making plans with other people; our skins were hardened by cancellations and last-minute pivots. "How far is it from here to Leavenworth?"

A month after returning from Leavenworth, I was in my workday cubicle, doing whatever very important lighting control work was required at the moment, when my Outlook pinged with a new message from Blankenbiller, Matt.

I realized … it's only three months until our house is Spooky Halloweened again! And then … turkey! And then … Christmas!

To have it all laid out like that made it seem as if my Year of Writing My Novel was already up. We'd hopped into autumn with a fit of pretzels and pumpernickel-hued Dunkel ale. We bumped Oktoberfest up before the Fourth of July—a proclamation of surrender. Who needs a summer?

October would sweep us into a fury of ritual: putting out the Halloween decorations, shopping for candy, canning apples. The gourds and pumpkins would bleed into Thanksgiving, and I'd barely set the table for dinner before the snowflakes and evergreen boughs shoved their way through.

My year was over. My work was not.

On the other side of the email message, staring at the same calendar, was Matt. Matt, who was not holding himself to a make-your-life-actually-matter deadline. Matt, who'd come to treasure the traditions we'd crafted in 11 years together. Matt, who didn't beat himself up if he fell asleep at 8 p.m. or went out to drink with friends instead of shutting himself into a writing room on a Friday night. Matt, who would quietly remind me on occasion, *There's a lot to be happy about. No one in the world is as hard on you as you are.*

Just as the email predicted, September 2016 dissolved into October 2016. Without book, without agent, it came just the same. On the first day of the month, we schlepped all of the Rubbermaid totes and cases of Halloween decorations into the living room. I gathered up the year-round baubles that normally adorn our house, like the cactus-shaped vases and mercury glass votive-holders, to replace with haunted house cloches and black, *Nightmare Before Christmas*-inspired garlands. The piles of macabre adornments, collected over my adult lifetime of loving the holiday, were overwhelming.

"Where the hell does all this shit go," I muttered to myself, my chipped nails caught in fake spiderweb gauze.

This is where my annoying cellphone picture-taking habit saves the day. I pressed the Instagram square on my iPhone, knowing there had to be a past set of "Hey, everyone, look at my spoooooky house!" pics saved for posterity. I thumbed through hundreds of photos uploaded over the last four years—1,300 tiny postcards from moments so easy to forget, rendered fully back in bursts of my past enthusiasm. Tabbouleh and Lebanese 'tacos' out on my parents' patio. The Black Forest cake that looked like a dream but was doused in an inedible amount of cheap kirsch. The dirndl I loved that didn't quite fit. The indent of Marilyn Monroe's Hollywood Walk of Fame handprints, visited during

AWP in Los Angeles. The Hello Kitty food truck, where Matt waited two hours in line with me for a box of Sanrio-themed macarons and somehow didn't commit homicide. Me, drunk outside the Portland City Grill in a fancy new coat and lipstick 10 shades too dark and purple. Our cats! Over and over, our cats.

Jessica Rabbit drag for Halloween.

Butternut squash soup.

Anniversary dinner lobster.

Sounders scarves embroidered with SEATTLE TIL I DIE.

Freshly canned cherries.

Starbucks mugs from the latest AWP tent pole stop.

My sweet, hulking Smith-Corona typewriter lugged from my writing office out to the patio in the summertime, because I cannot stop being ridiculous.

They blur as I scroll, a Skittle-hued collage of the last 12 months. So much more beautiful than I remembered. More beautiful than it likely was, the best of everything tucked away, collected, and shared. My posted social media evidence was a parade of little fictions, short stories I wrote with braided pie crusts and new shoes, coffee mugs turned just so, and even-numbered monumental page counts in the left-hand corner of Microsoft Word.

This year was good, I thought. Which was, I knew, a generalization. Life was not a curated highlight reel. But then again, was it the Parade of Fail I kept claiming to be stuck in? Did it feel more authentic to obsess on shortcomings instead of the shards of joy? If I had learned anything in the years since enrolling in Writer School and sending out my first messy, misfiring, ridiculously earnest essays and getting my first, "Yes, okay, we'll take this," and all the ebb and flow in the six years since, wasn't it that there was no waste? How many times would I have to learn that the only squander of time was deciding the project, the wild chance, the submission wasn't worth trying in the first place?

Here's the truth. I don't know if *Emily and Julia* is ever going to grow from 35,000 messy, spark-flash words to 80,000 precise, gleaming ones. I don't know how long that will take, or if that story is still one I need to tell. The fact that I wonder suggests the answer. A scene from Jess Walter's novel, *Beautiful Ruins*, keeps repeating in my head. In it, an old man has been toiling his entire life to write the epic, all-encompassing war novel he has poisoned himself into believing must be told no matter how long it stalls out (forever). He cannot get past the single chapter he has written. Finally, a friend says, "*Maybe it's finished. Maybe that's all there is.*" And that comment gives the old man permission to go on with his life.

I have carried that scene with me for five years. I remembered it when my first agent couldn't sell my first book. It resurfaced when my second book proposal crash-landed. And when I think back on the joy of writing that first chapter of *Emily and Julia*—of describing how I would feel if my same old dream came true, and I were accidentally thrown back in the same room with my long-lost best friend, of the laughter and understanding from the women in the Sasquatch House with their own failed relationships and collected heartbreaks, and I weigh it against the stall-outs and dead ends the subsequent pages have tangled into —I can't help but think, *Maybe it's finished. Maybe that's all there is.*

Sometimes the hours and the efforts and the word counts don't add up to a book. So often they end here, facing another direction, holding something you did not expect.

For me, this year of writing wasn't a magical time when my Great American Novel materialized. Instead, a series of essays emerged about trying to work and eat and survive between ambition and reality. They started as missives I typed into emails on work lunches and late nights as 'breaks' from that monumental task I was supposed to be doing, and were eventually published here and there. They were the pieces I enjoyed writing. I slowly embraced the work that didn't feel as fancy or splashy, about how I wrote and ate and how often I messed those two loves up, but I couldn't let them go, because they were everything about me. I gave myself a year to write a novel, and, as a 'diversion,' I wrote from my heart. At the end of one fruitless forage, I found an accidental feast.

If there's a lesson from these 12 months it's this: You can't force the story that you think you're 'supposed to be' telling. It will stall. It will stop. It will spin out in ridiculous tendrils. It won't stop working against you until you have either burnt yourself out in the madness of the fight, or you remember what I only write here so that I can remember each time in my life I am going to go on and forget. There is no pushing through the process. There is no scheduling the thing you were meant to create. This idea you imagine as the most prestigious, important, potentially successful creation, that hot hook that's going to make you famous, isn't usually the good work. The best work. The most honest work. Work that sparks to life without the hammering or the vain demand makes no promises. You can't plan it to life. There is no recipe for art.

Luckily, though, there is one for sauerbraten.

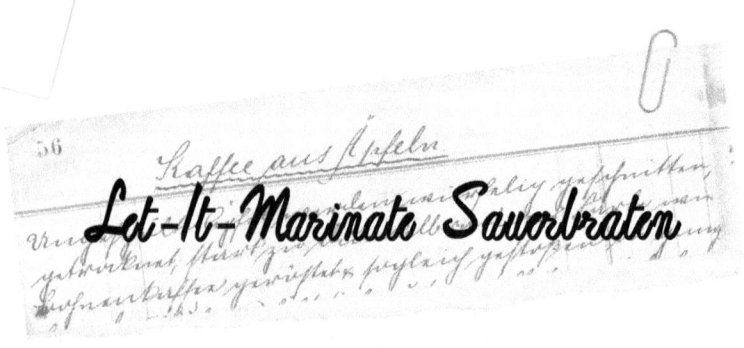

Let-It-Marinate Sauerbraten

hat separates a real German restaurant from mere brat-slingers? Answer: a menu that includes traditional sauerbraten and serves it with spaetzle, even though mashed potatoes would be easier to explain and source. If you're not brave enough to accept the wonder of spaetzle in your life, you don't deserve the miracle of sauerbraten.

I made it for the first time on Matt's birthday, a month after we returned from Leavenworth. It's not a quick weeknight dinner, since you have to let it marinate for several days and then cook all day before you serve it. You'll want to meditate on the joy that's about to unfold in your life. You will want time on your side.

- o   3 pounds beef chuck roast
- o   2 yellow onions, quartered
- o   1 cup red wine vinegar
- o   1 cup water
- o   1 tablespoon salt
- o   1 tablespoon pepper
- o   10 whole cloves
- o   3 bay leaves
- o   3 tablespoons all-purpose flour
- o   Vegetable oil
- o   1 cup gingersnap cookies, pulverized in a food processor[*]
- o   ½ cup raisins

2-3 Days before You Want to Feast

In a gallon-sized Ziploc bag, place the beef roast, red wine vinegar, water, salt, pepper, cloves, and bay leaves. Seal tight and massage to let the marinade distribute over the meat. Place in a Pyrex container seam-side up and refrigerate for 48 to 72 hours

---

[*] You can, and should, use cheap, super crunchy gingersnaps that come from the grocery store, or the Trader Joe's Triple Ginger version, but whatever you do, don't skip this ingredient. It makes the entire dish.

(the more time, the better). Massage and turn the roast each day. Matt and I have to do this with bacon before he smokes it, and we call the ritual Family Bacon-Flipping Time. I encourage doing the same. There's nothing like poking a future dinner to bring people together.

The Morning of Dinner
When it's time to cook, remove the beef from the bag while reserving all marinade in the bag (This is paramount!). Gently pat it dry with paper towels. Sprinkle the flour and additional salt and pepper over the meat. Heat 1-2 tablespoons of vegetable oil in a cast iron skillet (Please tell me you have one of these by the time you've finished this book; otherwise I haven't done my job as a persuasive writer.) over medium-high heat. Sear each side of the meat until it's brown and crusty, about 7 minutes per side. Place the beef in a Crock-Pot and cover it with the saved marinade (and yes, that includes the onions, cloves, and all that jazz). Set to low and cook for 7-8 hours. Cover the cast iron skillet with tin foil, reserving the bits that were left behind by the roast, and place in the fridge.

When you're ready to serve, remove the sauerbraten meat and keep warm on a platter while you make the gravy. Skim the solids out of the cooking liquid and discard. Pour the liquid carefully into the reserved cast iron skillet over medium-high heat, scraping the burnt-on little bits as it boils for a minute or two. Turn the skillet to medium-low and stir in the gingersnaps and raisins. Let this cook and thicken for 10 minutes, then pour over the roast. Slice and serve atop spaetzle. You're welcome.

About the *Author*

Tabitha Blankenbiller

grew up in Washington State and currently lives outside of Portland, Oregon. She graduated from the Pacific University MFA in Writing program in 2012 and has written essays for *Electric Literature*, *The Rumpus*, *Bustle*, *Catapult*, *Hobart*, *Brevity*, and other venues, and has been anthologized in the *Not My President* and *All That Glitters* collections. Her home is populated by her husband, Matt; her cats, Max and Mehitabel; and her prized dual oven, Doubles.

The *Author Wishes* to *Thank*:

*T*here are a multitude of people who not only cheered on the writing of this book in the midst of writing another, but who, throughout my life, have pushed me to take my words seriously. You are my world and my well, and I endeavor only to make you proud.

To my mom and dad, Scott and Kathy, who have worked hard every day of their lives in the hopes that their children would grow up and do what they love: you didn't understand why I was doing this crazy masochistic art thing, but you loved and supported me anyway.

To my sister and brother, Brianna and Zach, who cherished and created stories alongside me for many years.

To my husband, Matt, the love of my life, father to my kitty children, gracious eater of what I cook, good and bad: you have patience that transcends reason and a heart I'll never fully know, so very big is it. Thank you for bearing with me as I grow and fail and repeat.

Thank you to my first writing teachers, now friends—Brynne Garman, Kimberly Knutsen, Ceiridwen Terrill. Thank you for reading so many of my first stories I sent you high on excitement and novelty, and going above and beyond any professional obligation to read, comment, laugh along, encourage, and shove me in directions I didn't know existed.

Thanks to the entire Pacific University MFA community, including my advisors Judy Blunt, Rachel Toor, and Debra Gwartney: my two short years of studying with you are the best of my life, and I'm so grateful that you believed in what I was doing and were willing to share your tricks for how actually to get where I was headed. To Shelley Washburn, Colleen Sump, and Tenley Taylor, thank you for creating such an outstanding program. You didn't just transform my life: you saved it.

Cupcakes and thank you's to my writing group: Katie Martin, Sharon Harrigan, Charlotte O'Brien, and Stephanie Bane. You are always up for reading my drafts and my random manic emails that I know push against the boundaries of reasonable friendships. Every interaction we have is the highlight of my day, and you make the grind of being a writer glimmer with understanding and camaraderie. Special thanks to Sharon for fixing the sauerbraten.

To all of the editors who have published work and put faith in my pitches and submissions, you have made my writing career possible and rekindled my belief in myself over and over again, when I've needed it most. Special thanks to Aaron Burch, Erin Fitzgerald, Arielle Bernstein, Eileen G'Sell, Nandini Balial, Dot Dannenberg, Anna March, Nikki Gloudeman, Kelly Luce, Mary Breaden, and Diya Chaudhuri. A special thanks to *The Rumpus* for their ceaseless support of my writing and of this project. A special special thanks to Leah Angstman, Eric Shonkwiler, Paige M. Ferro, and all the staff at Alternating Current for giving my *Naked Lunch* column series a go, and liking it so much they wanted a whole book of them, which you now hold in your hand.

Thank you to my friends who tolerate my frequent panic and accept my Christmas cookies: a super shout-out to Christian Bishop (my Charlotte), Lisa Carlson (my Sister in Cheese), Tiffany Hauck (who doesn't like people but likes me), Kerrie Allen (my Work Wife), James Yates (Twitterfriend for life), Kendra Fortmeyer (Sailor Senshi sister), and Susan DeFreitas (Hustler Queen).

To all my readers, friends, mentors, and family. You are brilliant. You are my community. You are my favorite part of waking up in the morning. Thank you for letting me bask in your light.

Colophon

What you are holding is the First Edition of this essay collection.

The alternating title fonts are Reprox Script by Intellecta Designs and Whiskey Aged by Vozzy. The back cover Alternating Current Press font is Portmanteau by JLH Fonts. All other type is set in Calisto MT.

Cover artwork: "Picking Peaches" by Robert Skemp. The original copyright has expired and piece is now in the public domain. Cover art modified and designed by Leah Angstman and Michael Litos. Interior fruit, vegetable, and berry illustrations from Fruits & Berries Watercolor set by Natali Smolova and Watercolor Tropical Fruits set by Nereia. The peach section divider is isolated from the cover art. The recipe header is created by Leah Angstman from a German recipe card photo by Klaus Beyer.

The lightbulb logo was created by Leah Angstman, ©2006, 2018 Alternating Current. Tabitha Blankenbiller's photo was taken by and ©2017, 2018 Christine Hyatt of Cheese Chick Productions.

Other Works

from Alternating Current Press

 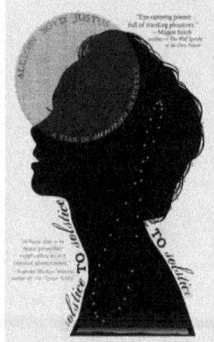 

All of these books (and more) are available at Alternating Current's website: press.alternatingcurrentarts.com.

alternatingcurrentarts.com